PRAISE FOR *BLACK WOMAN REDEFINED*

"On the page as she does on television, Sophia A. Nelson uses bold insights and no-nonsense observations to cut through the myths and misperceptions about what it means to be a black woman today. But this isn't just a book for black women. It speaks to everyone who cares about equality and opportunity, and especially to women, of every color, who are looking for a fresh perspective on everything from careers to dating to faith. Whether you agree or disagree with her, you'll find it hard to put this book down."

—Chris Jansing
Emmy-Award winning anchor and host of MSNBC's *Jansing & Co*

"The enduring legacy of any great work is that it touches our souls and causes us to reflect inward. It calls us to open our eyes, step out of the shadows of our pain, and to live life forward. *Black Woman Redefined* does that for us all. This brilliant, powerful book is not just about and for black women—it invites the entire American family to see black women more fully as people. Sophia A. Nelson is one of the most gifted analysts and writers of our time. She effectively rejects the centuries-old myth that black women's lives aren't worth discussing. The often painful stories shared in this book are still being told because they're still being lived. In the end, this book is a much-needed generational battle cry for recognition, release, and healing."

—Michael Eric Dyson
Professor at Georgetown University, radio host of the
*Michael Eric Dyson Show*, and best-selling author of
*Why I Love Black Women*

"Sophia Nelson, with her keen intellect, detailed research, and never before written insights, encourages all women, especially our strong and diverse black sisters to achieve new and unprecedented heights."

—Armstrong Williams
*Washington Times* columnist, author, and nationally syndicated
TV and radio host

"In her first book, Sophia A. Nelson gives us all great insight and information on some of the serious issues facing today's African American women. This book is bound to generate discussion across the social and political spectrum for years to come."            —Sean Hannity
Best-selling author, radio show host, and host of FOX News'
top-rated political program *Hannity*

"Each generation has a voice that is lifted at just the right time to grab hold of us and shake us from our slumber. Sophia A. Nelson calls on black women to rethink the way things are and change them. She has tapped into the pain and silence of her generation of 'sisters,' and approaches this important subject matter in a way that is compassionate *and* profound. Sophia carefully dissects

the continuing, yet often invisible, struggle of modern day black women when it comes to our image, the perceptions that others have of us, and that we have of ourselves."
—Terrie M. Williams
Author, *Black Pain: It Just Looks Like We're Not Hurting*

"Nelson uncovers the issues that are often hidden beneath the surface of black women's pain, and demonstrates to all how to live well and emerge victorious on the other side."
—Dr. Melody T. McCloud
OB/GYN- columnist *Psychology Today* and author
of *Living Well, Despite Catchin' Hell:*
*The Black Woman's Guide to Health, Sex, and Happiness*

"Think 'redefinition.' Sophia A. Nelson's new book *Black Woman Redefined* cuts through a mountain of myths, stereotypes, and negative thinking. The result is a treasure chest of new information, valuable insights, and inspiring advice for African American women—and for us, the men who love them!
—Clarence Page
Pulitzer Prize-winning syndicated columnist for the *Chicago Tribune*

"At a moment of profound economic and cultural change for America, *Black Woman Redefined* comes along at the perfect time. While Sophia A. Nelson knows her target audience, she's also aware of the broader, diverse world. With solid research and a smooth inclusive voice, Nelson has produced a book that that holds lessons for many."
—Robert A. George, *New York Post*

"*Black Woman Redefined* is a book that has been greatly anticipated because it was penned by a woman who for years has displayed refreshing analytical and political savvy first as an attorney on Capitol Hill, then as a lobbyist, and finally as a national TV commentator and columnist. This book encourages black women to do what Sophia A. Nelson has exhibited to us all for years: how to be a successful sister, wrapped with old-fashioned charm, endless grace, an unflinching determination, and a passion for serving others seldom seen in our modern times."
—Hamil Harris,
*Washington Post*, Emmy-Award winning videographer

"The research and insight in this book lend to a much-needed discussion of just how far African American women have come and how far they have to go."
—Mika Brzezinski,
co-host of MSNBC's *Morning Joe* and
author of *Knowing Your Value*

"*Black Woman Redefined* offers an urgent message that readers need to hear now: Put yourself first. The stories Sophia A. Nelson offers, coupled with thorough research and data, will make this read *a game changer*. Many conversations will begin about this book over many, many years and that's a good thing."
—*Essence* magazine

SOPHIA A. NELSON

*Black Woman*
REDEFINED

DISPELLING MYTHS AND
DISCOVERING FULFILLMENT
IN THE AGE OF
MICHELLE OBAMA

BenBella

BenBella

BenBella Books, Inc.
10300 N. Central Expressway, Suite 400
Dallas, TX 75231
benbellabooks.com
Send feedback to feedback@benbellabooks.com

Printed in the United States of America
10 9 8 7 6 5 4 3 2 1

Library of Congress Cataloging-in-Publication Data is available for this title.
ISBN 978-1-935618-94-2

Editing by Erin Kelley
Copyediting by Rebecca Logan
Proofreading by Jay Boggis
Cover design by Allison Bard
Text design and composition by Neuwirth & Associates, Inc.
Printed by Bang Printing

Dr. Dorothy Height photo: National Council of Negro Women Photo Archives
Sophia and her nieces photo: Janet Hitchen Photography
Michelle Obama photo: Official White House Photo by Joyce Boghosian

Distributed by Perseus Distribution
perseusdistribution.com

To place orders through Perseus Distribution:
Tel: 800-343-4499
Fax: 800-351-5073
E-mail: orderentry@perseusbooks.com

Significant discounts for bulk sales are available. Please contact Glenn Yeffeth at glenn@benbellabooks.com or (214) 750-3628.

# DEDICATION

There are so many dear sister friends, male friends, colleagues, and family members who helped to make this book possible. I will acknowledge all of these angels in my life in the back of this book. However, there were a few individuals who stood by me through thick and thin from the fall of 2006, when I first started writing up to the publication of this important work in 2011. This book is dedicated to them:

My mother, Sandria A. Nelson. *What would I do without you?* You are my gift from God. The best mother a daughter could have. My best friend, my confidante, my prayer partner, my spiritual role model, my federal reserve when I am broke (smile), and my strength when I am weary. Thank you, Mom, for all you have done and all you do. I love you dearly.

My mentor and sister friend Sheryl Hilliard Tucker, the woman who labored with (and gave up sleep), laughed with, and listened to me for eight weeks as we edited the first draft of this book. You were tough on me, but you made me reach deep to tell our story and helped me redefine myself in a way that would allow me to truly find happiness and fulfillment. Thank you, Sheryl. You are your sister's keeper.

To my sorors Linda J. Gill-Anderson and Therral "TJ" Haygood. *How blessed I am to call you both my friends and sorors.* Linda, you were the spark that got the fire started that day I lost my job back in 2008. You told me to seize the moment and follow my dreams. I did, and look at what God has done. TJ, you are the big sister I never had. You stepped up big time when the chips were down in my life in the fall of 2004 and again in the summer of 2010. I will never forget your counsel, generosity, and love. You model to me what being a sister in Christ is *truly* all about.

To my two *blue-eyed soul* sisters, Kellyanne Conway and Marty Wye. You two are truly blessings from above. Kellyanne, you stuck with me from the time I  first came up with the idea for this project, to the very end. You and your team gave a lot to this process for very little financial gain. But mostly you encouraged me and never allowed me to give up on seeing it through. Marty, what can I say to the woman who single-handedly saved my home and my finances and kept me encouraged when times were tough? You exemplify what it means to value your clients and work with them in crisis. You never wavered, and I am so grateful. Thank you.

To my two nieces, Alexandra (13) and Mikaela (8), I wrote this book so that you will not have to have this conversation about what it means to be a "black" or "bi-racial" woman twenty years from now. May you both have lives filled with true love, laughter, joy, happiness, health, success, friendship, family, marriage, children, and grandchildren of your own, and a faith that sustains you when the challenges of life test you.

And lastly, I dedicate this book to my co-literary agent the late Emanuel "Manie" Joseph Barron December 7, 1955–January 8, 2011. You embraced my gift when no one else saw it. I am so saddened that you did not live to see this book published. Rest in Peace, dear friend, and thank you eternally.

# CONTENTS

*Black Woman*
REDEFINED

# PROLOGUE

## THE AGE OF MICHELLE OBAMA:

*An Open Letter to the First Lady of the United States*

Dear Mrs. Obama:

Do you have any idea what you mean to us?

By us I mean the strong, independent, accomplished black women of America. I suspect that on some level you do, but because you are the First Lady of the United States, I know that you don't think along those lines, and you should not. I love that you embrace *all* Americans and that you are everyone's First Lady. But please allow me this small indulgence as I share with you how special you are to us. What I am about to say may seem a bit much, but it is important that you know—that everyone know—how much you have changed and are changing everything for present and future generations of black women in this nation.

"How so?" you may ask.

I'll tell you how: *You humanize us. You soften us. You make us invisible no more. You make us approachable, feminine, sexy, warm, compassionate, smart, affirmed, accomplished, and fun-filled all at once.* Your very nature most emphatically answers Sojourner Truth's 160-year-old question, "Ain't I a woman too?" *Yes, we are women too!*

In a national survey of accomplished black women (ABWs) conducted for this book, a whopping 87 percent of black female respondents credit you with "dispelling stereotypes" about the achievements of black women in America. You are our ebony Jacqueline Kennedy—our brown-skinned Eleanor Roosevelt. You are down to earth and yet surreal. We have waited for someone like you to come along and set the record straight. *And set it straight you have!*

Yes, many other phenomenal black women have come before you: Coretta, Rosa, Fannie, Shirley, Barbara, Oprah, Condi, and many other successful sisters whom Americans admire. *They made it possible for you to be where you are.* But no one has ever been the first black First Lady of the United States. And that is what makes you different.

Your very image and presence is captivating in a way that brings forth our pained history and our powerful triumph all at once. I had the unexpected privilege to meet you and the president at the White House this past Christmas. I was so moved and so humbled by the moment that I could not speak. Meeting the president was great, but I hope you will forgive me for standing there staring at you starstruck, in awe, and speechless as you reached to shake my hand and say a few words. I think you knew I was having "a moment," as they say, and thank you for the warm sister embrace that pulled me back to reality. I wanted to cry, but I dared not—I was so proud at that moment to be a black woman, standing in the house built by slaves, touching you and your husband, and so grateful to the elders who persevered to make it all possible. I was so hopeful for the future of our great nation and the generations to come, knowing that anything and everything is truly possible in America.

I don't know you, Sister Obama, but I know from what I see that you are far too humble to accept such accolades and praise. But I respectfully ask you to embrace your unparalleled title as "the sister who changed it all" for this present generation and the next generations of black women and girls who never thought they'd see someone like you living at 1600 Pennsylvania Avenue. You yourself have reflected openly on why you felt it was so important for you to do the historic *People* magazine cover shoot in March 2009 with these important words: "While I don't consider myself a fashionista, I thought it was good for my daughters and little girls just like them, who haven't seen themselves represented in these magazines, hopefully to talk more broadly about what beauty is, what intelligence is, what counts."[1] And although I know many now suggest we live in a "post-racial" America because your husband is the president, we all know that being the first at anything matters because it sets the tone for all those who come after.


We have all heard of the Victorian Age, the Age of Innocence, the Age of Enlightenment, and of course, the Elizabethan (Golden) Age. Each of these periods in history signified a cultural "shift," a new movement, a change of the public mind-set and morals, *a rebirth of the world*. I believe that right now in America we as black women are going through such a time. You can feel it in the air—there is something transformative, reaffirming, and fulfilling about our willingness to share our stories in cinema and reveal these mysteries in heartwarming prose. Myths and legends don't die easily. History teaches this lesson well. But I can't tell you enough how much you have contributed to *dispelling* misinformation about a certain kind of black woman in America and how much you are helping young women of a new generation to discover the possibilities for their lives beyond our much-heralded academic and career achievements.

Somehow, seeing you descend the steps of Air Force One in faraway places like India, Japan, or Africa, looking confident and full of grace, swells our hearts with pride. And that pride continues as we watch you step out onto the White House lawn from Marine One as you return from a short trip here at home. Some days you are glamorous and looking fierce as you await guests at the White House for a state dinner. At other times we may see you popping your fingers and dancing to Stevie Wonder as you entertain our nation's governors. And my favorite days are when we see you walking with your daughters hand in hand, your hair pulled back, sporting jeans and sneakers as Bo the pup tags along. This is why we love you, Sister Obama. *You are real.*

You make us proud every time we see you with our soldiers and their families, traveling abroad as an ambassador of goodwill, and talking to our kids here at home about citizenship and service. The images of you walking barefoot along the beaches of Panama City, and dancing freely with young girls in India as well as playing hopscotch in the streets were magical. You exude a laughter and warmth that is rarely ours.

Most important (and this is a big one), you show us how you *truly love your man* and you let him love and take care of you. You honor the passion and sanctity of your marriage by making time for date nights out, nuzzling in public (unaware of or unconcerned that cameras are snapping every move), and private weekends away with the commander-in-chief. You support him too; you are his total and complete helpmate.

This may sound a bit extreme, but I see this time in our American history with you as our First Lady as a time of rebirth, renewal, and redefinition for the American black woman. In that regard, I hope you won't mind my coining the phrase "the Age of Michelle Obama" because I believe that long after you are no longer in the position of First Lady, you will forever be remembered as the woman who changed the national perception of strong, educated, accomplished black women in America.

*Forbes* magazine seems to agree with me, as they dubbed you the most powerful woman in the world in October 2010.[2] And others concur about the extent of your influence. Research conducted by New York University business professor David Yermack that was published in the *Harvard Business Review* reveals that your style choices have contributed $2.7 billion to the retail sector.[3] He further concluded that American retail companies have seen a 2.3 percent stock gain when you wear their products—a value he says is worth *five times* that of a typical celebrity endorsement. Your poll approval numbers have continued to climb since February 2009 and remain consistently in the high 60s reaching 72 percent in January 2011—an average boost of over 23 points since the 2008 campaign, when your approval numbers were in the low 40s.[4]

*So how did you do it? How did you shift public opinion in your favor?*

Some have insultingly suggested that you were forced to undergo a political makeover. Others suggest that it is simple corporate "brand management." I say they are all wrong. I say you have always been the woman we see now, despite the fact that just three years ago, you were criticized as "angry," and "unpatriotic," by some like conservative columnist Cal Thomas. You were also accused of "emasculating your husband (by none other than *New York Times* columnist Maureen Dowd),[5] who also said that you were a potential "liability" to his run for the presidency.

What we all witnessed was a very familiar, open attack on a strong, confident, accomplished black woman and her right to express her opinions and observations. They dug into your college thesis, for goodness sake! They said you had made racially charged statements on a video at your former church. They caricatured you as a machine gun–toting, Afro-wearing, fist-bumping sister in the *New Yorker*.[6]

We all watched and prayed and quietly spoke words of encouragement your way. We understood because we have all been there on our respective college campuses, in our jobs, and in our day to day lives. We know about the stereotypes about feeling *invisible* when you are one of a few black women in any setting. We all know the impact of hateful words and demeaning stereotypes because we have all endured them. And, despite living in a so-called postracial, post-gender America, we endure them still.

Unfortunately, the barbs hurled at you back in 2008 have not stopped. Former vice presidential nominee and Alaska governor Sarah Palin has jabbed at you directly this past year in her newest book *America by Heart*, in which she resurrects your remark made during the 2008 campaign that you were proud of your country for the first time and asserts that it is indicative of your belief (and that of your husband) that "America . . . is a fundamentally unjust and unequal" nation.[7] She threw another punch in December 2010 on her TV series *Sarah Palin's Alaska*, when she accused you of wanting to rob parents and children of their right to eat dessert as she stuffed s'mores in her mouth.[8]

None of this comes as a surprise. This narrative of black women is played and replayed daily in the media, on YouTube, in the workplace, in the boardroom, in church gossip, and everywhere we exist. We are angry, overly opinionated, aggressive, controlling, emasculating, and generally physically unhealthy women—right? Yet, whether it is in the heat of a national campaign or in the course of your daily duties as First Lady, you take it all in and absorb the attacks and the smears with grace, humor, and an unflinching strength that we all know is the hallmark of strong black women everywhere. Whether you know it or not, you are teaching a powerful lesson on how to deal with conflict even under the glare of a spotlight that few of us will ever experience.

One biographer noted that your popularity has increased since the 2008 elections because you won over your harshest critics: conservative Republican women (i.e., mostly white women who supported Sarah Palin).[9] What you have done, Sister Obama, is ingenious: you gained their approval by deemphasizing your career achievements and instead emphasizing yourself as America's mom-in-chief. All one has to do is go to the White House website and look at your bio, where you make clear that your most important job is as "Malia and Sasha's mom."[10]

There is a powerful lesson here for us all: You don't have to shout back at your critics or crawl into the pit of mudslinging with them. The best revenge is success, and success comes with a willingness to constantly reinvent, reform, and redefine the rules of the game, how you play the game, and what you consider a "win" at the end of the game.

As I mentioned previously, I believe you are the woman you have always been; the difference is that you have now been given the platform and opportunity as First Lady to show the world what we have always known exists within our community: healthy, vibrant, powerful, family-focused sisters who take care of business on all fronts and do so in a way that truly empowers the lives of all who know them. You are teaching us to master the rules of the game as you publicly support your husband's policies while championing your own initiatives and always being a great mom, daughter, and wife. In this way, you represent the model wife that most women aspire to be and you exhibit twenty-first-century career-girl savvy. You remind us—gently—of your power in a very chic, feminine, endearing way.

*That is redefinition at its best, my sister!*

I still get misty-eyed when I see you on television, whether you're putting your arm around the Queen of England so endearingly or tenderly holding hands with a wounded soldier or sick child. I know firsthand that you have a tender heart because when a sorority sister's twelve-year-old daughter was dying of brain cancer in December of 2009, I asked your office if you could reach out to this little girl. You did so without a second thought, sending her a personal note and a picture of Bo. I want you to know that you made that little girl smile; you made her feel special, and she saw herself in your image as she died just two days later.

Yes, you will be the one historians write about fifty, seventy-five, and a hundred years down the road. You will be the embodiment of America's twenty-first-century accomplished, beautiful, balanced, healthy, and fulfilled woman. You will help us transition to what Sojourner referenced so long ago: we will just be seen as women—not as black or brown women to be limited or defined by our status. I believe with all my heart that you will single-handedly help erase generations of stereotyping about black women and, in so doing, break down barriers in the relationships between black men and black women, white women and black women, white men and black women, and others.

I know that what I am saying is true because in conducting research for this book we asked your fellow Americans (black, white, male, female, Hispanic, old, and young) how they see you, what you mean to them, and how you are changing their opinions about strong, accomplished black women everywhere.

So let me share some good news with you from the polling and focus group research we conducted from summer 2009 through 2010. We polled 1,000 Americans (±3) of all races and demographics, including over 750 professional black men (211) and black women (540) separately as well as in focus groups, both regionally and nationally. We asked about their perceptions of you and how you have positively affected the way Americans now view accomplished black women. The following is a very brief snapshot of what we found. All Americans, regardless of their race, education, or region, given a set of descriptive words and phrases to choose from, overwhelmingly chose these words as their top descriptors of you: *accomplished, inspiring, intelligent, role model*, and *wife/mother*.[11] Less than 10 percent of Americans viewed you as "made over" from the 2008 campaign image of you. When we drilled down in focus groups of your peers (educated, professional black women and men) and short survey anthologies with white professional women and men, again the results were very positive.

For example, 87 percent of the black women we surveyed felt that your very presence and image has helped to *dispel damaging myths and stereotypes* about us as black women. Black men concur; three out of four agree that you are "reconstructing" a positive image of black women in society. In fact, as you will see throughout this book, you come up a lot in how attitudes toward professional black women have shifted in the workplace and in relationships, and your presence is felt in our discussions about encouraging black men and women to build strong, healthy families once again. This is important because we know from census data, as well as from many studies conducted in the past decade or so, that the incidence of black marriage has declined dramatically since the 1940s. As a result, black children have suffered most of all.

More important to me, and for the younger women we polled and spoke with in focus groups, you show the world every day that strength, intelligence, and achievement alone don't make a life—they simply add to one's life. You have shown us all what it is like to shift and willingly redefine yourself not as a hard-driving career woman or policy theorist or outspoken political activist, but as a devoted wife, mother, and daughter first. You demonstrate for young women and middle-aged women who still aspire to marriage and family that balance is possible and that you can have it all—maybe just not all at once. In addition, we are very grateful that you love and support our nation's military families and that you have taken up the great cause of reducing childhood obesity, especially since it affects African American children most disproportionately.

*I'll ask again: do you know what that means to us?*

You model for us, and the many generations of sisters to come, something that we haven't seen in the media and culture for a long time: a loving, compassionate, attractive, smart, spiritual, nurturing, devoted, physically fit, temperate, classy, fun, married, strong, accomplished black woman. A sister who knows how to rest, how to take care of her mind and body, and most important, how to be comfortable in her own skin (and show that skin off in a tasteful, attractive manner). I'll end by echoing the words of Alice Walker in a moving letter she wrote to your husband on the day of his election to the presidency in 2008: "[Y]our smile . . . is that expression of healthy self-worth, spirit, and soul that, kept happy and free and relaxed, can find an answering smile in all of us, lighting our way, and brightening the world."

Thank you, Sister Obama, for your example and your smile, which is lighting the way and brightening the world for us all.

With Sisterly Love and Pride,
Sophia Angeli Nelson, Esquire

"Being strong can be also feminine. I don't think feminine equals being weak. Being strong is very sexy."

—ACTRESS SANAA LATHAN

# INTRODUCTION

## JUST WHAT DOES A "REDEFINED" BLACK WOMAN LOOK LIKE ANYWAY?

"If you don't define yourself for yourself then you will be crushed into others' fantasies of you and eaten alive."

—AUDRE LORDE

My Dear Strong Accomplished Sisters:

Many of you are likely asking yourselves, "Who is this woman on the front cover of this book, skin bare, all dressed up like something out of a Glamour Shots portrait, asking us to 'redefine' ourselves?"

More important, you are probably asking, "Why should we listen to her about discovering fulfillment in our lives?" Where does anyone get off asking a group of such accomplished, well-educated, savvy, worldly, power-brokering, and well-spoken women, who seem to have it all, to redefine or change themselves? That is a fair question, and I'd like to answer it at the outset of this book so that any doubts or reservations you may have about my own life experiences, qualifications, and intentions for this book are satisfied. What I want to share with you is too important to miss, so I hope you'll trust me to tell our story with candor, love, responsibility, respect, and integrity. I want you to take a journey with me to another side of yourself—a side beyond the educational degrees, the achievements, the titles, the material possessions, and the surface. I want to speak candidly with you about you, and about me.

I'll start by saying this: the first duty of a witness is to testify. I am a witness, and this is my testimony. I live my life as a black woman every day. This is not a book written by another well-meaning brother or others who frankly have no clue what it is like to be us. This is my love letter to my sisters, not based solely on my opinions and experiences but on what you told me mattered, what you told me was important in your life, and what the next generation needs us to give them so that they will have every chance to live happy, meaningful, and fulfilled lives.

Sisters, *I am you.*

This book is as much about me as it is about you. No one ever needed to redefine her life more than I did when I woke up at forty years of age and realized I was not happy and not living the life of my dreams. It finally hit me after many years of doing what others expected of me and covering up my emotions, burying my hurts, and living in the shadow of my true self that I was not *defined* by what I did or achieved in my life. I am *defined* by my love of others, my care of myself, my active and authentic faith, and my ability to flow with the winds of change in order to soar above the storms of life.

I also discovered that I was more than just a woman who always had to be "on" or who had to be clothed in the classic corporate power gear (e.g., pant suit, expensive shoes and handbag) to feel powerful. The image on the cover of this book is *me*, and it is *you*. Affirmed, fulfilled, attractive, relaxed, and ready for anything that comes my way. If Sister Obama can bare her arms, so can we; if she can be healthy and fit, so can we. Until Mrs. Obama came along, we did not see many images of ourselves in such a way. Maybe it's time we brought glamour back, sisters—it's okay to be and feel *sexy, sensual, and sacred* all at once.

Now, at forty-four years of age, I have never looked better, felt more attractive, or been more open to the possibilities of my life. Oh, how I wish I had figured this out when I was twenty-five. Somewhere I had lost myself in all of the pursuits of my life. I was a stressed out, overworked, wound-up girl who was buried beneath a rubble of business, religion, and regret. *I am glad to be reintroduced to myself.* My authentic, transparent self. She was missing for a long time. But life has a way of forcing us to rediscover who we are at the most inconvenient times. And it is usually when we believe that all of our hopes, dreams, and desires are lost that we realize our life is just beginning.

This writing journey started for me in the fall of 2006. Like all of you, I was growing weary of the portrayals of black women both in the mass media and in everyday life. The problem was not that some of the portrayals were not based in reality (sadly); it was that they had become commercial. Our pain and drama seemed to have captured the interest of a broad swath of America, and we were the brunt of cruel jokes, lyrics, internet videos, articles, nationally televised specials, and the like. And that troubled me greatly.

At the time, I was working for a law firm of over 1,200 lawyers that had only a few black female partners. I was very unhappy in my career, and as a result, I had started an organization dedicated to the emotional, relational, spiritual, physical, and career wellness of professional black women (I Am My Sister's Keeper, Inc.) two years earlier. I was starting to see some disturbing trends and patterns with us that I knew deserved a deeper look. I was not interested in exploring what was wrong with us as much as learning how we get past this and make happiness, fulfillment, and love part of the equation.

Before some of you jump on me, *know that I know* many of us *are* happy, affirmed, and fulfilled. We are not hiding from our pasts; nor do we hold grudges. We are in positive and healthy relationships with men; we are mothers, wives, and partners; we love our families; we honor our elders; we are faithful women of God; we take care of our bodies; and we love our fellow sisters. We treat people with respect, and we in turn respect ourselves.

But, sisters, if we are going to be honest—*really honest*—we all know too many of our girlfriends, sorority sisters, colleagues, and family members who are not living the lives they are capable of living, and perhaps we are in the same boat ourselves. We are burdened, buried, walled off, and oftentimes downright "hard." It's time for us to make a bold move forward so that our generation and the next generation do not have to be limited anymore. I want better for the young women coming behind me. They need to know that we are more than the sum of our hurts. We are not broken. We are not damaged. We are special, and we are worthy of love, respect, and adoration.

I just had my twenty-fifth high school class reunion in 2010. If someone had told me on graduation day in June of 1985 that I would be my age now, not married, with no children, I would have laughed. I had a whole other life planned. Now I am living "plan B" for my life, and I am okay with that. My point is this: If I can emerge from my past, my pains, and my disappointments to rediscover and redefine my life in my early forties, *so can you.* If I can find the courage to resolve that I will not give in to feeling sorry for myself, depression, or health challenges, and if I can move past the belief that I cannot be happy because I didn't check off every item on the list everyone told me I had to complete by the time I was thirty-five, *so can you*. If I can leave one profession at age forty and pursue the profession and passion of my dreams, and actually find myself just three years later living the exact life I always wanted, *so can you*.

You see, sisters, for too long we have allowed ourselves to be defined by others' versions of who we are and how we are to act, feel, and exist. That has got to change because the truth is that it is not working, and it has not worked for a long time. This book is for the sisters of Gen X and Gen Y, whom I have spent the last seven years of my life traveling around the country talking with, listening to, working with, supporting, and being supported by in all of our triumphs and tragedies.

Let me explain why I wrote this book *about* and *for* strong, independent black women. First, we are all well aware of the media's newfound interest in successful black women. Some of it is positive, inspired by our fabulous First Lady, Michelle Obama. But disturbingly, much of it is driven by an implied social pathology that, somehow, something is wrong with the 44 percent of African American women who have never been married and the 70 percent of us professional sisters who are currently not married. Second, much has been written about us—how we feel, think, act, and respond to life's challenges. Yet much of what has been written and said about us has not come from us. Nor has it been accurate, fair, flattering, compassionate, or helpful.

I wrote this book because everyone seems to have an opinion about strong, accomplished black women, and sadly it is not very good. I think we can all agree that the American black woman has gotten a bad rap for too long. Some of it, perhaps, we have earned, and we need to take responsibility for that. But most of it is nothing like the women we really are, and it's time we told the other side of the story and released ourselves from the stereotypes and negative images and narratives that often depict and limit us. It seems almost daily that some video clip poking fun at us goes viral on the internet. I, for one, am tired of it, and it's time we set the record straight. It's not that we don't have a sense of humor—we do—but it seems that everyone has an opinion about who we are and what ails us *but us*. I want to ensure that our story is told from a firsthand and multidimensional perspective.

To help me in this quest, I've explored personal experiences, gathered expert opinions, and read with great interest a 2010 study conducted on black women, published in the *Journal of Experimental Social Psychology*, by Amanda Sesko and Monica Biernat that examined the intriguing idea that black women are socially invisible.[1] I also commissioned a ground-breaking national research study, convened a unique set of focus groups, and conducted interviews with women and men across America. I have scrutinized the media coverage of African American women (especially black professional women), and culled seven years of dedicated experience dealing with the issues and challenges that confront today's successful black woman. I also spent considerable time with our wise "elder sisters," who ranged in age from fifty to seventy, to provide a more holistic and historical perspective of black women in America.

I promise that you will find some part of yourself in this book, whether you are twenty-five, thirty-five, or forty-five, single or married, a mother or childless. For sisters over age fifty, this book will help tune your antenna to the new language, dating rituals, workplace rules, and challenges confronting your daughters, granddaughters, and younger sister colleagues. I wrote this book specifically for all of you sisters who've done so many things right in your life, but are still constantly told you are not enough as you struggle to find joy, love, intimacy, and a general feeling of well-being.

For those of you who are not black women, I hope you read this book, because you need to know the real us. You may not be a black woman, but you know one. You need to see beyond the myths, legends, and stereotypes of us. I invite you in to take a look at us unveiled and ready for redefinition. My hope is that by going where few books have gone before, I will reveal to the world that we are a beautiful butterfly waiting to emerge from the cocoon, despite the troubles we have faced.

Let me state emphatically, however, that this book is not every black professional woman's story. It serves as a road map to help readers confront and deal with the significant challenges facing the majority of college-aged and career black women in America—relationally, spiritually, emotionally, physically, and professionally.

While working on the book, I realized how well Michelle Obama embodies so much of what black women in America treasure—qualities we don't always incorporate into our own lives. We all acknowledge how intelligent, confident, and beautiful she is. But it's her warmth, compassion, grace, and playfulness that have dazzled the world. Her unapologetic black womanness is extraordinary. Her smile invites you into her world.

My goal for this book is to pull off the proverbial mask. I'm determined to end the guesswork and stop the blame game. So right up front, I'm asking you to forgive me for breaking the "sister code" about "keeping our business to ourselves." Trust me, I'm not interested in fueling the media's debate on what's wrong with successful black women. I'm inviting you to join me on a journey exploring five core goals that accomplished black women must achieve if we want to live the life we truly desire:

1. **Positive, multidimensional relationships** expressed as strong, happy, supportive, and meaningful bonds with men, women friends, family members, and colleagues
2. **Satisfying, successful, and flexible careers** that we truly enjoy
3. **Balanced and emotionally rewarding lives** that nourish us and allow us to forgive, grow, and dream
4. **Good health** that's grounded in conscious choices and a lifestyle with little stress
5. **Spirituality that doesn't reject sexuality**—a deep, rich spiritual life that embraces us as sensual human beings who desire love, intimacy, marriage, and family

I invite you to come with me on a journey, sisters. A journey to putting the past behind you. A journey of forgiveness, healing, good health, emotional balance and wellness, financial security, self-love, sisterly love, romantic love, and reconnection with your spiritual side that will allow you to embrace *all of you* in all of your splendor and majesty.

PART I

# Dispelling the Myths and Discovering the Truth about Who We Are

"Each of us has the right and the responsibility to assess the roads which lie ahead, and those over which we have traveled, and if the future road looms ominous or unpromising, and the roads back uninviting, then we need to gather our resolve and, carrying only the necessary baggage, step off that road into another direction. If the new choice is also unpalatable, without embarrassment, we must be ready to change that as well."

—Maya Angelou,
*Wouldn't Take Nothing for My Journey Now*

# 1

# WHO WE ARE AND WHAT WE'VE ACCOMPLISHED

*"To conquer oneself is a greater victory than to conquer thousands in a battle."*
—BUDDHA

*S*ome say we have conquered the world as accomplished black women; I say that we have yet to conquer ourselves.

Sisters, it is time we had a candid and meaningful conversation about just how far we have come and how far we have yet to go in valuing the things that truly matter in life. Black women have survived the unimaginable, and many of us have *thrived in the midst of it all.* We come from good stock, sisters, and we should never forget that truth. We must honor those who came before us, who sacrificed their hopes for ours, who could not dream as big as we can, and who gave us their extraordinary examples to dare us to be more, do more, and achieve more.

The twenty-first-century successful black woman is brilliant and tenacious and not afraid to flex her intellectual, spiritual, or financial muscles. She has accomplished, earned, and owned more than black women of any other generation in American history. Just forty years after the civil rights and women's movements of the 1960s and 1970s, successful black women have rapidly scaled the ladder of success to the top. Today, against all odds, we stand proud in corner offices throughout corporate America, in partners' meetings at law firms, in hospital operating rooms, in academia's ivory towers, in trading rooms on Wall Street, in the studios of media and entertainment conglomerates, in the research labs of prestigious scientific institutions, in the halls of Congress and the White House.

Think about it: we now have *three generations* of amazing black females in the White House. There was no way Mrs. Marian Robinson could have ever dreamed in 1964, when her daughter was born, that she would join Michelle and her granddaughters, Sasha and Malia, to call 1600 Pennsylvania Avenue home.

Wherever you look in the second decade of twenty-first-century America, you will find a sister at the top of her game. You know her when you see her. There's an invisible "S" tattooed on her chest, just beneath her camisole, for "Superwoman." She is strong, independent, and ready for any challenge in the workplace. She's sharp and confident, sports fine shoes and the best handbags, drives a nice car, and loves the Lord. She's politically active as well. That's why, as a group, black women were the largest and most reliable voting block for candidate Barack Obama during the 2008 presidential election.[1] She's the pillar of her church and the committee chair of her sorority, and she is the most important community fund-raiser. She is well connected, highly visible, and always on call, ready to help a family member or friend in need. She's the go-to on everyone's speed dial, for volunteers, for mentoring, for money, and for comfort.

Today we celebrate a growing cadre of accomplished black female superstars, such as Xerox Corporation CEO Ursula Burns, media mogul Oprah Winfrey, former secretary of state Condoleezza Rice, U.S. ambassador Susan Rice, NASA astronaut Mae Jemison, model-turned-TV-star Tyra Banks, Tony Award–winning actress Viola Davis, Academy Award–nominated actress Taraji P. Henson, Brown University president Dr. Ruth J. Simmons, Rear Admiral Michelle Howard, the Honorable Ann Claire Williams (U.S. Court of Appeals Judge for the Seventh Circuit), and sports icons Venus and Serena Williams, just to name a few. Everywhere you look you can see sisters making an impact—moving and shaking, and reshaping the world around them.

*Yet there's something amiss.*

When did our achievements start to trump our fulfillment? Somehow, a significant slice of this intriguing community of women has disconnected from what our mothers and foremothers valued. Somehow, far too many of these highly successful sisters who have achieved the

American Dream have replaced love, relationships, and family with ambition. Somehow, our strength has been transformed into a galvanized coat of armor, shielding us from our pain *and* depriving us of an authentic and joyful life. In spite of all we have accomplished, everyone around us—friends, family, coworkers, brothers, and even our younger sisters—have decided that we've become too hard, too aloof, too independent, and too strong. As one twenty-eight-year-old sister told me this past spring, "I admire the accomplished, older black women in my life so much professionally, but I don't want to be like them—alone, and childless at forty."

Life as a strong black woman, who is always independent, always a survivor, always a caretaker, always on, and mostly doing it alone, is hard and lonely. And Lord knows, armor gets really heavy when you're forced to wear it 24/7. Eventually, the strong black woman (or what we call in our studies "ABW" for "accomplished black woman") lifestyle can take its toll on your psyche and your health.

## *Is Our Image Really Changing?*

IT WAS JUST fifty years ago that the only images we had of black women portrayed us as vulnerable, uneducated, and oppressed. We were largely viewed as self-sacrificing matriarchs who would do anything to assure our family's survival, the invisible domestic who served as surrogate mother to her white family's children, the God-fearing, sexless sister who was a pillar of the church and was there for her siren sister, the tragic mulatto. Beneath such stereotypes rest the lost stories of our grandmothers, mothers, aunts, and family friends. Harlem Renaissance writer Langston Hughes so aptly gave voice to these women in his legendary poem "Mother to Son": "Life for me ain't been no crystal stair."

Over time, the media enshrined new stereotypes of black women—the angry black activist; the promiscuous unwed mother; the child-selling crack addict; the take-no-shit, more-man-than-woman black bitch; the beat-the-system welfare queen, and the hypersexual video vixen. We've been accused of being both unfeminine and oversexed *at the same time.* Too visible, and yet invisible. It just doesn't add up.

But such one-dimensional stereotypes have been laid to rest in postracial America, right? Let's consider the impact of two controversial movies on our present-day image of black women: *For Colored Girls,* released in

2010, and the Academy Award–nominated *Precious*, released in 2009. *For Colored Girls* is the on-screen adaptation of the 1975 play *For Colored Girls Who Have Considered Suicide When the Rainbow is Enuf*, written by Ntozake Shange. The movie earned $22 million on opening weekend (driven in large part by sisters) and a whole lot of unexpected anger from black men at how they are portrayed. It reminded me of similar outcries from black men about *Waiting to Exhale* and *The Color Purple*.

Nominated for Best Picture, *Precious* is based on the novel *Push* by Sapphire and is a story about a mentally unbalanced  black mother who physically and sexually abuses her obese, illiterate daughter. The girl is also raped by her father, gives birth to his two children, and is infected with HIV. *Precious* won a Best Supporting Actress Oscar and Golden Globe for Mo'Nique and six 2010 NAACP Image Awards. While the fight to give voice to the victims of sexual abuse and mental illness in our community should not be minimized, many challenged how this film, directed by Lee Daniels, was valuable. (Daniels also produced the controversial *Monster's Ball*, for which Halle Berry won an Oscar.) To be candid, I too asked myself what "image" in the movie was actually worth celebrating.

The images in *For Colored Girls* were even more upsetting because I know (as do all of you) at least one sister in that movie who is *like us* or *like someone we know*. I lost a professional, upwardly mobile sister friend to domestic violence in 2009. I have a sorority sister who left her husband because he was sleeping with other men. I have girlfriends who sleep around like sex-crazed wildcats. I know sisters who have had abortions or contracted  STDs  and still suffer the physical and emotional scars. I had one young sister come to me  and share that she was raped by two men, and when she told her mother, her mother blamed her for being in the wrong place at the wrong time—told her to "man up" and move on. Like you, I have read the stories in the news about black women standing passively by while their husbands or lovers abused or beat their children to death. And we all know sisters who have lost themselves in religion so deeply that they have missed the true meaning of faith and spirituality.

Yet black men were deeply offended at the movie's portrayals of them and said they were false. My retort to the brothers (I wrote a few op-eds on the controversy[2]): Are you kidding me? Art often imitates life, and sadly, these characters are not made-up folks. Furthermore, do you think the images of black *women* in these movies are any better? I mean, come on, how often do we see black women who conquer racism, sexism, and discrimination to build healthy, happy, and prosperous lives with husbands and families intact? Rarely! *Yet we know they do exist!*

So, although there is some accuracy to the portrayals of black women in *Precious* and *For Colored Girls*, America is still lacking the other side of the story—a balance that we can achieve only if we can show instead all those healthy, fulfilled black women we know are out there.

Today, the media spotlight has turned on the most successful segment of our community—upwardly mobile black women—but the story isn't much better. We should be celebrating that America has finally discovered the successful black woman, but the media, through distorted lens, tends to focus on black dysfunction, and has managed to be blind to our good qualities. Why can't the media talk about what we do well? Does the media care about what we have to offer as lovers, wives, and mothers, and how we are building businesses and institutions, educating minds, and changing the world? No! Talk shows and news headlines ask, "What is wrong with accomplished black women, and why can't they find love and fulfillment?" Despite our brains, gifts, and forbearance in the face of extraordinary challenges, we are still viewed through the prism of age-old definitions and stereotypes of us that do not begin to scratch the surface of who we truly are as people.

In the past two years, we have been bombarded by news articles, television shows, blogs, sociological studies and special forums dissecting the lives of successful black women. From ABC News *Nightline* to a jabfest on a Russian television show, to a ground-breaking 2009 Yale University study, to debates on Historically Black Colleges and Universities (HBCU) campuses nationwide, everyone is asking: "Why can't successful black women find a man?" "Are black women invisible?" "Why don't black women have as much wealth or save as much financially as other professionals?" "Why are black women struggling, as single heads of households, with depression, with obesity, and now with alarmingly high rates of STDs and HIV?"

Surf the internet, and you'll find books written by black men with titles like *Why We Hate Black Women: Deconstructing the Paradox of Black Female Masculinity* (Hasani Pettiford), *Why Black Women Are Alone: The Truth Revealed* (Hank Bullard), *Why Black Men Love White Women: Going Beyond Sexual Politics to the Heart of the Matter* (Rajen Persaud), and more disturbing, *Why He Hates You!: How Unreconciled Maternal Anger Is Destroying Black Men and Boys* (Janks Morton).

You all remember when the proverbial shit hit the fan in 2007 after radio shock jock Don Imus called the black women on Rutgers University's basketball team "nappy-headed hos" and his sidekick added that these coeds looked like the Toronto Raptors.[3] *Really?* They looked like male Canadian basketballers? Or was he referring to the vicious, carnivorous dinosaurs?

More recently, Grammy Award–winning musician John Mayer likened his penis to the notoriously racist Ku Klux Klan leader David Duke when asked about dating black women.[4]

The bitter reality is that it has been open season on black women for quite a while in our own community. It's proven by thirty years of rap lyrics, hip-hop chart toppers, and their music videos. It should be no surprise that those outside our community have jumped on the sister-bashing bandwagon too. Some observers stand on the sidelines and simply report on the war between the brothers and sisters. Mort Zuckerman of *U.S. News & World Report* weighed in:

> Imus, it has been said, was doing no more than spewing the language of sexual and racist aggression mouthed by African Americans in rap and hip-hop (and talk radio, movies, TV, etc.) which is, by the way, financed by corporations. If you look at the current top 10 rap albums, they relish the "N" word and insult "ho's" and "bitches." That does not make the revealing language acceptable. In fact, it takes us back to a core issue: why the increasing stature of African American females seems to have caused the male culture to demean them.[5]

Journalist Allison Samuels wrote in *Newsweek*:

> Sadly, even though an initial public outrage had Mayer apologizing via his Twitter account and found him crying on stage during an apology, my guess is Mayer will suffer little for his comments. And the reason is very simple. He clearly said out loud what a large majority of mainstream men in power feel in private. I'm referring to those invisible men in the corner offices with the influence and power to put women in movies, on magazine covers, and television shows. The ones who decide what beauty looks like, how much it weighs, and what age it should be. The ones who, just like John Mayer, have deemed black women as just not good enough.[6]

Even some rap artists have admitted to distorting realistic images of black women in their lyrics and the impact of that misrepresentation on black women. Jay-Z, who has made tens of millions being a top rap artist, laments in his first book, *Decoded*, that his demeaning of black women weighs on his conscience. He admitted in one interview with the *Wall Street Journal*, "Some [lyrics] become really profound when you see them in writing. Not 'Big Pimpin,' That's the exception. It was like, I can't believe I said that. And kept saying it. What kind of animal would say this sort of thing? Reading it is really harsh."[7] Another rap artist, Dr. Dre, has been quoted as saying, "Black women are the strongest, most hard-working people on earth. The shit I talk on records about black women is just that: shit." How magnanimous of him to admit that his lyrics are just "shit talking"! What he doesn't understand is that his lyrics influence how our culture perceives black women's value, and they drive the raw emotions and demeaning actions of generations of young men.

How is it that an entire race of women—so successful, so beautiful, so intelligent, and so powerful—can be so *devalued, vilified, neglected, unwanted, disliked, misused, increasingly misunderstood,* and *blatantly abused*? And why and how has this onslaught of nastiness been intensi-fied now, as we celebrate the ascension of our beautiful, accomplished black sister, Michelle Obama, into the White House? Thinkers, bloggers, and conspiracy theorists in our community are debating whether all this media motion is some type of devious plot hatched to keep ambitious black women in our stereotypic place—at the bottom of the achieve-ment ladder. Others see it as way to further destabilize black families and the black community.

I want to be clear, though: the media is only reporting what we allow them to see of us. You can't shoot the messenger. Certainly, I am not pleased with how the media and social networking feeds into the anti–black woman feeding frenzy, but we all need to take responsibility for the fact that what is being reported about us is often, sadly, rooted in reality. I hate to admit it, but when our younger sisters consider it a badge of honor to be called a "bitch" and seem to have adopted a new code of honor that includes being "hard" and "gangsta," what can we expect? Worse, how can we expect the media to show our kinder, gentler side more often when we openly attack each other in books (for example, Helena Andrews' slam of former employer Sheila Bridges in her book *Bitch Is the New Black*[8])and music (for example, the ongoing rap war between Nicki Minaj and Lil' Kim[9])?

Someone once said to me, "Sophia, we teach people how to treat us." *I agree.* Unless and until black women in America get tired of living up to only a very low set of expectations and feeding into negative myths and stereotypes, we can stop complaining about the media reporting on our bad behavior.

No matter why this is all happening now, it's time to tell our side of the story. In doing so, I hope we will shed some much-needed light on the question everyone, including many of us, seem to have on our mind: *Just what is going on with successful black women in America?* It's time we found the courage to answer this question for ourselves and dare to redefine the ways that we have been portrayed for the last four decades by the media, by our own community, by our men, and sometimes, sadly, by ourselves.

## My American Dream Life

LIKE MANY OF you, I am a never-married, well-educated, *forty-something* high-income-earning professional African American woman with no children. I live in a big house in the suburbs of Virginia surrounded by neighbors and friends who are seemingly living the American Dream. They appear to be successfully balancing their career ambitions, marriages, families, and dreams. Sometimes I wonder, *Where did my American Dream go?*

I played by all the rules I was taught to obey. I did exactly what my mother told me to do. I went to college and then law school. I worked on Capitol Hill and at prestigious law firms, bought my own house, exercised regularly, and always stepped out the door with my "beautiful sister" face on. But somehow, I'm not living the life I aspired to when I was in my twenties and thirties. Like many of my sisters, I look at our nation's First Family and am filled with pride. The example of achievement that Mrs. Obama is setting for generations of young black girls—accomplishing success in marriage, motherhood, and career with extraordinary beauty from the inside out while consistently exhibiting the virtues of respect, grace, humility, compassion, and faith—is awesome. Many of you know of what I speak. I am no different from millions of beautiful black women who feel this way. And we wonder, *Why can't I have that too?*

Although my story is not every professional black woman's story, what I found in my research on black women—conducted through small groups, national focus groups, and an extensive survey—is that sisters have at least two things in common: *our legendary strength and our desire for better and more well-rounded lives*, including emotional and physical well-being, meaningful relationships (with men and our sister friends), financial security, family support, and spiritual centeredness.

I hope that by sharing parts of my own life's journey, and those of other phenomenal black women, I will clear the air and spark a much-needed national conversation across race and gender lines about who successful black women really are—at home, at work, at church, in our hearts, and in our personal lives.

Writing this book has been a difficult journey for me that started many years ago. I have carried this book in my heart and soul for years because I love black women. I love them because I am a black woman, and I know we have a uniquely positive, powerful, and life-transforming story to tell.

*Remember, this book isn't meant to reflect the story of all black women.* Although I've talked with a broad swath of successful sisters, I am focused on those who have achieved major accomplishments in their careers, their church, and their community, only to be left facing a painful question: *Is that all there is?*

To make sure that this book reflects more than my particular view, I tapped the expertise of my friend Kellyanne Conway, president and CEO of the Polling Company/WomanTrend. We conducted regional and national online focus groups, a nationwide online research study of professional black women, and a 1,000-person nationwide phone poll of all Americans. To bring black men into the discussion, I enlisted Dr. Silas Lee and associates of Xavier University in New Orleans to conduct a nationwide poll of college-educated and working black men and moderate an online focus-group discussion with black men from around the country. I also put on my journalist hat and interviewed dozens of experts (psychologists, psychiatrists, doctors, spiritual leaders, sex therapists, and academic researchers). And of course, I talked to scores of black, white, and Hispanic men and women to make sure to capture the full story of accomplished black women in America today.

### The Successful Twenty-First-Century Black Woman: Who She Is and Why She Matters

So just who are America's accomplished black women (ABWs), and why has it been so challenging for many of us to achieve the American Dream?

The research* for this book focused exclusively on college-educated professional black women. They hail from every region in the continental United States, with the majority (59 percent) from the South Atlantic region.[10] Slightly more than one-quarter (27 percent) graduated from a four-year college, while over half (58 percent) hold postgraduate degrees. The vast majority (75 percent) of the respondents identify themselves as professional/executives or business owners, while 25 percent hold "white-collar" positions.[11]

The age range of the survey respondents is truly cross-generational, with 26 percent belonging to Gen Y (ages 25 to 34), 37 percent belonging to Gen X (ages 35 to 44), and 26 percent being baby boomers (ages 45 to 54). Only 10 percent of the respondents are age 55 or older, and fewer than 1 percent are under age 25.

Overall, the group we surveyed is affluent. More than half of respondents (53 percent) report having yearly household incomes of over $90,000; 41 percent of this group top $100,000. These women are extremely proud of their accomplishments but are concerned about advancing up the career ladder. More than two-thirds (68 percent) say this is more of a problem for black women than other groups. However, only 38 percent cite "lack of opportunities to be promoted" as the biggest barrier to their ability to succeed in the workplace, and only 29 percent believe that "being treated unfairly because of my race" is the biggest barrier.

The ABWs who responded to the survey (as well as participated in the national and regional focus groups) are acutely concerned about the negative image of strong black women and especially that we're stereotyped as being angry or pushy. They are also offended by the portrayals of black women on TV and in music videos. They are tired of endless dissections of black women and are interested in solutions that will help

---

*A convenience sample is a sample of study subjects taken from a group that is more readily accessible to a researcher. The advantage of a convenience sample is that it is easy to access, requiring less effort on the part of the researcher. In all forms of research, it would be ideal to test the entire population, but in most cases, the population is just so large that it is impossible to include every individual. This is the reason why most researchers rely on sampling techniques like convenience sampling, the most common of all sampling techniques. Many researchers prefer this sampling technique because the subjects are readily available. Still, convenience samples can provide you with useful information, especially in a pilot study. To interpret the findings from a convenience sample properly, you have to characterize (usually in a qualitative sense) how your sample would differ from an ideal sample that was randomly selected. This has been done for this book in Appendix A.

us achieve the things we desire most: love, relationships, financial security, wealth, happiness, and spiritual connection.

Like most of us, these sisters are still celebrating having a black First Lady in the White House. They believe her presence is helping black professional women overcome stereotypes or misperceptions about their ability to raise a family while successfully pursuing their career. However, a majority of these women are pessimistic about their chances of finding their own "Barack": a whopping 66 percent say they'd rather be alone than settle for man who doesn't meet their standards or expectations, but almost half (42 percent) also admit that their expectations are too high. That may be why 42 percent of this group have never married.

Most ABWs in our survey believe that black men are intimidated by them (67 percent), a statistic that brothers firmly reject in interviews, focus groups, and our online poll of black men. These women think brothers see them as "too independent and self-sufficient" (70 percent), "standoffish" (51 percent), "arrogant" (48 percent), or "angry" (30 percent). In fact, about a third (31 percent) of female respondents agree that black women often limit our potential for new relationships by holding on to past hurts. The men surveyed put that number much higher, at 59 percent. These are just a few indications of the *deep disconnect* between what black women and black men see as the barriers to their love connection, a topic I carefully explore in Chapters 4 and 5. In a rare instance of agreement, however, almost half of black men and black women (49 percent and 46 percent, respectively) say that differing career and/or life goals is why we have a difficult time finding a compatible black man.

The good news is that of the one-third (35 percent) of the black women in our survey who identify themselves as married, a majority of them (66 percent) say they are happy in their union and sexually satisfied.

The black women we polled for this book are women of great faith, attending church services regularly and turning to prayer and meditation to deal with life's challenges. But unfortunately, our faith doesn't set our spirit free when it comes to dealing with our sensuality, our sexuality, and difficult issues from our past. Interestingly, less than half (46 percent) connect their overall sense of well-being to being in an intimate, loving, committed sexual relationship. Many of the women of faith I interviewed have deeply conflicted feelings about our sexuality that is rooted in "sex is dirty" teachings from their childhood. For almost half of the women, brutal sexual experiences as girls or young women may contribute to their uneasiness about sex: a heart-wrenching 46 percent say they've been a victim of sexual molestation, sexual abuse, or rape. Unfortunately, from what professionals tell me, that number is likely underreported, which is why I devote an entire chapter (Chapter 7) to the topic of sexual abuse and black women.

Our faith also challenges society mores about sex. It would have us reject the "new rules" of dating, by which sex (and a whole lot else) before marriage is the norm. However, married or not, only 2 percent of respondents claim they are virgins. More than half (56 percent) have engaged in casual friends-with-benefits/jump-off sex, but we're not feeling good about our choices.

Our faith also isn't helping us be more forgiving. The study shows that the more religious a woman considered herself, the *less likely* she was to forgive when presented with four hypothetical scenarios of wrongdoing. (See Chapter 8.)

Despite our enormous strides and achievements in life, accomplished black women still feel that we are facing bigger challenges in life than white women. For example, 78 percent feel "finding a suitable husband" is more of a problem for black women, and 66 percent think we face more difficulties providing for our families. (No wonder 60 percent cite financial pressure/debt as the problem most likely to damage our emotional health and give us a case of the blues.) Almost two-thirds (64 percent) say we're more likely to suffer from stress-related diseases than our white peers.

## The State of Denial

THE RESEARCH FOR this book confirms what many of us have long suspected: A very large number of successful black women are neither happy nor fulfilled. Too many of us are living in *the state of denial.*

We are in denial about the poor state of our emotional health and wellness. We are in denial about the fact that many of us are angry, bitter, and broken down by our own inability to forgive those who have wronged us. We are in denial about the way we really see each other and the way we treat each other as black women. We are in denial about the generational rule book being handed down to us, full of behaviors and myths that are rooted in slavery, poverty, and racism.

We are in denial about the hardships of going it alone; we think it is somehow a badge of courage, or we tell ourselves that it is God's plan for our lives. We are in denial about how much self-imposed pressure we feel to perform in the workplace and the toll that it takes on our physical health. We are in denial about the hidden land mines that threaten the union of our spirituality and sexuality. We are in denial about our responsibility to speak honestly as we are called to mentor and encourage the next generation of young black women.

We are in denial about the mounting financial and family pressures we face in a very fragile U.S. economy. We are in denial about our roles and responsibilities in the many interpersonal relationships that we have shattered, lost, or destroyed along the way. And most critically, we are in denial about how much we need each other and how much being connected to other black women is central to our survival. As a result, we are like pressure cookers ready to blow our tops at people—that is, if we haven't already pushed them away.

*Is it any wonder that we are often perceived as difficult?* If we are not walking around aggravated, many of us are riddled with anxiety. We are hurried, harried, worried, and stressed. We often feel straitjacketed. As a result, many of us have retreated and drawn inward. We may appear put together on the outside, but inside many of us are deeply troubled. In short, sisters, we need to muster the courage to face the truth and redefine our lives.

In the chapters that follow, I shed a bright (and sometimes painful) light on the significant issues—good and bad—that are affecting and shaping the lives of successful black women. I do so in a way that I hope is compassionate, factual, enlightening, and inspiring. My goal is to provide some new insights and perspectives, solutions, and strategies for how sisters can successfully redefine our reality to become the well-rounded, happy, satisfied, loving black women we want to be. It's time to reflect on how to build *a fulfilled life* based on good physical and mental health, strong friendships, meaningful intimate relationships, a loving family, an exciting career path, service to the community, and, most important, a well-nurtured soul.

My quest in this book is to find out two things: (1) If black women are as strong as the portrayals of us suggest, why do so many of us feel angry, depressed, isolated, weary, and lost? (2) What is really working in the lives of happy sisters who are thriving professionally, emotionally, physically, and relationally?

Let me be clear on one important point. Although I want to make an honest assessment of our situation, the last thing that black women need is more criticism and condemnation. That is why I wanted this book to offer fresh research, diverse expert opinion, and clear-eyed advice on how to make our lives richer, more rewarding, and more fulfilling on all fronts.

Some of my sisters out there will find *Black Woman Redefined* deeply disturbing. They will self-defensively try to debunk the book's research and negate the challenges that many of us need to explore if we want better lives. That is to be expected.

Many younger sisters are quick to quip that they are "sexy, single, and satisfied," and perhaps at times we are all of those things. These are the girls who see being called "bitch" as a compliment and not a reproach, as it was when my mother and I were coming of age. But, baby girls, let me tell you this: life begins to look different as we age. Some women like living in denial, and that is fine. Let them continue to cover, duck, and dodge the very truth they must embrace if they plan to be free of what is really holding them back.

I invite all black women to be brave enough to *accept responsibility* for some of our unhappiness. That will require some serious self-examination and reflection. Sisters, this book is not the *be all and end all*. Rather, I see it as a serious conversation starter for black women, with ourselves, our sisters, our families, our men, and our community.

This book is my testament to those of us who have *seemingly conquered the world but have yet to successfully conquer ourselves.* So what does it mean to conquer oneself? It means that you know your worth and your value. It means understanding that *you* are the most important asset in your life and that you only live once—so you had better live the hell out of this life while you have it!

# BLACK WOMEN, STRENGTH, AND OUR BEGINNINGS

*M*ost stories of black women's lives under slavery have never been told. Slave masters routinely brutalized black girls and women, justifying their dehumanizing treatment by labeling them 'sexual savages.' Stripped, beaten, raped and forced to work as 'breed sows,' black women suffered a double burden under slavery because of their sex.

Carla Wilson,
"Black Women's Narratives of Slavery,
the Civil War, and Reconstruction"

# 2

## OUR CONTEXT FROM SLAVERY TO THE WHITE HOUSE:

### Why It Still Matters

"People are trapped in history and history is trapped in them."

—JAMES A. BALDWIN, *Notes of a Native Son*

*I* know what you are all thinking right now: *Oh no, not again. Why is she talking about slavery? What does that have to do with me or my life as an accomplished black woman right now?* Or if you are not a black person, you are bristling for some kind of guilt attack. Don't.

We all know that discussions about race and slavery in America usually spark great division and deep resentment. One only has to look back at the summer of 2009 and the Henry Louis Gates dustup with Officer James Crowley in Cambridge, Massachusetts, for a vivid example of racial controversy. As another example, in April 2010, Gates wrote a very controversial piece in the *New York Times* titled "Ending the Slavery Blame-Game," in which he calls on our first black president to end the nation's sense of responsibility for the legacy of slavery. Gates argues that the fact that Africans themselves were complicit in the slave trade should negate the responsibility of the United States government to pay reparations or apologize for the evils of slavery.[1]

As you can imagine, his article caused great outcry and resentment from black scholars and the black media. According to historian and author Barbara Ransby, who wrote the award-winning book *Ella Baker and the Black Freedom Movement*, "Gates' essay fits conveniently into the new discourse on post-racialism. Slavery was long ago, the story goes, and Black Americans have come such a long way. So, we need to stop embracing 'victimhood,' get over it and move on. We need to stop complaining and 'end the blame game,' with regards to racism. After all, doesn't the election of Barack Obama relegate racism to the dustbins of history?" Ransby goes on to refute these ideas, countering that "'the past' is not so long ago. . . . [W]e don't have to go back to Jim Crow to see the ravages of American racism, a racism that took hold under slavery."[2]

I think Ransby is on point. We seem to be living at a time in which any discussion of race and our complicated racial history is viewed as politically incorrect or divisive. It is as if we now operate in a state of moral blindness that allows us to all get along peaceably on the surface until the next racial firestorm starts and we all take sides and start yelling at one another from the fringes. Without a doubt, the biggest blight on our history is slavery. And I think we need to talk about it again and again until we bring healing to our nation and to the people who still suffer under its odious legacy.

"Slavery," as former secretary of state Condoleezza Rice once said, "is our nation's great birth defect." The late, great historian John Hope Franklin, on the sixtieth anniversary of his book *From Slavery to Freedom*, said, "America had not yet confronted the issue of slavery." This is a troubling truth, considering that this nation confronted the *question* of slavery in the form of the Civil War way back in the 1860s.

Given this backdrop, why is it that when we raise the issue of slavery as a legitimate basis to explain some of our current social, familial, relational, and financial challenges, we are immediately dismissed as wanting to remain perpetual victims or, worse, as wanting our white counterparts to feel guilt for what their ancestors did to ours? I want to be very clear that that is *not* my intention in writing this chapter. I am *not* interested in blame. I am *not* interested in victimhood, I am *not* interested in reparations, and I am *not* interested in apologies. *Those are political issues.* I am interested in healing for my sisters. It is time that we helped black women understand that we have a very unique context and a very cruel beginning here in America and that, *like it or not*, we are still feeling the effects of that context.

As I mentioned at the outset, sisters, I am on a mission in this book to change the national dialogue surrounding black women. I want to turn the conversation from one about all that is wrong with black women to one about all that is right with us. We need to talk about our context in an open and candid way that helps us all (regardless of race or gender) move beyond the "definitions" of black women that are deeply rooted in the institution of slavery. Every one of us has a context—a beginning, a root—and it is key for us, as we seek to redefine the images of black women over the past several centuries, to explore our roots so we can address these definitions and move beyond them.

My goal in this chapter is to address *four issues* that I think may help us gain a better understanding of our historical context as black women and the deep issues confronting us as a new generation of powerful black women in America. The first issue I discuss is how slavery and its aftermath have left black women with a poor self-image and how we still see ourselves as "beasts of burden" who are undeserving of love and happiness. The second issue I address is how slavery still has an impact on black women and black men relationally today. The third issue I address is the vestiges of slavery and how are they still affecting our lives economically and socially in the year 2011. Fourth, I examine how slavery shaped the black family structure in America, how that influence plays out today in our community, and what we can do to move beyond the struggle.

For a long time, when our nation has focused on the "black community," the attention has been rightly centered on the plight of the black man. Conferences, news articles, government programs, and media attentions have been focused on black male difficulties and challenges since the 1980s. For the record, I support that attention and think it is important; however, in our efforts to save our black men, we have neglected the backbone of our culture, our race, and our families: the strong, independent black woman.

Until now, America has paid little or no attention to the worth and value of black women (beyond Oprah and some other luminaries). In many respects, no matter our accomplishments, we were simply invisible or, at best, told to be seen and not heard, lest we be perceived as too aggressive.

*Enter Michelle Obama.* There can be no doubt that First Lady Michelle Obama is the culmination of generations of strong black women, and our elders' greatest hopes and dreams for us as black women. She has achieved it all: a world-class education, a successful career, financial security, a handsome and successful black husband, beautiful children, a strong faith in God, an abiding love for her mother, and a passion for the well-being of the next generation of young people in America.

What is rarely discussed about our First Lady is that she is a fifth-generation descendant of slaves. Her maternal great-great-great-grandmother, Melvinia Shields, was an illiterate slave girl from South Carolina who was sold for $475.00 to a plantation near Rex, Georgia, when she was just six years old. As a young teenager, she was impregnated by an unknown white man and became the mother of Michelle Obama's great-great-grandfather.[3] History may never tell us who Michelle's great-great-great-grandfather was, but given Melvinia's situation, we can surmise that she was likely forcibly raped or coerced into her first sexual experience. "No one should be surprised anymore to hear about the number of rapes and the amount of sexual exploitation that took place under slavery; it was an everyday experience," said Jason A. Gillmer, a law professor at Texas Wesleyan University who has researched liaisons between slave owners and slaves.[4]

We all know of the president's mixed heritage as half African and half American, but what I find of greater interest is the unobvious mixed heritage of our First Lady. Why? Because, unlike Barack's lineage, which does not include slaves, it highlights the fact that America was born from a complicated history of miscegenation, bred most often by sexual violence against black women, that still flows unsuspected in the bloodlines of many African Americans. The reason I raise this delicate issue is because I want us as black women to understand that our First Lady, though she is an accomplished, strong black woman, is also a product of the ugly history of slavery in America. And if she can overcome that legacy and her humble roots by becoming the most powerful and fulfilled woman in the world, so can we.

I know that many of you younger sisters out there don't believe that slavery (or its vestiges) has anything to do with your existence as an educated, sophisticated black woman of the twenty-first century, but I would venture to say it has *everything* to do with who you are and how you see yourself as a woman. I don't say this to downplay your personal responsibility for your own choices in life or to somehow make excuses for our own shortcomings and issues as black women. But it is so very important for anyone reading this book to stop and truly understand the historical forces that have shaped black women and are the root of some of the most pervasive and damaging stereotypes about us as black women. Thus, I would be remiss if I did not begin telling our story by taking a look back at from whence we came.

Sisters, this is where our journey to discovering fulfillment must begin if we are to truly grasp what has happened to our self-image over the last several centuries right up to today. So let's have some straight talk on this sensitive subject.

First, narratives and myths about any group of people that have gone uncorrected or unchallenged for centuries have power. And once something has power over you and defines you negatively, it is very hard to get out from under that power and definition in a way that allows you to be your best self. Second, as you will read in the chapters that follow, some of the problems that black women struggle with most are rooted in slavery, Jim Crow, and a dysfunctional tradition of covering our hurts, not being allowed to acknowledge our pain, and suffering through life even when we appear to have it all together on the outside. This has made many of us hardened, broken, and unforgiving.

I believe we have some collective work to do. We need to identify the generational "curses" and legacies that many of us have inherited from our own families, dating back to our great-great-ancestors, and we need to learn to forgive. Some of us are carrying generational pain, and it's time to let it go. *I know. Trust me.* This context is why we have such a hard time feeling truly valued, loved, and worthy of the rest, self-care, compassion, and respect that all human beings deserve. And why we tend to hold on so tight when someone or something wounds us.

## *How We See Ourselves and Where It Starts*

MY DEAR SISTERS, despite all of our successes and accomplishments, we have been *defined* for generations by someone else's version of history and our role in that history. We have been defined by outright mythology that started on the plantations of the Deep South several hundred years ago and persists to this very day. That mythology has painted us as the always happy and robust Aunt Jemima, the always sexually available and complicit Sally Hemings, the always strong runaway Harriet Tubman, or the always dutiful and obedient Mammy, like Hattie McDaniel's Oscar-winning character in the movie *Gone with the Wind*.

None of these images paints us as who we truly are at our core: soft, feminine, sacred, valued, vulnerable, and sensual. Sisters, you cannot outrun your history. None of us can. All we can do is stare it down, dissect it as best we can, learn from it, and choose what we do with it from there. Our value as humans was diminished from the moment we boarded the slave ships for the transatlantic crossing to America in the early 1600s. Our value as women was crushed from the moment we became sexual objects on those slave ships and later in the dark, dank corners of southern plantations, subject to the cruelty of strange men who violated our bodies, our minds, and our spirits over and over again.

*Sisters, don't miss this:* slavery dehumanized black women by robbing them of the ability to fulfill their most basic emotional needs—love, value, and personal power. Through the rape and abuse by their white male owners, and because of a legally sanctioned system that prevented them from marrying and having functional families, they lost their personal dignity, their humanity, and their worth as women. When they bore children, they endured the worry of not being able to protect their children from the evils of slavery.

As women, one of our contexts has to do with our image of beauty and our value. For the American black woman, that image began during the time of slavery. I know that people want to dismiss this as silly; how could we still be affected by events that occurred over three hundred years ago, right? Well, think of it like this: regardless of our race or gender, we can all agree that the family teaches us our first life lessons, and those lessons get passed down from generation to generation. In black families, some of the most common lessons go something like this: "It has always been this way in our family" or "This is how we do it." "We don't air our dirty laundry." "Your daddy was no good." "Your great-grandmother liked the lighter grandchildren more than she did the darker ones."

We have all heard these types of things in our families, for better or worse. I interviewed one sixty-year-old black woman who was born and raised in the Washington, D.C., area who told me that her mother had twelve children by twelve different men, and she kept the lighter-skinned kids and gave the darker ones away to their grandmother. This woman was one of the darker kids, and I could still feel the pain of her experience in her voice as she shared her story with me. She, in turn, had children by several men, and now her granddaughters are emulating the same patterns. Someone has to break the cycle of hurt and pain.

In her narrative *Incidents in the Life of a Slave Girl*, Harriet Jacobs (originally using the pen name Linda Brent) chronicles her experiences as a slave and the various humiliations she had to endure in that unhappy state. She also deals with the particular evils suffered by women of her station. Often in the book, she will point to a particular punishment that a male slave endured at the hands of slaveholders and comment that, although she finds the punishment brutal in the extreme, it cannot compare to the abuse that young women like her faced while still on the edge of girlhood.

More impactful is her suggestion that "beauty is a curse" to female slaves and her observation of how unnatural it is that "that which commands admiration in the white woman only hastens the degradation of the female slave."[5] Beauty usually meant being mulatto or light-skinned. But even those slaves who were not deemed beautiful suffered, because they too often lost their innocence at the hands of their white male owners.

Jacobs presents a stirring portrait of nineteenth-century slavery, under which female slaves were sexually abused and the white women were left with intense resentment, degradation, and embarrassment because of their husbands' open adultery and sexual abuse of these slave women. In her jealousy and rage, the white mistress often didn't recognize, or refused to acknowledge, that these sexual episodes weren't consensual and had nothing to do with romantic love.

The white women, as Jacobs writes poignantly in her book, were forced to find their dignity in the degradation of black women, reminding themselves that these women were not truly a threat, because at the end of the day, they were "just slaves."[6] So white women, much like black women, were also powerless, but sadly it was the black women who felt the wrath of their frustration. By positioning the issue of sex as an unspoken but constant dividing line between white women and black women, slavery damaged the natural affinity these women should have had for one another, and that division perhaps persists today.

So how do the abuses that black women suffered as slaves affect our lives as black women now? In her famous rant "Ain't I a Woman?"[7] freed slave Sojourner Truth highlighted the paradox between how women were supposed to be treated and the stark reality for black women of her day. Women are supposed to be cared for, doted on, and honored by the men who love them. Yet for many black woman in America, this has never been our reality. To the brothers reading, please pay attention; this is important.

Our first experiences as innocent slave girls had to do with being abandoned, violated, and treated like farm animals to be bred and sold off. The physical intimacy that we experienced was based not in love or admiration but in raw physical lust and abuse. We were never adored or loved. In fact, we weren't viewed as women but as sex objects to be used at will, beaten, and raped. Not only could our owners sleep with us at will, but any man visiting the plantation as a guest could sleep with us without our consent. We were forced to service the white men who owned us and endure the frustration of the black men we loved. Our men could not protect us and consequently became broken, emasculated, and angry. And they often directed their anger toward us.

Unfortunately, violence by black men is not just a thing of the past. Many accomplished, professional, well-educated black women (in our survey, almost 50 percent) have been the victims of rape, sexual abuse, or sexual violence in their lives at the hands of black men. What does that say about how far we have come from the slave narratives above?

To better understand what our elders endured, I took a personal journey to South Carolina this past summer (where my paternal grand-mother's family is from) and spent several days at a three-hundred-year-old plantation near Charleston. Many of you have seen this plantation, with its famous Avenue of the Oaks, in Alex Haley's miniseries *Queen*, starring Halle Berry, or in the epic Civil War miniseries (based on John Jakes's trilogy) *North and South*, starring the late Patrick Swayze. I wanted to truly feel my own words. I wanted you as the reader to feel them also. If I was really going to understand our context as black women, I could not think of a better place to do this than at a southern plantation where there are original slave cabins still standing.

Our collective context as black women existed in Africa long before America, but our American history is more recent and perhaps more poignant. I felt that sitting in the slave cabins, walking the plantation grounds, and taking in their still-palpable energy might bring me a step closer to a better understanding of myself and of all of us.

*Close your eyes, and be still. Now imagine you are here with me.* If you listen closely, you can hear them walking about, doing their chores, tending to their babies, cutting wood, washing clothes, cleaning the mas-ter's mansion, picking cotton and rice, singing hymns, and wondering when, if ever, a new day will come. But imagine that you are not a visitor from the twenty-first century. This is no historical reenactment or imag-inary exercise. Imagine that *you were sold here. You work here. You live here. And it is here (if you are not sold off) that you will die.*

*Tears come to my eyes because I can feel the spirits of these women.* I can feel the strength and faith that it must have taken to survive such unimaginable and unnecessary cruelty. I can feel their hopelessness and the senseless inhumanity they endure each day. I cannot fathom, however, the emotional steel it must have taken to endure the endless rape, humil-iation, and beatings at the hands of the white men who owned and had power over them. It all started here on the plantation. This is where our mothers, grandmothers, and aunts *taught us how to survive the worst that life had to offer.* They taught us to be strong—so strong that, hundreds of years later, many of us have become hard and impenetrable.

There was *nobody* to comfort these black women. *Nobody* to wipe their tears. So they learned to take care of themselves. They learned to turn inward. They learned to be *strong.*

Sound familiar?

Buckle up here, because this may get rough.

You see, until we have this conversation in the *open*, and *stop* dis-missing the power of our history—how we came to this country, how we were treated, how we were viewed, and how we have been defined ever since—we (and others) will not grasp why many of us are still struggling with self-esteem, self-love, self-definition, and self-worth.

We can learn powerful lessons from the plantation. This is where we became hardwired to cope with life's challenges and disappointments. I would venture to say that our legendary strength is now a part of our DNA. As I sat there on the cotton dock near the river and further took in the sights and sounds of the once robust plantation, I could see myself in the women who once lived there. They too were strong, fierce, loyal, compassionate, hardened, tough, smart, and yet isolated in many respects. They too must have longed for the devoted love of a good man who could cover them, lessen their burdens, and protect them. They too must have hoped for a better future for their sons and daughters.

Slavery was about power and economic prosperity for white male land-owners. For black women, it solidified our place on the last rung of the ladder to personal prosperity and freedom. I submit to you that we are still feeling the effects of this legacy today, and therefore we need to redefine our beginning. We need to rewrite the script and define for ourselves who we are and who we want the world to see us as in this new millennium.

But our past does not end at slavery, folks. As America entered the period known as "Jim Crow" after Reconstruction in the 1870s through the 1960s, the strong black woman faced new challenges. She endured working long hours for low wages as a housemaid, nanny, or cook to wealthy southern whites. She was often a critical financial stake-holder in her family as the black man struggled to find work against the backdrop of racism—a situation that marked a turn away from the prevailing patriarchal American culture of that time. Worse, many historic accounts and interviews from that era tell us that black women continued to be the victims of domestic violence, incest, sexual abuse, verbal assaults, and powerlessness—not so much at the hands of white men, however, but at the hands of black men. Many times we covered up our abuse—and still do—because we feel responsible for the black man's unhappiness and pain. We cower in silence to protect him because we understand how unkind life has been to him at times. But we need to recognize that the time has come for us to love ourselves. Sisters, you don't owe anyone your life or your peace of mind. You don't have to do what great-grandmamma did to survive the times in which she lived. You are free now. You are free to be loved, cherished, adored, and valued. *Embrace it.*

Our narrative needs to change from one of being "sick and tired" to one that says: "I am worthy of rest. I am worthy of happiness. I am worthy of fulfillment in my life."

We are the women who carry it all, do it all, handle it all, and have to *be* it all for everyone *all the time.* Unfortunately, when we are in need, or when we ache, there is rarely a shoulder to cry on unless we are still blessed enough to have our mothers, aunts, or grandmothers with us. Perhaps that is why so many of us shrink back from asking for help or accepting it when it is sincerely offered. We have come to depend on ourselves over everything and everyone else because too many of us have been disappointed and hurt by life, by our men, by our friends, and mostly by our own choice to try and be *all things to all people.*

Many of us have said that we feel both blessed and cursed to be a strong black woman. Once again, I think this is where we need to redefine ourselves. The *blessing* of being a strong black woman is that, if not for our strength and courage, we would not have survived the horrors of our past. The black race would likely not have survived either. The *curse,* however, is that we have become so conditioned to being strong all the time that we have forgotten how to turn it *off* and be rested, still, loving, well-loved, gentle, compassionate, life-giving souls that speak life into one another and into ourselves.

Our context as slave women gives us a framework for understanding the events that have shaped us as successful black women. The bottom line is this: being a black woman in America has never been easy. Being a professional or otherwise accomplished black woman in America can be downright difficult. It is not that we are not up to the task; nor is it that we feel incapable of succeeding in the most challenging of circumstances. Quite the contrary. But in our subconscious, we are still "less than," we still have to work twice as hard, and we still have to prove our worth. We still feel that incessant need to cover, deny, go it alone, and be strong at all costs. In the workplace, many of us feel isolated and at times invisible, which I will address at length in the next chapter. We silently fight against damaging stereotypes, such as those most often cited by our black men, that paint us as uncompassionate, unloving, hard, too strong, and too independent.

## Why He Hates You: Understanding Black Male-Female Relationship Dynamics

THE MOST ENDURING and damning legacy of slavery is that it changed the natural order of black male and female relationships from the way they were originally formed in Africa. Before African men and women were brought to America as slaves, the African man was in many cases a strong warrior, provisional farmer, brave hunter, or a tribal leader. All stations were respected and honored in the homeland. He courted his wife-to-be, families lived together in villages, and women were revered and honored as precious jewels, helpmates, and partners. As a proud African man, he was his woman's strength, her protector, and her lover, whom she respected and loved in return.

All that changed during the course of slavery. The black man was rendered powerless to protect, provide for, and uplift his female counterpart—something his African culture had taught him to do from the time he was a boy. Now, he was like a fish out of water. He was lost, stripped of his masculinity, which was held in high esteem and made him honorable in African culture. In America, black men were called "boys," "niggers," or worse. They had no authority, no education, and no ability to make a life for themselves or their loved ones outside the plantations on which they labored.

During slavery and the Jim Crow era that followed, black men were routinely brutalized, lynched, and emasculated (in the presence of their wives and children), and they were often helpless to protect their loved ones from harm. We've all heard the term "angry black woman," but I think we need to discuss the evolution of the "angry black man" for a moment.

While conducting the research for this book, I interviewed a number of black men who came of age in the 1970s, and they said one of the things that disturb them about the modern-day interaction between black men and women is that upwardly mobile, educated young black women have no protectors. One successful Harvard Business School graduate in his late fifties said, "If somebody messed with a sister on campus, the brothers would get together and go deal with that person, be he white or black. At one point in my undergraduate days at another Ivy League school in the east, we actually burned down a white fraternity house on campus because a sister had been sexually assaulted."

"There are no consequences now for bad behavior against black women," said Dr. Floyd Hayes, professor of political science and coordinator for the Center for Africana Studies at Johns Hopkins University. "In the 70s, if some black woman was accosted by a man, we would go after him; if someone was mistreated, we protested. Now we submit because we do not want to lose our 'stuff.'" Hayes said in our interview that this is a direct result of the 1980s Cosby decade excesses. "Parents in the 1980s and 1990s stopped teaching our young people about race and racism because they assimilated. We had no models There has been a breakdown in the transfer of values and mores over the past twenty years, and we are reaping the results of that failure on our part."

One of the most enlightening and challenging interviews I conducted for this book was with well-respected author and independent documentary filmmaker Janks Morton. Morton is the author of the book *Why He Hates You!: How Unreconciled Maternal Anger Is Destroying Black Men and Boys.* The very title of this book stopped me in my tracks when I saw it. I read the book cover to cover in about two days. I asked Morton to share with us why he wrote the book and, more importantly, what he sees as the root cause of the seeming complexity, hostility, and difficulty of black male and female relationships. Morton said, "The root is between black men and their mothers. Not their fathers, as everyone presumes." He continued:

I know because I resented my mother for years, until I finally found the courage to confront those emotions and not push them down.

There is pathology on the souls of black folks. One of the most debilitating yet unspoken issues in the black community is the "deification" of the black female matriarch. Black men are not held in high esteem anymore because they are largely absent from their families' lives. We as adult black people are allowed to confront the disappointment we feel with our fathers—it's encouraged by our culture—because fathers are less valued. But if we have issues with our mothers and the things they did to us, or if we question the choices they made that caused us harm, we are damned to hell if we speak up about it.

The primary authority figure in our community is black women, and this dates back to slavery. And to be frank, it is a doubled-edged sword. Think about it like this: for the past forty-five years in particular, more black women have been primarily responsible for the socialization and rearing of our young black children, particularly our black male children.

Morton's point is this: black males often harbor resentment toward the all-black, all-female structures in which they were reared. Many black boys grow up without a father in their lives at all, and the rejection, frustration, and hurt they feel turns on the women who are raising and caring for them.

A recent *Grio* article describes how single black moms now have to take their sons to baseball games and play catch with them. The article pointed to single black female parent households as one of the major factors keeping African American boys away from baseball. According to data compiled by the U.S. Census Bureau, nearly one in three black households (29 percent) are headed by single mothers, many of whom can't afford to take their kids to baseball games played in today's expensive ballparks. Traditionally, baseball has been a sport that boys learn from their fathers, but the numbers suggest that that father-son interaction is on the decline: in 1974, black men made up 27 percent of professional baseball players; in 2010, that number was less than 10 percent.[8]

I asked Morton some deeper questions about the issue of how black boys are growing up with a lot of anger toward black women and why in our modern relationships we see so many examples of black male violence against black women. He said:

One of the vestiges of slavery that is most pronounced is the suppression of black male emotions. Most black men I know, and have worked with in my clinical observations, are existing in what I call a "childlike space" because they are not reconciled with their mothers. I know what I am saying is taboo, but it has to be said. If black women are going to continue to be the primary caretakers of black male children, then we have to open up a dialogue and create a safe place where they can express their emotions in a constructive way that brings healing.

## The Economic and Social Vestiges of Slavery

ONE ONLY NEED recall the vivid images of displaced, poor, and homeless black people during Hurricane Katrina in 2005 to know that America still has a long way to go before black people achieve economic parity and, in some cases, possess even the most basic of human needs, like housing, food, and transportation. Although slavery ended in 1865, followed by Reconstruction, which ended in 1877, freed slaves, who had spent their lives being told what to do and were conditioned to follow orders rather than initiate thought, were left to their own devices to face "freedom" without resources, or that forty acres and a mule.

In his book *The Ethnic Myth*, Stephen Steinberg writes, "Ghettos are nothing less than the shameful residue of slavery."[9] Many scholars blame slavery for the pathologies in the black community such as homelessness, single-parent households, and youth violence.[10] Black scholar and Georgetown University Professor Michael Eric Dyson puts it like this: "The effect of slavery continues to exert its brutal influence in the untold sufferings of millions of everyday folk." He continues by saying that slavery is responsible for the prevalent residential separation between blacks and whites today.

But, as mentioned previously, when this issue is raised, it is dismissed with "Get over it," or "Black people need to help themselves." Part of the challenge, however, is not that America at large does not want to have this discussion but that many black folks simply do not want to acknowledge or talk about what slavery truly did to our history and our families. This is clear baggage that we carry as black women and as black people. Dr. Floyd Hayes explained it to me like this:

What happened out of the nineteenth century is that black people saw slavery as so humiliating that they wanted to escape it altogether.

They saw the end of slavery and the coming into the twentieth century as a period of opportunity and being industrious. Unlike our Jewish counterparts, who have embraced the mantra "never forget" [in reference to the Holocaust], our ancestors decided they would not talk about the past and instead move forward. Our mantra ironically became "We must forget." We learned to not be truthful with ourselves within our historical context. Segregation's impact on us as a people was enormous. [But] black people made a mental leap that we were not Africans but Americans, and we wanted to be part of the American community, so in many ways, we shed our culture and or our desire to know our culture. We made a decision on a subjective level that white is better.

## How Slavery Shaped Our Families

IF SO MANY of our ancestors, who survived the brutality of slavery and endured the degradation of legalized segregation, were able to migrate and find work, build lives, and nurture their families, why are our modern families in such disarray? As noted sociologist Dr. Andrew J. Cherlin suggests, "A black child had a better chance in slavery of being with both of his parents than he does in the present day."[11] Wow! If that does not wake us up, nothing will.

I spoke with Dr. Floyd Hayes about whether slavery is to blame for what appears to be the demise of the black family, and he had this to say:

Slavery has *some impact* in terms of our consciousness but not all. What black people have taught themselves is to be here-and-now people, with no appreciation of the past and no preparation for the future. But *slavery is not the culprit*—we have to look at the last thirty to forty years as being where the real damage was done. I think the challenge is that black parents stopped modeling for their kids and teaching them anything—it is an intergenerational disconnect. Post civil rights, many black parents abandoned their children [unconsciously] by striving for monetary wealth, and so we lost our foundation. Families were about pursuing wealth most clearly in the 1980s—the Cosby decade—so the origins of our modern-day drama are in more recent phenomenon versus slavery.

## *How Do We Move Forward and Overcome*
## *Such a Powerful Legacy of Pain?*

I KNOW MANY people will simply not want to see the critical connection that exists between us now in 2011 and our history as slaves. I will let those individuals stay in their place of denial, but I will maintain that there is stark, unsettling evidence that black women and men are still wrestling with the consequences of slavery, as is our entire nation.

In the chapters that follow, I hope to bring to light each of the critical issues that are affecting us both positively and negatively as accomplished black women. My goal is to provide some new insights, solutions, and strategies for how those of us who are over forty can successfully reinvent and reposition ourselves and how those who are under thirty can best prepare to become well-rounded black women of true success—the success that comes with building *a balanced life* that is based on loving relationships, a good education, good physical and mental health, an exciting career path, a family, service to one's fellow man, and most importantly, care of the soul.

# PART II

# How We Work and Love

"Your best individual work-life balance will vary over time, often on a daily basis. The right balance for you today will probably be different for you tomorrow. The right balance for you when you are single will be different when you marry, or if you have children; when you start a new career versus when you are nearing retirement."

—Jim Bird,
worklifebalance.com

Our deepest fear is not that we are inadequate. Our deepest fear is that we are powerful beyond measure. It is our light, not our darkness, that most frightens us. We ask ourselves, Who am I to be brilliant, gorgeous, talented, fabulous? Actually, who are you *not* to be? You are a child of God. Your playing small doesn't serve the world. . . . [A]s we let our own light shine, we unconsciously give other people permission to do the same. As we are liberated from our own fear, our presence automatically liberates others.

Marianne Williamson,
*A Return to Love*

# 3

## CHANGING THE GAME:

### Redefining Ourselves
### in the Twenty-First-Century
### Workplace

"A successful woman is one who can lay a firm foundation with
the bricks others have thrown at her."

—DAVID BRINKLEY

*D*on't hate the player; hate the game." We've all heard that
famous phrase, and nowhere is it more on point than in the twenty-first-
century workplace. Sisters, the time has come for us to master the rules
of the game—*and play to win.*

When former CNN White House correspondent Suzanne Malveaux
accepted the 2009 Essence/Southern Company Congressional Black
Caucus Journalist of the Year award, she offered a powerful perspective
on the new game board that we're all operating on. In her remarks, she
recounted her interview with then presidential candidate's wife Michelle
Obama during the 2008 campaign. I remembered watching that interview with pride and awe as these two phenomenal sisters easily conversed
and at times gently sparred over important issues of the day.

Malveaux explained how during the interview both women realized
the pivotal historical roles in which they'd been cast. There sat two confident, Harvard-educated black women on national TV doing their jobs—
one asking the questions and the other answering and representing the
man who would become the next leader of the free world. These were not

two black women on the outside looking in. Here was a well-respected black journalist and the wife of the Democratic presidential candidate (an accomplished professional in her own right) deeply embedded "in the game."

Citing the lineup of impressive black women in the Obama administration, Malveaux expressed optimism that the rules are changing and barriers are falling. She encouraged all of us to take hold of this unique time in history and build a new set of rules, new respect, and new opportunities for ourselves as black women.

I could not agree with her more. Accomplished black women must openly discuss strategies that will advance our careers far beyond where we stand today. It's too bad that careers don't come with a playbook, outlining the do's and don'ts of navigating the workplace gridiron. This chapter explores the established rules that we are expected to play by and the high cost many of us pay to stay in the game. We'll also explore the real secret to workplace success—relationships and how we handle them. A study published by the Carnegie Institute of Technology confirms that 15 percent of financial and career success is due to technical competence and 85 percent is due to interpersonal skills. This means that no matter how many degrees you've earned, what schools you attended, who you know, or how many mentors you have—it all comes down to how well you relate to people.

Years worth of well-documented professional studies and research have shown that most people who lose their jobs or find themselves stalled in their careers end up in these situations because they had high rates of absenteeism, exhibited unprofessional behavior, or did not "play well" with others, as defined by the workplace culture they were a part of. This is important to grasp, sisters: you are more likely to lose your job or get stalled in your career because of personality conflicts or workplace politics than you are because you are incompetent or unqualified for a job.

One story comes immediately to mind to underscore this point; a woman shared this story with me in our focus group, and I found it simply jaw-dropping. This woman was hired to come in at an executive level to a major defense contracting company, and she was the first black woman to be hired by that company at that level. During her first month on the job, she was flown in to meet the executive team at their annual meeting. She was introduced, all was well, and people were welcoming to her, until this very accomplished, well-credentialed sister raised her hand and spoke up at the meeting to share some important information with the team to protect them from a possible liability. She was informed a few weeks later by another senior executive of color (a black male) that her comments were not welcomed and that she was expected to be seen and not heard at this meeting. Her much older, white, male superiors resented her sharing information that they were not aware of first, and they felt it made them look bad. They met after that meeting and decided she did not fit in with their "culture." She lost her job shortly thereafter, and the company had to pay a fairly large out-of-court settlement to cover its deeds.

So what am I saying, sisters, is this: While racism, sexism, and discrimination are very much alive, and black women are in the crosshairs, the bigger issue we have to deal with is how to handle ourselves in the workplace from the lowest levels to the highest. The problem in the executive's story had more to do with her not knowing the "rules of the game" than her being incompetent or incapable of succeeding at her job. She rubbed the old boys wrong, and they wanted her out. A little mentoring or coaching of the culture she was entering into would have likely caused her to (1) not take the job, or (2) learn how to strategically navigate the terrain and begrudgingly win the respect of her colleagues.

More important, however, is the fact that even though African American women represent an important and growing source of talent, year after year Catalyst researchers report that black women represent only 1.1 percent of corporate officers in Fortune 500 companies.[1] Despite the fact that black women are graduating from college and professional schools in record numbers, the pipeline isn't clogged with young sisters climbing to the top. Just 27 percent of African Americans age sixteen or older work in the management or professional arena, and less than 1.2 percent of black females are executives in corporate America.[2]

Interestingly, these numbers seem virtually stuck at the same levels they were a decade or so ago. *How is this possible?* This dilemma has ignited a wide range of sophisticated research studies and helpful career-advice books targeted to sisters trying to find their way through the tricky corporate landscape. Before we get into the intriguing research findings and excellent insider's advice, consider these six probing personal questions. Your answers will be invaluable touchstones as you read through this chapter.

1. **Are you ready to reposition and redefine yourself as a first-class professional?**
2. **Are you willing to move beyond evaluating your station in life through the distorting prisms of racism and sexism?**
3. **Are you brave enough to listen closely to what professional colleagues and management are really saying about professional black women?**
4. **Are you prepared to take risks and move outside of your comfort zone to form strategic alliances with the power players in your organizations, no matter what race or gender? Specifically, are you willing to cultivate working relationships with senior-level white male executives?**
5. **Are you committed to leveling the playing field by mentoring, coaching, and sponsoring professional peers and younger African Americans through difficult workplace challenges and opportunities?**
6. **Are you ready to challenge second-class corporate citizenship and step up to a team leadership role?**

## *The Power of Definition*

SISTERS, WORDS ARE powerful. Words can define us *if we allow them to*.

When I think of accomplished black women, I think of Marianne Williamson's quotation that opens this chapter; and one line strikes me most of all, "Your playing small doesn't serve the world." So many times we have to play it small to make someone else feel big. We as black women are so often viewed through the lens of unflattering stereotypes. You've heard them all before: we're *angry, aggressive, pushy, hostile, too strong*, and *too independent*; we have *bad attitudes*, and we're *not team players*. These judgments subtly force us to turn inward and question our value. As powerful as any punch in the gut, they can make us question ourselves and shy away from who we are uniquely designed to be.

Whether we feel these descriptions are true or not doesn't matter. *Perception is reality*, and perhaps there is always a bit of truth embedded in stereotypes. Contrary to what we might think, though, our ABW research suggests that negative stereotypes of successful black women may not be as prevalent at the upper echelons of power. That could be good news, since this is the arena where most professionals and corporate leaders want to play. However, researchers caution us from being too optimistic, because senior executives simply may be less willing to admit their biases.[3] Either way, groundbreaking studies (including our research) reveal the complicated realities of the achieving black woman and expose a much more intricate set of barriers keeping us from breaking through the glass ceiling—and it's up to us to fix them.

## The Invisible Black Woman

CONSIDER THESE FINDINGS from a 2006 report by the American Bar Association (ABA) Commission on Women in the Profession titled, "*Visible Invisibility: Women of Color in Law Firms*":

> Women of color experience a double whammy of gender *and* race, unlike white women or even men of color who share at least one of these characteristics (gender or race) with those in the upper strata of management. *Women of color may face exclusion from informal networks, inadequate institutional support, and challenges to their authority and credibility.* They often feel isolated and alienated, sometimes even from other women.[4]

As the study clearly states, employees who are black and female carry *the burdens of both but the benefits of neither* of those distinct classifications.[5]

I nodded in agreement as I read this report. Why? One of its central themes is that black women and women of color in the legal profession often feel *invisible. How ironic.* As one blogger wrote on angryblack-woman.wordpress.com, "We [black women] are intensely scrutinized while remaining completely invisible." My take is that even though executives may not describe their accomplished black female col-leagues using the demeaning stereotypes I discussed previously, gen-eral perceptions of us make it easy to dismiss black women as unable to be power players. That, coupled with the fact that there are so few of us in the high-paying professions, not only makes us *feel* invisible; to a third of the American workforce, we truly *are* invisible. I found it fascinating that 39 percent of the white poll respondents in our ABW study did not work with any black women, compared to just 11 percent of black and 24 percent of Hispanics. This is a huge indicator of how little interaction still exists between black women and others in the workplace.

The validity of these findings was backed up in a new 2010 study conducted for the *Journal of Experimental Social Psychology*. Researchers Amanda Sesko and Monica Biernat examined the intriguing idea that black women are socially invisible by conducting a series of tests with photographs and conversations. In the experiments, participants were asked to recall who they saw in the photographs and who they remembered hearing in group conversations. In each instance, black women were the most likely to go unnoticed among white men, black men, and white women.

When discussing this reality with a friend, she recalled a comment made by the legendary African American economist Andrew Brimmer (the first black governor of the Federal Reserve Board): "The primary goal of a corporation is to make money, not to make [its] employees feel good." *Okay. I get that.* But the goal certainly isn't to make a significant segment of its hardest working, dedicated, and competent team players feel bad, *right? I know. I know.* I'm preaching to the choir, here. *It is what it is*, and we need to deal with it, so let's start with the issue of perception. How others perceive us can be a powerful catalyst in how we choose to use (or not use) our God-given talents and abilities.

What do black professional women want? We want what every career-minded professional wants: an equal opportunity to be part of the team, to compete, to deliver, to excel, to advance, and to grow into successful professionals regardless of race or gender.

As a new generation of black female professionals, we must take ownership of poet William Ernest Henley's credo: "I am the master of my fate: I am the captain of my soul."[6] This mind-set demands that we take a hard look at ourselves and what we may be doing to contribute to stereotypes and negative perceptions about successful black women. We also need to read between the lines in reports like the ABA's. For example, it's up to us to initiate the liaisons we'd like to make with important people in our organizations and professions.

*I know this will not sit well with many of you out there, so sisters, let me be direct*: It's easy to point the finger, lament, and get swallowed up in the long-standing workplace inequities, biases, professional humiliations, racial ridicule, ugly stereotypes, and gender discrimination that we *all* endure, in and out of work. It's distressing to hear what people are thinking about black women—and knowing that it comes from all fronts: Caucasians, Hispanics, black men, and even other black women. *So hear me out.* I am not blaming black women for responding to the racism and sexism with anger or outrage. We must fight discrimination and prejudice together whenever possible. Diversity and inclusion are important efforts to rally around. Making sure that our institutions and corporations hire and advance enlightened executives, corporate leaders, and progressive human resource departments is critical to racheting up the woeful numbers of people of color in senior-level positions. However, this chapter is designed to help you fine-tune your individual game plan for success. As I have said over and over again (and will keep saying), *we must conquer self first.*

We must take control of our own destiny and stop wasting energy trying to change racist or sexist people who refuse to recognize our value. We may be able to enlighten a few, but the only one each of us can change is herself, and that's where our reassessment and redefinition must begin. How we respond to workplace slights, attacks, and unpleasantness will have a huge impact on how we are perceived in the wider workplace. A positive approach to such workplace realities is imperative for black women on the success track. Plainly put, we must be more *strategic* about who we are, what we bring to the table, and what we want from our professional lives. We must take stock of our professional battle scars and transform them into a powerful force for change. Our sights must broaden to spur collective as well as individual victories. We must play down our weaknesses and better leverage our strengths, achievements, and leadership skills. And we must build stronger, more diverse networks and alliances. Above all, we need to take better care of ourselves and each other physically, mentally, and spiritually.

Unmanaged stress, combined with the heavy baggage we're carrying up the career ladder, is a toxic combination. As unfair as it may be, this lethal combo is fueling much of the hostile attitude everyone's talking about. (Come on, we know it's true.) And it's making us sick. As we explore further in later chapters of this book, illness brought on by unexpressed emotions and workplace stress is serious.

We can't fight the good fight until we are battle-ready, sisters. Let's admit this right now so we can move on: The strong, frustrated, lone sister thing isn't really working for us, is it?

Frankly, I think we're still working through the post–civil rights era.

Granted, our challenges are not the same as what our parents and grand-parents endured during the Jim Crow era and the civil rights movement. They laid the groundwork for us to be the successes that many of us are. They marched so that we could ride. They sat so that we could stand at the gates of opportunity and become doctors, lawyers, actresses, profes-sional athletes, engineers, architects, scientists, film producers, college presidents, news anchors, journalists, and heads of state. But we still have our struggles. The "isms" that we face today are far subtler and more nefarious than they were during segregation and the women's move-ment of the 1970s. For example, rarely does discrimination play out by way of racial epithets or the obvious signs of bias that were so prevalent when my parents were growing up. You don't see signs saying, "No blacks or women allowed." Instead we deal with inherited gender bias, uncon-scious bias, or microinequities (concepts that suggest we all engage in stereotyping often without realizing it). For example, did you ever start a job at the same time as other younger or male colleagues, only to realize that you were the only one who didn't get a *plum* assignment right away? Remember the reason? Perhaps it was: "We're going to let you ease into this job." Or maybe you found out through the grapevine that you weren't placed on the slate of potential team leaders because you're a single mother and you probably need to leave work earlier than other candidates.

## How Others See Us—It's Better Than You Think

LIKE SOME OF the polling and data trends I reviewed of generations past, our research reveals that some long-standing attitudes about black women in the workplace may be shifting for the better. In a national research phone poll of 1,000 Americans (black, white, male, and female) conducted for this book, respondents were asked to choose from a list of descriptors to describe professional black women in their workplace. Fifty-seven percent view the black women as "capable" and "skilled," 57 percent view them as "intelligent," 54 percent see them as "independent," and 49 percent consider them "accomplished." Only 15 percent view professional black women they know as "controlling," and 13 percent view them as "angry," "arrogant," or "unfulfilled." (See Table 3.1.) Don't get me wrong. I'm not stuck on word games. But knowing where we stand is necessary to move forward.

ourselves and the next generation of black women professionals. We must be sleek, subtle, and sophisticated in how we wage our workplace battle. To help you get started, I've excerpted key findings from two well-regarded studies on professional black women and women of color in my profession: the law. These reports clarify one of the main reasons so many black women (like me) leave private practice and go elsewhere— simply put, the stress and strain of fighting is often just not worth the price you pay in health and wellness.

The 2006 ABA report *Visible Invisibility: Women of Color in Law Firms*, mentioned previously, offers these insights:

> The career experiences of women of color in this study differed dramatically from those of their peers and from white male counter-parts in particular. Nearly half of women of color but only 3% of white men experienced demeaning comments or harassment. Unlike white men, many women of color felt that they had to disprove negative preconceived notions about their legal abilities and their commitment to their careers. . . . Women of color had mentors, but their mentors did not ensure that they were integrated into the firm's internal networks, received desirable assignments (especially those that helped them meet required billable hours), or had substantive contacts with clients. . . .
>
> Women of color often became stuck in dead-end assignments. . . . Nearly one-third of women of color but less than 1% of white men felt they received unfair performance evaluations. Sometimes their accomplishments were ignored by the firm or were not as highly regarded as those of their peers; sometimes their mistakes were exaggerated. Many women of color complained that they received "soft evaluations" which denied them the opportunity to correct deficits and gain experiences that could lead to promotions and partnership. Twenty percent of women of color but only one% of white men felt they were denied promotion opportunities.[9]

A 2009 study by the Executive Leadership Council provides a realistic snapshot of how we are perceived at the highest levels by our peers and, in particular, by white male executives and managers.

In a study of 132 senior executives and corporate leaders (which included black female executives, white male CEOs, and peers), one of the key findings was that black women executives/professionals do not

suffer from a lack of networking but instead from a lack of "comfortable, trusted, and strategic relationships at the senior level with those who are most different from themselves, most notably white males."[10] When white peers of black women were asked to explain their perceptions of black women executives, they made some very helpful observations worth sharing here:

- Black women tend to form more *support* networks than *strategic* networks.
- Black women collaborate well among themselves but have some difficulty feeling comfortable in an environment with white men.
- White men and black women have not formed close enough working relationships to understand each other. This needs to change.
- White men do not make it easier to cooperate when their discomfort level is heightened because of race and gender factors. One executive reported that some men in her business won't even have lunch or dinner with women, let alone black women.
- White men don't have a frame of reference. Most of them don't know any black women in the corporate setting. Black women need to be aware of this and work on it. It's up to them to take the lead here. The burden is on black women to navigate the environment successfully by creating their own map.[11]

If reading the findings of these reports upsets you, don't let your emotions get in your way. These important findings can help us rethink how we maneuver in a workplace that was designed without us in mind. As James Brown sang, "It's a man's world," but the workplace is becoming more female and more diverse each year. It's up to us to make this shifting trend work for us.

## Debunking the Myth of Affirmative Action

ONE OTHER ISSUE that we studied in our national sample was related to affirmative action programs. There is still a wide perception by a majority of whites that black women have benefited the most from this government-mandated program that was started under President Kennedy in 1961 and expanded by President Johnson to include women in 1965 (see Table 3.2).

TABLE 3.2: How much of a factor is affirmative action in advancing black women in the workplace?

| RESPONSE | PERCENTAGE OF RESPONDENTS |
|---|---|
| A very big factor | 22 |
| Somewhat of a factor | 38 |
| *Total affirmative responses* | 60 |
| A little bit of a factor | 13 |
| Not at all a factor | 17 |
| It depends | 3 |
| Don't know/unsure | 7 |
| *Total negative and neutral responses* | 30 |

Interestingly, the facts tell a different story. *White women have benefitted most from affirmative action programs across all academic and economic/ professional sectors.* The numbers don't lie: black women make up less than 2 percent of corporate executives, less than 2 percent of lawyers, and less than 1 percent of doctors, as opposed to their white female counterparts, who are also less likely to be unemployed, who make more money, and who have attained greater parity and success in the corporate ranks and professions, such as law, medicine, and higher education.

## The Grass Isn't Greener for Black Male Professionals

WHO KNEW THAT black men are *more* likely to perceive themselves as victims in some of the occupational categories than black women? One unanticipated revelation in our research on professional black males is that 73 percent of professional African American men cite "stress-related challenges" as the number-one obstacle they experience in the workplace, followed by being "stereotyped as angry or threatening," at 66 percent, and "hitting the glass ceiling and being denied advancement at work" and "providing for [their] family" at 46 percent each.[12]

This sentiment was further endorsed in our black male national focus group when a majority of the participants expressed exasperation with carrying the "black man's burden." "Every mistake I make as a black man I feel is counted doubly than if I were a white man," lamented one participant. A concept historically applied to the experiences of women in the workplace, the "glass ceiling" emerged as a contributor to lack of career mobility for 46 percent of the professional black male respondents. Surprisingly, more black men think "being denied advancement at work" is more of a problem for them than for black or white women. Only 38 percent of the respondents said black women have more challenges; 2 percent said white women do.

The value of our key findings on black males is that we know they also feel a great deal of stress related to overcoming stereotypes and perceptions about them in the workplace. Yet we know from various studies that black men have often helped to negotiate and translate the barriers between white men and black women in the workplace.[13] The one advantage that black men have over black women is that black men are male, and this sometimes helps them connect better with white men. That's why black men and black women in the workplace need to form more strategic and tactical alliances, and should work together more as a support system, because both are fighting to overcome similar individual barriers and obstacles. The question for many black men is how far they are willing to go out on a limb to help support and advance black women in the workplace when they themselves have to overcome similar stereotypes and barriers. Unspoken career tension leading to increased competition between black men and women may be a major contributor to the deterioration of black male and female personal relationships over the past twenty years.

When I interviewed white women in small groups and asked about their perceptions of the black women with whom they work, they were mostly positive, and the participants felt that black women and white women faced many of the same struggles and should work together to help one another advance in the workplace.[14] Although I agree that we should work together as women to help support, collaborate, and advance one another, it's important to distinguish those of us who feel the sting of gender *and* race bias in our society in general, as well as the historic social issues that apply uniquely to black professional women. My hope is that this chapter will help bridge that gap of understanding.

## Mentors, Coaches, Sponsors, and Allies

To be at the top of our game and stay there requires patience, skill, good instincts, a deep knowledge base, an understanding of how to get and use the best resources, and a well-connected and informed support system. It's not surprising that, without these on-ramps to success, many upwardly mobile, high-achieving black women who started their careers with a bang find themselves fired or their careers stalled or derailed after a few years. We've all celebrated when a college friend or soror landed a highly coveted corporate, law firm, hospital, or government position, only to later find ourselves consoling her as she recounts how isolated, stifled, and humiliated she felt when she was terminated or quit her job.

What happens to us in the workplace?

The American Bar Association and Executive Leadership Council studies are something we should really take to heart, sisters. Even when we're in the game, we're still treated like outsiders and not the leaders, big thinkers, and strategists that we can be. We don't connect with each other well, and we don't have a sophisticated network of advisors, according to the research.

It takes a broad and diverse village for black women to succeed in the workplace. And that includes white men most of all. Your achievement village must include advocates who are invested in your career success and are willing to put some skin in the game. Almost without exception, the successful black women I've encountered have dedicated mentors, coaches, and sponsors who advocate on their behalf with higher-ups.

No matter what you may call it, your personal "board of advisors" has a specific role to play in your professional life. You want to have bosses who are invested in your career. You need an advocate who lobbies to make sure you get critical assignments that demonstrate your skills and expose your work to senior executives. These opportunities give you access to clients and provide honest, empowering, and transformative feedback through formal performance reviews and informal comments. A good boss can also be a great *coach*, providing ongoing insights and strategies to improve your performance.

You want knowledgeable *mentors* (inside and outside your workplace) who can help you by sharing their experience. Mentors teach you how to read between the lines, anticipate challenges, troubleshoot, and provide unfiltered feedback on what you do and how you're perceived by others. A good mentor may introduce you to key players and possibly let you tap his or her network. According to Ella L. J. Edmondson Bell, PhD, author of *Career GPS: Strategies for Women Navigating the New Corporate Landscape*, mentorships are where "the personal meets the professional."[15]

One of my longtime mentors, Ray Cotton, a partner at Mintz Levin Cohn in Washington, D.C., told me in a recent conversation that a "mentor has to be engaged and [has] to see your potential." He also believes that "there should be a reward for mentoring, either with compensation, or billable hour credit, because human beings respond to self-interest, particularly when we are all so challenged with managing our time."

There's nothing like having a powerful *sponsor* on your side who can open doors and help move you up the ranks, or perhaps start a well-placed whispering campaign on your behalf. Sponsors are not your personal friends, explains Dr. Bell, an associate professor at Dartmouth's Tuck School of Business. They're not the ones you should confess your fears and weaknesses to. They function outside of your advisory sphere, managing your reputation and looking out for opportunities to promote you.

It's important for us to make the distinction between the different kinds of advocates. I had a so-called mentor at my firm, and he was a truly great guy. But he had been a personal friend for years before I joined the firm as a lateral hire, and our prior friendship got in the way of him being a true advocate. We had monthly luncheons, mostly initiated by me, but we never talked "turkey"—no strategy—no plan to help me advance, meet my billable hours, and get me on top assignments. Do not fall into the trap of believing you have a workplace advocate when what you have is simply a friend at work, sisters. That is not the role of your mentor. That is the role of your "war council"(after this book we are going to call them the "love council" in our efforts to redefine the language we use to define other black women).

The bottom line is that strategic allies throughout the company, your profession, or around your industry or city help keep you informed on several fronts and help connect the resources, people, and channels to move you ahead. As noted in the Executive Leadership Council study findings, the onus is on black women to develop strategic relationships with white males and other managers and executives, not the other way around. This isn't easy, but with finesse, it can be done. There are lots of resources out there to tell you how. Dr. Bell's book is one. Many black professional associations (e.g., the National Black MBA Association,

Greek and fraternal organizations, and local business groups) as well as the National Bar Association and the National Medical Association have networking seminars on how to find and attract mentors and sponsors. However, the best insights you can get on this subject come from asking people who are mentoring or coaching others, or people who are bene-fiting from these relationships. Don't just ask how he or she got a mentor. Learn how to build better relationships that work for you.

I can think of no better way to amplify the critical importance of men-toring than to share my interview with Martha Barnett, former Amer-ican Bar Association president and senior partner (and the first woman to be hired) at my former law firm, Holland & Knight LLP. Martha, who is a white woman, was raised in the 1950s in the rural, segregated South in Lacoochee, Florida, not far from Rosewood, Florida, site of the infa-mous Rosewood massacre. Her father was a doctor who often treated black residents in Lacoochee. While at Holland & Knight, Martha helped to successfully lobby the Florida legislature for a $2.1 million reparation package on behalf of the Rosewood victims, after her colleague argued the case before the Florida Supreme Court.[16]

I asked Martha about the importance of a having a mentor in a young professional woman's life, because I know of the mentor relationship she had with her famous, older, white male colleague, the late former ABA president Chesterfield Smith.[17]

She said:

> Having Chesterfield as my mentor changed my life. Without his influence in my professional life and my life in general, I would have had a good job, sure—but not a great profession. I did not have to seek him out or win his approval. He saw something in me—not sure what it was, but he did, and he took a genuine interest in me as a person; he guided me, gave me wisdom, and most importantly, he transferred his personal credibility to me by taking me with him to meet clients, giving me work, exposing me to people like his good friend U.S. Supreme Court Chief Justice Warren Burger. Chesterfield used to call me his lawyer. Bottom line—he taught me to "do good" with my life. He had the heart of a real mentor—he invested in me, and it made all the difference in my success.

Martha enjoyed the support of an ideal mentor. I have had many *wan-nabe* mentors in my legal career, but there is a big difference between someone you meet with for coffee once a month or who buys you lunch once in a while to discuss your career progress and someone who takes a committed, vested interest in you as a human being. Professional black women must learn to build these kinds of relationships early.

I have watched African American male and female colleagues rise or fall in their respective professions because of whom they were connected with as mentors or with whom they directly reported to in their workplace hierarchy. In one of our focus groups, one participant shared how her mentor pushed her to pursue an advanced degree. She emphasized the importance of an advanced degree, *especially* for black women, as this mitigates the need to repeatedly demonstrate our capabilities.

> I was told by my master's advisor, who is one of my mentors—he's Latino—he said to me that I had no choice; I had to get my PhD I asked him, "Why, why, why are you pushing me?" He said that no one understands the way you understand the things about our communities, and we need your voice to be there and to impact policy. And so, here was someone who has lived the challenges that many of us as black women have experienced. But his championing of me was overwhelming.

Her mentor's encouragement helped her make the decision to return to school and earn her PhD, which has been invaluable to her career success.

Survey participants feel that it is somewhat harder for black women to find mentors. Some commented that older white males seem to have more ingrained stereotypes about African Americans generally, and especially about black women. This can cause ABWs to feel the need to prove themselves time and time again. A friend's twenty-seven-year-old daughter, who works as a diversity professional at one of the nation's most prestigious law firms, lamented to me recently that what she finds most troubling is that *women*–black and white—who reach the top of the ladder seem to be less interested in "reaching back and helping to mentor" the younger women in the firm. "They simply do not feel a sense of obligation . . . to help other women make it." But, in general, our survey respondents believe that there are people in their offices and industries willing to help, including ones outside their gender or race. What's more, one focus group participant believed that "women are open to being mentored," suggesting that as mentors become more available and continue to increasingly recognize potential in African American women, this relationship will develop into an important force in the workplace. As our ABW research shows, fully 89 percent of professional black women age 34 or younger "agree" that they value direction or advice from older black women in the workplace, and the majority (62 percent) "enthusiastically agree." Three-fourths of the women over 35 years old (the most likely mentors to these women) feel that young black women respond well to mentoring.

## How Feedback Can Make the Difference

THE BIGGEST COMPLAINT that many black women have over the tenure of their careers is that they're not given the same candid feedback that others receive. The experts are concerned that white men (and women, perhaps) are reluctant to tell a black associate that her work is not up to par for fear of being seen as racist, sexist, or both. Or they anticipate that their black colleague will get angry.

This is most unfortunate because it creates a huge barrier to successful learning and improvement for black females. Over the years, I've sometimes been given outstanding job performance ratings and bonuses, only to be told later that something I'm doing isn't working or that I'm weak in a particular area. As one Time Warner executive explained, black women must learn how to "decode the language" used in informal and formal performance reviews as well as in feedback on their day-to-day projects. I agree: evaluations do not amount to a hill of beans, sisters, if the folks evaluating you are not candid, invested, and willing to help you do better.

Thus, young black women want and need the feedback of older, successful black women who are further along in their careers—the most likely people to give them honest feedback. Although this makes perfect sense to me as a black woman who *longed* many days for the support, guidance, and mentorship of other black women in my firm, I was often disappointed because in many cases those women were not able to give me work, mentor me, or even guide me because they were struggling to keep their own heads above water. This is a problem that I'd like to see experienced and savvy black women work on more so that we can help each other and younger women better navigate the rough terrain ahead. (I address this topic further in the next section.)

*Now here's the tough love.* Feedback and performance reviews are often influenced by perception, biases based on stereotypes, and past relationships that our bosses and colleagues had with other black women. *Unfair?* Yes, of course. Nevertheless, this is a fact of life. For example, you may be accused of being angry even if you think your reaction merely demonstrated hurt or surprise. This accusation, often based on a stereotype, really sets us off—even when it's true. As one sixty-year-old educator said in our Washington, D.C., regional focus group, "If we are angry, many of us have good reason to be." While I don't disagree with her, we have to find ways to better channel our anger and use it to our advantage.

Our lifestyle choices are often questioned as well and may color how we are perceived. For instance, you may be very conscientious about completing your projects on time and on budget and providing more than was requested. However, if you're a single mother, leaving at five o'clock every day may trigger concern over your commitment to work. If you're a mother who never married, your character or judgment might be questioned. If you're single and attractive, no married man with good sense will come near you and want to mentor you or invite you to meet the wife for drinks. If you wear dreadlocks or Afrocentric clothing, your look or demeanor might not be considered professional. If you're overweight, you may be quietly chastised for not being disciplined. Are any of these opinions or reactions justified? No. But these are just a few of the perceptual challenges we face.

I'll never forget a conversation I had with a white male partner at my former law firm. I asked him why a certain black male attorney had not yet been elected to the partnership when he seemed to have the billable hours and skill. He looked me dead in the eye and explained that making partner takes more than having the right numbers. He said, "What's often more important is how the person fits in our corporate culture, with our clients and influential people in our industry and community. Firms assess how responsible potential partners are in their personal lives. And everyone knows this guy sleeps with the secretaries, is not committed to anyone, and is all about himself." There are behavior rules and codes of ethics in all professions and business. Some can ignore these conventions. We cannot do so if we want to succeed. This hearkens back to what our grannies said: "You have to be twice as good."

Learning when to duck, when to dive, when to advance, and when to simply run for cover requires well-honed emotional intelligence (EI), which is simply the ability to accurately perceive, properly assess, and successfully manage the emotions of the people in your sphere of influence. Although we like to think that people get hired, fired, promoted, or given plum assignments purely because of their skills and experience, allow me reemphasize that your ability to get along with others is often as or more important. Corporate studies also report that some people get fired not because they're incompetent but because they have serious "personality conflicts" (real or perceived) with others in the workplace.

## The Strengths and Challenges of the Corporate Sisterhood Networks

I CAN'T TELL you how many times my closest black girlfriends and I have been on the phone or sitting down over drinks venting—even yelling—about how much we "can't stand," "don't like," and "hate" dealing with other black women. Many of us are sick of the petty nonsense and drama surrounding our so-called enlightened sisters. We trade stories about black women backstabbing and undercutting each other (see Chapter 11, sisters, because we are going to deal with this issue once and for all and work it out).

One seasoned seminar leader related a situation that occurred in her "Managing Anger in the Workplace" seminar at a national conference of black professionals at a Fortune 50 company: "When discussing how black women deal with each other at work," she explained, "one woman stood up, shouting, 'Not only am I angry at the black women who don't help each other out, I'm really pissed at that bitch specifically!' as she pointed to a colleague in the room. You can imagine what happened after that."

Sisters, buckle up here, because this is a serious point. We innately expect other black women to have our backs—to support us and encourage us at work. When this fails to happen, we get very upset. We'll cut a sister off quickly if she gets into our business or says something that just rubs us the wrong way. Or we'll distance ourselves if she stumbles, makes a mistake, or falls out of favor. Or we'll give feedback that's more hurtful than helpful—just like so many others do in a competitive atmosphere. Perhaps some of us could benefit from polishing up our conflict resolution skills. We've got to learn to separate the personal from the professional.

We are tough on ourselves and tougher on each other. *You know what*

*I'm talking about.* What's wrong with a little sisterhood in the workplace? Let's face it—we all need a support system that boosts our confidence. The good ol' boys network sure has worked for white men, and women's networks among our white colleagues are quickly gathering steam. And whether you want to believe me or not, your workmates are watching and asking themselves, "If she can't get along with other black women, how can I expect to get along with her?"

I came across an interesting example of this sister pettiness in our single professional black women's summer focus group. One beautiful former foundation executive, who was now in her early fifties, lamented about how shocked she was to find out what her colleagues really thought about her. She had been tasked with building and launching a new foundation at a Fortune 50, and build it she did. Everyone was amazed at the job she did with very few resources and little support. Yet, like many of us, after having experienced great success in her role, she found herself suddenly out of a job and packing up her things.

Unbelievably, about six months after she had been let go, a younger black female colleague approached her to provide her with some insight into why she lost her job. She started the conversation with, "You know what your problem is?" According to this young sister, her problem had nothing to do with competence. Her problem was that she "intimidated others" with her ability, her confidence, and most of all, her quiet power. In short, the young woman was suggesting that my friend needed to shrink back in order to make everyone around her feel more comfortable. As I think about it, I'm sure this young woman meant no harm. But shrinking back is a dangerous box for black women to crawl into. Being reactive rather than proactive in managing perception is not usually the best strategy for repairing a damaged reputation.

Clearly, this conversation did not sit well with this woman, and she was stunned that a younger black woman would speak to her in that way, especially without factoring in all the issues that may have contributed to her demise. The younger sister spoke without asking questions or offering support, which was unfortunate, because the confrontation ultimately ended their friendship.

Although unvarnished feedback from other sisters can be critical to success in the workplace, we need to be careful how we dole out our critiques. We also can't shoot the messenger when we don't like the news. As smart black women, let's commit to learning how to dish it out with love and take it in with courage.

As for this smart, savvy executive, she ended up like far too many of us who are viewed as a "threat" or as "too much" to handle: she was simply phased out of her position.

Unfair? Yes. Surprising? No. Had I checked into the situation, I probably would have discovered that her network at the job didn't include those critical mentors, sponsors, and strategic allies that are key success factors, according to the two career studies I discussed previously.

This sister's story reminds me of something that happened early in my own career. I was twenty-six years old and thrilled to land my first job out of law school working for former governor of New Jersey Christine Todd Whitman's administration. My white, male, Republican mentors in the legislature paired me up with an older black woman who they thought would show me the ropes. I couldn't believe my good fortune. She was in her late thirties at the time and at the top of her game. She even had another sister as her second-in-command. I felt covered, protected, and blessed to be working for two dynamic, fabulous sisters in authority.

Along the way, I had a major ideological run-in with some heavy hitters in the Republican Party regarding the dearth of African Americans in the GOP. (This is a fight I picked often and a problem I still lament in my columns to this day.[18]) When the Republican National Committee leaders screamed for my head, my boss refused to speak to me. Then, instead of explaining to me why my direct approach was not the best way to be a change agent in the party and offering up some better strategies, she berated me in a crass and demeaning way that I will never forget. She suggested that the way to success for a young black woman in the world was to find someone of power, "crawl up their butt, and stay there." I am not making this up.

I was stunned, speechless, and mortified that my boss (and mentor, I thought) was giving me such limiting, offensive advice. I paused and then asked her a question: "What happens if they take a s***?" Bad move on my part, but I was twenty-six. Still, I think you see my logic. What kind of advice was that to tell a young woman starting out in her career? And what happens when people tire of you, or you are no longer of use? Then what?

I paid a heavy price. She phased out my job several months later and blackballed me. I was young and didn't understand why this black woman I admired was so angry at me and wouldn't give me a second chance, like so many of my white colleagues who had stumbled on the job in far more egregious ways and were given a pass. My bold move cost me dearly. I went from being a well-respected and emerging young leader in the GOP, long before I met this sister, only to have her take me out. It was a very sobering experience for which I paid for years. To this day, it still brings sadness to my heart.

Looking back, I realize that my boss came up the ranks the hard way without someone of color looking out for her. She toughed it out, making work her life and leaving little room for anything else; she never married and never had kids. I made some mistakes, and I understand that now. But I was a quick learner, and perhaps with a little coaching from her, this could have turned into one of the best lessons of my life. White men do this all this time for each other.

My point in telling these stories is this: Black women must take stock of how much we've internalized some of the junk that's been thrown our way. It's time to be accountable for how we spew our life experiences and hurts onto other black women. We also need to "get real clear," as my aunt Debbie would say, about our strategy for being successfully recruited, retained, and advanced in the twenty-first-century workplace. That starts by getting rid of the baggage that we bring to the workplace—our own troubles and the conflicts we have with each other. (I take a deep dive into this topic later in the book, in Chapter 11.)

Face it: we can be our own worst enemies in the workplace. We have all had to deal with some angry sister who either verbally abused us or maligned our reputation. We have all had a hard time keeping our personal dramas out of the workplace. More than other social groups, we feel weary and tired of dealing with "us." Truth be told, we know better than anyone just how difficult we can be to deal with.

Usually when these discussions come up in the context of work-related projects, sorority, or professional associations, we collectively just shake our heads and say, "I know girl, I know." Instead, what we should be doing is confronting, teaching, and helping each other to grow. If we are going to successfully redefine, coach, mentor, and prepare the next generation of black women for leadership, we'd better step up and come correct. And we'd better examine our perceptions of each other before we start pointing fingers at others and how they see us.

In our national and regional ABW focus groups, we discussed in detail the stereotypes and pressures black women feel in the workplace. There was a marked difference between how unmarried professional black women under forty viewed themselves and how successful, married, older black women with families viewed themselves. The younger, single set didn't feel as accepted in the workplace, believed they were victims of racial stereotyping, and therefore were less confident they were viewed as executive material. Experience (and perhaps the love and strong support of a spouse) clearly fueled the positive outlook and confidence of the older, married women in the groups. They were much less likely than their younger, single counterparts to be distressed by evidence of stereotyping and career ups and downs. Mothers in the group, for instance, often found common ground and connection with colleagues around their children and family activities. These women were proud of their accomplishments and quick to talk about the value they bring to their work. One married, successful businesswoman in her early fifties, for example, commented about the sea change in the experience of being a black woman in America since the 2008 election:

> I think it's exciting today that we can be a role model to all people. At one time, we were just a role model for ourselves. I think it's just that everyone is open to watching everything we're doing, and that leads to a higher level of respect for ourselves, for our families, for our men, and for our children.

## Winning at Work: Strategies for Success

LIKE THOSE WHO have gone successfully and not so successfully before me, I've learned many valuable lessons in my fifteen years in the professional workforce. If only I'd known then what I know now, my life would most assuredly be on a different path. I'm not complaining, because I think all things happen in their proper season if we allow ourselves to learn from our mistakes and shortcomings. Fortunately, I was able to successfully shift, pivot, and turn my career path to where I wanted it to go at age forty—which is, admittedly, rare—and now I'm writing, on the speaking circuit, and tapped for my insights on black women, politics, the law, and social justice across national media outlets. My hope, however, is that I, and other women like me, can pass these lessons on to the next generation of professional black women so that they can perhaps skip some of the hurdles many of us have faced and put their careers on a successful path much sooner than in their forties. We must better educate and prepare women of color to be visible at all levels within private firms and corporations as well as in the fields of the arts, sciences, and technology.

If America is to move forward and reach its full potential, it must reflect the diversity of society. As Ray Cotton (who also has a master's degree in public health from Harvard and many HBCU clients) told me:

> Diversity programs and sensitivity training are fine, but the challenge is that they happen at the end of the line. We must start earlier with focused outreach and development of women of color in secondary and primary education if we want to see their numbers expand in corporate America, academia, medicine, industry, and in large law firms by the time they reach their twenties and thirties.

That's a job we all can take on.

The change starts with you. Take time to carefully review all the guidance offered throughout this chapter. Pay special attention to the advice on building strategic relationships and networks that include white men and women. And then take a look at the following easy ways to boost your chances for advancement in any job. These strategies are based on my personal experience and extensive interviews with men and women (both of color and not) who have worked as professionals for fifteen years or more.

1. **As a mentor and dear sister friend of mine likes to say, "Show up ready!" Every day**. This means that you come to work on time, and you go to your superiors and let them know you'll work harder, faster, and smarter—that you're prepared to be an excellent employee. Affirm that you want candid feedback, support, and—yes—guidance when necessary.

2. **Read the latest career advice books, and studies available including those on the following list.** These books were written by successful and well-respected black women who navigated all types of mazes and land mines to build their impressive careers. These experienced, savvy corporate veterans ask and answer the questions we really need to explore.

   - *Expect to Win: Proven Strategies for Success from a Wall Street Vet* by Morgan Stanley managing director Carla Harris
   - *The Little Black Book of Success: Laws of Leadership for Black Women* by Elaine Meryl Brown, Marsha Haygood, and Rhonda Joy McLean

- *Career GPS: Strategies for Women Navigating the New Corporate Landscape* by Ella L. J. Edmondson Bell
- *The 10 Laws of Career Reinvention: Essential Survival Skills for Any Economy* by Pamela Mitchell
- *From Visible Invisibility to Visibly Successful: ABA Commission on Women in the Profession.* Prepared by Arin N. Reeves, J.D., PhD (The 2008 updated strategies report from the 2006 ABA report cited earlier in this chapter).

3. **Deal with your prejudices.** We all have hidden biases. If you're intimidated by or resent taking orders from someone because he or she is a man, a woman, white, black, or other, get help to learn how to get past your bigotry. Learn to be more tolerant of differences. Your success as a black woman in the workplace may rest on how authentically you learn to work with white males and white females in corporate America. It's important to discover common interests and build personal relationships from shared experiences.

4. **Tap your network of friends, sorors, church members, children and teenagers, and other people you respect and trust inside and outside your workplace for honest feedback.** You want to hear their opinions about your skills, your attitude, your ability to work in a team, and your leadership capacity. This is called a 360-degree evaluation and is a staple evaluation tool for corporations looking to develop their high-potential staff and other valuable players.

5. **If you work in a diverse environment, ask your reviewers to comment on how well you get along with African Americans and people of different races or faiths.** Encourage your friends and family to be honest. Above all, you must be open to hearing the good, the bad, and the ugly. Remember: *don't shoot the messenger.* You need this information to be the best you can be on all fronts. If your company offers this type of feedback, ask to be included. The responses are usually anonymous, sometimes brutally candid, and often very revealing and helpful.

6. **Develop strong relationship-building skills.** Being friendly, positive, honest, gracious, and spiritually centered will serve you well. Let the wall down; even just a little bit will help. Become more approachable. Learning the art of small talk can work wonders in breaking the ice with colleagues, new clients, and people who are very different from you. Listen to what your colleagues talk about at lunch, before and after meetings, and around the coffee station.

7. **What's so hard about keeping up with how your local sports teams are doing?** Who's still standing strong on the hottest reality show? What new restaurants are getting all the buzz? Bone up and then chime in. Be willing to share funny stories about your weekends, your children, your dog, or your mother. These are subjects that everyone relates to.

8. **Develop collegial relationships with your peers, managers, executives, and staff.** Celebrity publicist and author Terrie Williams wrote an excellent book called *Personal Touch: What You Really Need to Succeed in Today's Fast-Paced Business World.* Williams is a strong advocate of handwritten thank-you notes and giving small gifts to colleagues who've helped and supported you along the way. I agree. As my former colleagues will tell you, I never missed an occasion to say "thank you" and let people know I appreciated what they were doing on my behalf.

9. **Cultivate a reputation as an outstanding team player.** No task is too small; no job too menial—you'll do whatever it takes to serve the team's interests and the corporate goals. When you start a job, take on an unwanted but important project that's driving your boss nuts. He or she will appreciate your thoughtfulness and will always remember you for doing this favor.

10. **Secure the education and training you need to be competitive.** This is especially critical if you're in (or aspire to be in) a leadership position. When it's time to put your career advancement efforts into overdrive, all your education and training ducks must be in place. As mentioned previously, an advanced degree is key, *especially* for black women, to help mitigate basic questions about our capabilities.

11. **If you're deemed difficult to work with (you know who you are), master good business etiquette, and take classes to smooth out your people skills.** Be especially vigilant about learning how to give good feedback, conduct constructive performance evaluations, be an effective negotiator, and handle tough conversations gracefully. If you have problems dealing with conflict or confrontation, look into programs addressing conflict resolution and how to be a better listener. As Time Warner attorney and coauthor of *The Little Black Book of Success* Rhonda McLean says, learning the "art of listening" was especially important to her career. There are numerous workshops, seminars, books, and webinars on these topics.

12. **Come to work ready to observe, listen, and learn.** As a boss once told a know-it-all colleague of mine, "It must be tough always being the smartest one in the room." No matter how skilled, experienced, and intelligent you are, there's always room to learn more, explore new ideas, and try different techniques. No one enjoys working with a rigid, stubborn, or difficult person. Your staff, your colleagues, and your supervisor will appreciate your flexibility and openness.

13. **Don't skip the "me" time.** Not just time with the girls but time alone to think, meditate, pray, and have fun.

14. **Set aside quality time to be with your boyfriend, girlfriend, husband, kids, parents, friends, and other loved ones.**

15. **Build your own special brand ID that people will come to appreciate about you.** It could be the creativity you bring to problem solving, your skill as a consensus builder, your ability to develop talent, or your determination to close the deal without giving away the store—anything that sets you apart from the crowd and makes your colleagues notice you for your skill set.

16. **Don't be a grumbler or allow yourself to be labeled the office complainer.** *Smile.* Don't get into petty conversations. Don't dump on other sisters. *Never* talk negatively about your colleagues or put down others. *Never ever* put in writing anything negative about anyone, any project, or any client's company.

17. **Do not bring your personal problems to work.** That's why you have sorority sisters, friends, family, and social networks. Use them properly—don't keep hurts inside or suffer in silence. Find people who share your life experiences and who can support you and surround you with love and concern. Seek out others who come from different circumstances so you can broaden your perspective.

18. **Most of all, be resilient, sisters!** Having the right stuff to succeed also means being able to bounce back from failure, disappointment, and missed or blocked opportunities. You won't help yourself by wallowing in self-pity or playing the blame game when things don't go your way.

No matter what, never let them see you sweat. If you are in a hostile, unhealthy work environment and can't remedy the situation, muster up enough self-love and respect to *leave*. I know leaving a good job is very difficult, but I'm going to ask you to hear this and hear it well: if you're as good as you think, you'll find your way. Sometimes fate is trying to move us in a new direction.

It happened to me. Though an attorney by training, I was holding on to a profession I no longer enjoyed. Once I tapped into my core interests and strengths—writing, public speaking, and leading thought-provoking discussions at seminars and workshops—I figured out how to put them to work for me. Then I started to soar. You can, too!

# Unveiling the Secret Soul of a Strong Black Woman:

## The New Landscape of Twenty-First-Century Love for the Successful Sister

### "Wild Flower" by New Birth[*]

She faced the hardest times you can imagine
And many times her eyes fall back the tears
And when her youthful world was about to fall in
Each time her slender shoulders
For the weight of all her tears
And a sorrow no one hears
Still rings in midnight silence in her ears

CHORUS:

*Let her cry*
*For she's a lady*
*Let her dream*
*For she's a child*
*Let the rain fall down upon her*
*She's a free and gentle flower growing wild*

[*]Third party license granted by Music Sales Limited; 14–15 Berners St; London W1T 3LJ, for Wildflower Lyrics, RCA.

And if by chance that I should hold her
Let me hold her for a while
And if allowed just one possession
I would pick her from her garden to be mine

Be careful how you touch her for she'll awaken
And sleep's the only freedom that she knows
And when you look into her eyes you won't believe
For the way she's always paying for a debt she never owed
And a silent wind still blows that she can only hear
So she goes

She's my free and gentle flower, growing growing growing wild
She's a free and gentle flower
Growing growing wild
She's my flower,
Growing growing growing wild
Growing growing growing growing wild
She's my free and gentle flower

# 4

## WHY CAN'T A SUCCESSFUL BLACK WOMAN FIND A MAN? ACTUALLY, SHE CAN

"Whatever the case, we men are no longer connecting with that special part of you that makes you a woman—that thing that makes you so very beautiful to us, and that also happens to make us feel more like men."

—STEVE HARVEY, *Act Like a Lady, Think Like a Man*

*L*ike a flower tossed and blown by the wind, our loving nature as black women can sometimes be overwhelmed with all that we've had to weather and absorb in modern life: the broken hearts, the disappointments, the betrayals, and the weariness from waiting for the right man to come along. Many of us are like the woman described in my favorite 1970s love song, "Wild Flower"; we have faced the hardest times you can imagine as we bravely held back the tears. We have carried the weight upon our shoulders while we pushed down all of our fears.

I am asking us to take a long, hard look at ourselves to assess what it is that we truly want, need, and desire from a love relationship with a man. I can tell you that I wasted precious years of my life with regret, fear, and worry about all the things I lost, the things I did not have, and the love I felt I was unworthy of when it came to dating and relationships. In doing so, I robbed myself of love and the opportunity to be loved in a whole and healthy way. I was too cerebral, too analytical, always thinking, analyzing, and dissecting. *Love is not like that.* Love opens us up, warms our hearts, and drives us to be our best selves, and in turn, we radiate light and love to all who know us. But without love, we wither and die. We shrink, we withdraw, and we hide. And everyone around us, no matter how well we think we are covering it up, can feel the fear, and it pushes them away instead of drawing them to us. I know, sisters; I have been there, and so have many of you.

Comedian-turned-best-selling author Steve Harvey wants us to act like ladies but think like men;[1] author and former NFL wife Shanae Hall rejects Harvey's premise and instead wants us to act like ladies and still get the man.[2] Actor-turned-author Hill Harper wants us to have a conversation,[3] and ABC's *Nightline*[4] and a host of other media outlets and publications want to know what is wrong with successful, educated black women and why we can't find a man.

Well, the short answer is this: We can, many have, and many of us are thriving in good, healthy, loving relationships and marriages. Once again, our First Lady Michelle Obama exemplifies that you can have it all in love. She is the quintessential successful sister, and *she has a man at home*, to borrow from an old Chante Moore song.[5] We can learn a lot from Sister Obama because she makes the seemingly impossible dream a reality for us all.

Let me be clear, however, that I am in no way suggesting that the relationship situation facing this generation and future generations of black women is not real or serious—it is. But I am convinced that we can have the love we seek if we will work on us *for us* and stop listening to the noise surrounding us *about us.* We have to get past the media coverage, past the dreadful black male-to-female ratio that we are all sick of hearing about, past the "should do's" and "should not do's," past the books written by men telling us how we should think and act, past the broken hearts, past the disappointments, and past the unhealed wounds that have stopped many of us from taking a second chance on love. Again, the path to fulfillment and love starts with the woman in the mirror, and just as we need to be healthy, rested, and centered to thrive in the workplace, we likewise have to bring those qualities to the relationship table.

Many of us are familiar with the 2009 Yale University study that found that fewer black women with advanced degrees are getting married and having children.[6] "In the past nearly four decades, black women have made great gains in higher education rates, yet these gains appear to have come increasingly at the cost of marriage and family," said Hannah Brückner, professor of sociology at Yale University, codirector of the Center for Research on Inequalities and the Life Course, and the study's coauthor. "Both white and black highly educated women have increasingly delayed childbirth and remained childless, but the increase is stronger for black women."[7]

The study, which was the first to review longitudinal trends in marriage and family formation among highly educated black women, found that black women born after 1950 were twice as likely as white women never to have married by age forty-five and twice as likely to be divorced, widowed, or separated. The gap in the percentage of black and white highly educated women living with a spouse has grown over the decades, increasing from 9 percent in the 1970s to 21 percent between 2000 and 2007.[8] "Highly educated black women have increasingly fewer options when it comes to potential mates," Brückner said. "They are less likely than black men to marry outside their race, and, compared to white and black men, they are least likely to marry a college-educated spouse."[9]

These findings sparked an intense debate about whether successful black women are truly suffering a so-called marriage penalty. Well, yes we are, but not when compared to less-educated black women, according to a lesser-publicized study from the Council on Contemporary Families. University of Pennsylvania professor and coauthor of the study Betsey Stevenson reports that the disparity (or penalty) is evident when the prospects for highly educated black women are compared to those of highly educated white women. But we have to look at the numbers in context, because if we compare college-educated black women to those who are not educated, the better-educated women fair better at marriage, but if we compare college-educated black women to their white female counterparts, the black women are at a distinct disadvantage.[10] It's all relative.

So enough of the statistics that we're all sick of hearing about; what we really want to know is this: Why is mating and marriage between the brothers and sisters so challenging?

The relationship rift between black men and black women has been going on for decades. *Ebony* was reporting on the problem back in 1977: "Black Men/Black Women: Has Something Gone Wrong Between Them?" featured an interview with renowned African American Harvard University psychiatrist Dr. Alvin Poussaint, who had this to say:

There is a kind of crisis in that relationships have been changing so much and so rapidly for Black females and Black males in the past decade that it is hard for them to get or develop answers. I think that is showing up in strife in relationships and in an increasing number of problems in marriages. Black women, being members of this racist society, have been conditioned not to see Black men as valuable, as reliable and so on. They fear that they are being exploited by Black males, that Black males can't keep a job, that they are insecure and so on. Black males have the same problem of being conditioned against the Black female. They accuse Black females of being too dominating, coming on too strong, being too materialistic, etc. All these stereotypes enter into their personal interactions and interfere with their relationship.[11]

*Sound familiar?*

Fast-forward to a 2003 *Newsweek* article written by Ellis Cose titled, "The Black Gender Gap." Cose was one of the first journalists to expose that the ranks of unmarried, accomplished black women were rising.[12] According to *Newsweek*, 42 percent of this group was unmarried when the story was published. This revelation partly inspired the 2006 movie *Something New* starring Sanaa Lathan and Simon Baker. This light-hearted love story hit on the ups and downs of interracial dating between a black woman and a white man. Interracial dating has now become a hot-button issue for sisters in pop culture, in books, and on the blogs and is something I discuss in detail later in this chapter.

Let's not forget the so-called man-sharing conference held in 1981 at Howard University. The gathering was based on an idea Dr. Audrey Chapman introduced in *Essence* magazine—that, for some women, the best way to cope with the pain of black men's infidelity might be to simply accept it and opt for a shared relationship.[13] Back then, the sisters were alarmed that there just weren't enough faithful, college-educated black men to marry. At that time, *The Cosby Show* was very popular, and the bar for what black women wanted in a black man was raised considerably higher. These days, black women want the ideal black man (IBM)—the Will Smith/Barack Obama/Denzel Washington types who sport the total package: good looks, a great job, and a big bank account. The problem, say the women we've surveyed and interviewed, is that these prize IBMs are no longer interested in the strong, independent, high-achieving black women who want them.

Why not? Although I'm not happy about it, I think I found one really good answer in an article titled *"Black Women: Successful and Single"* by the relationship editor of Mybrotha.com.

> When we explore the reasons why an independent black woman—who seemingly has it all—can't find a deserving black man, the answer is both simple and startling. Most black men are not looking for a woman who has it all. In fact, men are less comfortable with the brazen woman who wants to be on top of the world, and more comfortable with the laid back woman who looks for a leader. "It's a turn-off in many ways," says Travis Luxon, an environmental engineer from Lansing, Michigan. "I definitely support a black woman doing her thing, but I don't think it's natural for a man to desire that. When a black man sees a woman like that, we immediately think she's high-maintenance." Black men, like men of most ethnicities, are conditioned to be leaders and providers. From hustling in the streets, to managing a corporate meeting, a responsible man will do what it takes to provide for his family. Finding ways to provide physical and financial security for a wife and family has always been the goal of men. It may sound like an oversimplification of roles, but almost everything a man strives for in life—career, money, status, power—is based on his desire to keep a wife and support a family. Even in its simplicity, this is how a man shows love.[14]

## Desperate Love—How Did Your Assets Become Liabilities?

So LET ME get this straight: according to some black men, we are unloved, unlovable, and unworthy of love because we are educated, successful, and financially secure? Wow! Since when did such assets become a liability? In fact, 41 percent of black women in our study said that relationships with black men were challenging because black women "earn more money/have more financial security" and "have achieved a higher level of success." As a result, 78 percent of professional black women polled believe they are more likely than white women to have major problems finding Mr. Right.

This is a dangerous outlook for our young women, causing many of them to question whether going for a graduate degree or a big job is worth the risk of not getting married or having children—the circumstance of many older professional black women they meet.

But our "having it all" is only part of the black love dilemma, according to Joy Jones, author of *Between Black Women: Listening with the Third Ear*. In an article titled "Are Black Women Scaring Off Their Men?" Jones offered the following insight.

> Being acknowledged as the head of the household is an especially important thing for many black men, since their manhood is so often actively challenged everywhere else. Many modern women are so independent, so self-sufficient, so committed to the cause, to the church, to career or their narrow concepts *that their entire personalities project an "I don't need a man" message* (emphasis added).[15]

That's a very tough message to swallow for women like me who were raised to take care of ourselves, make our own money, and call the shots for the life we want to lead. However, it's something we all need to seriously reflect on if we want to move beyond the frenzied media debates about our love challenges.

Curious as to when black love (or the lack thereof) became such a hot media topic, I did a little pop-culture research. Surfing the web, I found one point of view posted by a brother reacting to a March 2002 *Ebony* magazine article titled "The Biggest Lies about Black Male and Female Relationships." He wrote:

> Yes, Black relationships are painfully complex, and we are in need of a renaissance of empathy between the sexes, but the media have enthusiastically magnified and complicated the issues even further. The media has delighted itself in highlighting the desperate plight of Black relationships and painting a picture of impending doom.[16]

Then I queried the legendary black advertising guru Tom Burrell, founder and former CEO of Burrell Advertising, for answers. His take: these hyped-up televised free-for-alls have become the go-to topic for networks looking to boost ratings. "Relationship issues are on everyone's radar—whether you are in one or not," explains Burrell, the author of *Brainwashed: Challenging the Myth of Black Inferiority*. "Black women, who drive media consumption, are interested in the weather report on black relationships. And non–African Americans are curious about what's going on with us."

Every time we see, hear, or read one of these discussions about what's wrong with us as successful black women, there is a frenzy of angry and defensive response on blogs and social networking sites, but this does nothing to help us move closer to the love we seek. We need to spend our energy working on us, making sure that our wants, needs, and desires are based on what truly turns us on and not some fantasy of what having it all is supposed to look like. There's a great distance between settling on a man and choosing a life of solitude. Spending our lives alone is not what God had in mind for us, and it's not what we wanted for ourselves. The telling news is that 66 percent of the women we surveyed say that they'd *rather be alone* than be with someone who did not measure up. On the other hand, 42 percent believe that we are alone because we hold unrealistic standards and expectations.[17]

A perfect example of how we might often miss golden opportunities in love is exemplified with two of my good friends and *Essence* bloggers Ronnie and Lamar Tyler (founders of BlackandMarriedwithKids.com). Their love connection flies directly in the face of all of this "settling" talk and men not measuring up to our status expectations. Lamar was in his early thirties and a newly unemployed IT specialist when he met his wife, Ronnie, who was a single mother with an MBA and her own home. She was a sister doing it all on her own and doing it well.

Lamar was very interested and felt an instant connection. Concerned with his economic situation at the time, Lamar was up front about living with his mom and his job prospects. He even showed Ronnie his credit report and the deed to his home he'd just sold to show that he was worthy of her consideration. This blew Ronnie away, and she had to take a second look, not because of what he had or did not have but because he was honest, transparent, and making a full-court press to win her affection. Had she dismissed him because he was not her economic equal at that time, she would have missed her husband completely.

On the other hand, I know a sister, fabulous, fine, and financially independent, who once broke up with an equally fine, very nice brother who adored her because she did not like the way his feet looked. Sisters, I only wish I had made that story up! We have to look for better reasons than this to break up with potentially good mates. I mean, come on, ladies.

I know many of you might have been secretly wishing that I would write the official successful sister rebuttal to brothers-turned-relationship-gurus Steve Harvey, Jimi Izrael, or Hill Harper, and come back at them with a litany of what is wrong with black men and why we are sick of their nonsense. That is not going to happen. It is not happening because brothers aren't the only ones who have issues; *we all have issues.* Waving our fingers in the faces of black men won't advance this conversation or help us find the love we seek. It's time for us to focus on us, sisters.

Black women and men have to grow up and face this radioactive topic without resorting to name calling and rolling out overblown generalizations. We have to deconstruct the problem step by step if we want to have genuinely productive discussions about how we mate, marry, and move forward. I don't know about you, but I'm ready to advance the conversation and get off this sociological-pathological track that we appear to be stalled on—and stop worrying about how the brothers feel about black women. *Sisters, all you need to find is the right man to love you.*

There are good men out there, and not all of them are going to be black. There are good men out there, and not all of them are going to be the IBM with a six-figure income. There are good men out there, and not all of them are six feet tall. But, sisters—particularly those of you who are so anxious, so pressed, and so willing to compromise your values just to have a man in your life—know this: there are a lot of good men out there, and you can attract one if you are willing to work on yourself. If we can stop the attacks and blame, and instead learn to embrace the virtues of mutual respect, friendship, intimacy, and genuine communication, I think we can have it all.

I dare you to have this conversation with the men you want in your life. One-on-one—without the drama, recriminations, ultimatums, and demands. I'm challenging you to ask yourself the tough questions and to benefit from what we've uncovered in our research, the opinions of experts, and the experiences I've shared from my own life. The goal is to inform your quest for a more meaningful relationship with a man who is ready to receive and honor your love.

To that end, it is my fervent prayer that we will all reexamine lives ruled by texting and sexting, jumpoffs and friends with benefits, and the cold, callous computer-generated and speed-dating rituals that reflect the plugged-in but disconnected world we live in. Too many good sisters and strong brothers have been left behind, and many feel empty and forlorn. We don't have to exist this way any longer. We can choose a better way, a new path.

## A Vote of Confidence for Marriage

AFTER INTERVIEWING RELATIONSHIP gurus, religious leaders, psychologists, and numerous men and women from other walks of life, I'm convinced that, despite the drama and the disconnect, affluent, educated African Americans value committed relationships and marriage. And for the most part, we want to marry each other.

Avis Jones-DeWeever, PhD, executive director of the National Council of Negro Women, has observed:

> We value [marriage] so highly that sometimes we delay entering into it . . . till the person we are considering has the job, has the career, and has everything in place. So we take longer to marry, if we marry at all. And sometimes we think of divorce as such a bad thing; we choose not to get married until we feel everything is perfect. For some people, that perfect situation never occurs.

For much of my life, that sounded just like me: always waiting for the perfect time that never came. I spent too many years fooling myself that there was a perfect man just for me, when in reality there were many men who would have made great mates if only I had been more willing to look beyond the surface. (I did not say "settle," sisters, before you wince.) *Does this sound familiar?*

Black women must stop romanticizing about the ideal black love based on impossible standards. Likewise, black men must stop fantasizing about the Beyoncé wannabe, long-legged, 36-24-36, with long flowing hair. (Okay, let's be honest. She is gorgeous.) Furthermore, we need to stop abandoning our relationships at the first sign of a difficulty or problem. Most of us don't live in Hollywood; nor are we celebrities. I would suggest that we stop comparing our mates to the retouched images we see in magazines that just aren't real in our day-to-day lives. The sooner we grasp this reality, the closer we will come to looking at the heart of a potential mate and not his or her physical attributes alone.

I had to laugh out loud thinking about what one of my older, wiser sister friends said to me: "This is not rocket science, Sophia. Relationships require that we be intimate, vulnerable, show love, share closeness, and be open—not all this other stuff your generation has bought into." Amen.

## Finding Our Way Back to Love

BEFORE WE START defining a more workable model of what twenty-first-century black love can look like, let's preview four critical findings of this book. These issues are definitely causing some big-time complications for us in the love zone. Left unchecked, they may prevent us from opening up our minds and our hearts to take our relationship conversations to a new level. Addressing these big life challenges is the only way to free your mind, body, and spirit to find love.

1. Too many of us have wielded our legendary strength, as one male friend told me, "as a hammer seeking to drive a nail." It's like we're building walls around us to keep others out. So instead of drawing people to us, we repel them. And when we're with a man, some of us are known to be too domineering and too controlling for our own good.
2. Many of us, including the scripture-quoting sisters among us, dwell too much on our past hurts and disappointments. We're stuck in a place of bitterness and anger, which leaves us unable to forgive. And it shows, sisters—everyone sees it but us.
3. Even more upsetting is the fact that far too many of us have been the victims of sexual abuse, sexual violence, or sexual trauma as children or as young adults, and we've carried these bricks of pain in silence for years.
4. Too many of us were taught that sex was somehow dirty, unnatural, or ungodly. Or we buy into the overgeneralization that all men want from us is sex. Thus, we are conflicted about how to be deeply spiritual, sensual, and sacred, all at the same time. As a result, we hide our beauty, deny our natural human desires, and replace them with disconnected, short-term, casual sex that leaves us feeling empty and alone.[18]

## What Black Men Want

SISTERS, STOP FOR a moment and digest the list you've just read. How on earth can you possibly allow someone to delve past your *MAC* and into your *soulscape* carrying so much emotional pain, baggage, and conflict?

Trust me, I know of what I speak. I have lived on this merry-go-round, as have many have of you, and it has prevented me from recognizing good men when they showed up. Instead, I either stayed in unhealthy, damaging relationships because they were familiar and I wanted to prove my own misguided theories, or worse, I shut down, as I told one brother who asked me on a date when I was in my early thirties, and just stopped dating altogether.

What the research tells us is that in the world of romance, women (black or otherwise) who are overburdened with such heavy baggage can be tough to love and are usually perceived as unapproachable.[19] Men tend to want women who are open, compassionate, happy, fun, secure with themselves, smart, and yes, somewhat independent. No one wants to start a relationship tearing down walls to get past your anger and pain. Some of us, says *Essence* dating guru Demetria Lucas, "can't even muster up a smile." Sadly, she is dead-on. I see our unsmiling faces all the time in my company, iask; in my sorority; and in church. Sisters, why can't we smile? Smiling is actually good for your blood pressure and your health.[20]

Men just aren't hardwired to project beyond the person standing in front of them to imagine what the future might hold. Men just aren't that deep. Very few guys want to stick around through lots of drama and antics to keep digging until he finds the real sweet, sensuous woman that may be buried somewhere beneath. That's just unrealistic. Why should they? They also don't want to go out for an evening on the town with you suited up looking (and acting) like you're poised to negotiate a megabucks deal. They're not looking for a hoochie-mama either. Let's be real. There are too many smart, attractive, easy-to-get-along-with women out there who won't make a man work so hard or give him such a hard way to go.

And finally, let's put to rest the popular misconception that black men are *too intimidated* to date independent black women. Two-thirds of the ABWs (67 percent) we surveyed report that "men are intimidated by them" as the primary reason black women have such a difficult time finding a compatible black man. Interestingly, black men in our sample view it quite differently. And for the record, so do I. More than half (55 percent) of black men say that the biggest barrier to dating successful sisters was that they had suffered "past hurts at the hands of other black men," and 49 percent identify the biggest barrier as differences in career and/or life goals. Another 37 percent said that we carry baggage from disastrous past relationships. However, when we probe a little deeper into the barriers to dating successful sisters, one-third question whether they can "enhance the quality of life for a professional black woman" (35 percent) or "make her happy" (33 percent). In another telling finding, older men are more likely to acknowledge the need to make compromises in relationships with successful black women. Good news for the mature set, but more challenging news for younger couples struggling to find neutral ground during their turbulent twenties and thirties.

Here's where our survey hit pay dirt: over 70 percent of the black men in our national sample say the most important trait they want in a black woman is "a pleasant personality," followed by "emotional stability" (69 percent), compassion and caring (65 percent), and good work-life balance skills (64 percent). *There was nothing in these studies that indicated that what men value in us is how successful we are, how much we have, what we do, or how much we earn.* Nor do they focus on our physical attributes. Sisters, are you listening? They want a positive, kind disposition, they want us to be less stressed, and they want us to stop working so much. Consistent with the emotional needs of men, the top four out of five qualities of women that attract black men are not related to physical characteristics. The ranking reaffirmed that men value the intellectual, emotional, and spiritual essence of women.

*Men also want to be respected.* The prioritization of the qualities they desire in a woman suggest that **the path to marriage does not start in the bedroom but begins with the mutual elevation of the mind, spirit, and body, and the ability to understand your partner.** Men want a woman who listens to their concerns. This not only distinguishes her but places her on the emotional superhighway to his heart. (See Table 4.1.)

TABLE 4.1: Qualities men desire in the woman they want to marry

| QUALITY | PERCENTAGE OF RESPONDENTS |
|---|---|
| Intelligence | 89 |
| Would be a good wife and mother | 83 |
| Refreshing/fun to be around | 83 |
| Sexual compatibility | 82 |
| Emotional stability | 82 |

## *Do Brothers Prefer White Women to the Sisters?*

To ADDRESS THE growing concern that black men are abandoning sisters to date women of other races, we asked a series of questions about interracial dating, specifically with white women. Out of our sample, 54 percent of the respondents have dated a white woman, and 46 percent have not. When we broke out the responses by income, marital status, and level of education, the story of who dated white women was quite revealing: 90 percent of single black men, 67 percent of brothers who earned more than $60,000 a year, and 67 percent of those with a college degree.

Even more interesting are the reasons black men date white women: skin color, and even hair texture and length (yes, I asked that question, and only 2 percent of brothers said it was a factor), *are not* major factors. Personality is the top attraction for 62 percent of the men polled. More than half (57 percent) cite physical appeal, 36 percent stress sexual compatibility, and 33 percent say white women are more compassionate and caring than sisters.

Delving further into the controversy, we asked black men who was more sexually conservative—black or white women: 45 percent agree that white women are *less conservative* sexually than black women, and 35 percent are neutral on the topic.

But author Janks Morton says that black men are naturally going to seek out white women (or other women—an idea that seems to be supported by Census data statistics showing that black men marry outside their race more than any other race of men) as an escape from the perceived control that black women have over their lives. "Black men on one level love their mothers, don't get me wrong, but they are also very conflicted about the emasculation of black men around them growing up, and the strength that black women must exert in the family to keep it together." Morton's take reminds me of Bill Bellamy's character, Brian, in the 2001 movie *The Brothers*, starring Shemar Moore and Morris Chestnut. Brian, a successful attorney, is skeptical of dating equally successful sisters because he finds them to be "mean," "controlling," and "crazy." But as the movie plays out, we learn that the source of his pain and frustration with sisters traces back to his untrusting and unaffectionate mother, who will not even hug her sons or tell them she loves them.

According to our survey, 51 percent of black men feel that black women are more likely than white women to let their devotion to their religion interfere with intimate relationships. Almost two-thirds (63 percent) of men making over $80,000 a year agreed with this statement, as did 55 percent of the younger men, ages 35 to 44. (I discuss this in greater detail in Chapter 6.)

After hearing from the brothers, I now have a much better understanding of what they want from us. They want our intelligence, compassion, laughter, and effervescence, as well as sexual and emotional compatibility. Sure, there will always be some insecure souls out there who can't deal with anyone who is more successful than they are. However, I'm now convinced that "intimidation" is *not* the main reason many black men have opted out of our lives.

I'm more inclined to side with attorney Jam Donaldson, who posted on her blog an entry titled "He's Not Intimidated, He Just Doesn't Like You: The Intimidation Doctrine." Ms. Donaldson implores African American women to look inward at the characteristics that may be driving away men. Rather than placing the blame elsewhere, she asks women to assess how their "I can do it all by myself" attitude comes off to men. Her premise: black women who take responsibility for their role in relationships and apply high standards to both their partner and themselves are the women who attract and maintain healthy relationships with successful black men.

> Because the "single" designation is such a source of anxiety as you get older, we oft find the need to justify our status. We have these little reasons that we tell ourselves we're alone to make us feel better. And it's time for it to stop. If I hear one more woman say that men are intimidated by their success and/or independence, I'm going to scream. I call this the *Intimidation Doctrine*. . . . As long as we believe that most men are intimidated by strong successful women, we fail to look at ourselves for the reasons we cannot maintain successful relationships. The Intimidation Doctrine keeps us looking outward for fault. It relinquishes us of all responsibility. And I think it's holding us back.[21]

Ladies, if you're wedded to the notion that a man is intimidated by black women, you risk limiting your own growth and potential for a deeper and more meaningful relationship. It's not about us having more; it's about men not knowing where they fit into our lives. Here's what one recently divorced brother and father of four in his late forties (who married a wonderful sister in the spring of 2010) told me:

Men at our very core are dragon slayers; we are hunters, and we want to be seen by the women we love as such. The problem that we face now is that women are now the hunters. Women now own the castle. Women in many cases outearn us. Outperform us at work. And you know what? That is as it should be. However, the problem with this is that men no longer know where we fit or what we are supposed to be in relation to a woman. There has been a huge paradigm shift and for black men; the ramifications have been enormous. In fact, if the truth be told, women are running circles around men in every aspect of our lives. Men have been feminized in our culture, told to be *metrosexuals*, to groom themselves and *manscape. That is not who we are, ladies.* And nowhere is our confusion with who we are showing up more than in our relationships with fabulous, accomplished black sisters.

*The brother's point is powerful.* This man is not saying he wants a woman to walk behind him or not pursue her career. The challenge is that times have changed both our expectations and our comfort levels. Fortunately, there are some young black men who understand that this new reality calls for a new mind-set. One of them spoke out at a Howard University standing-room-only discussion where I was the keynote speaker addressing the ABC *Nightline* news program, "Love, Marriage, and a Baby Carriage." When I was finished speaking, I asked the brothers in the audience about their thoughts on black love on a campus where the women greatly outnumber the men.

Maybe it's time men realized that things have changed with women. We are still trying to date in a 1950s/1960s context when women had less options, stayed at home, and were not as educated or independent. That time no longer exists in our culture, and black men must learn to compromise, be more flexible, and not see her success as a threat to our manhood or our ability to lead the relationship or marriage. We must learn to be proud of the sisters' accomplishments and work with them as a team.

Now that is what I am talking about, young man! I agree with him. It is time for us to *redefine* how we approach dating and love. Maybe our outdated notions of what dating is supposed to look like are what are causing so much distress. So if any of these points or dated misper-ceptions about black men ring true for you, consider the advice in the chapters to follow on how to unearth a new, happier, more approachable, sensuous you. Then join me in a fascinating journey exploring, redefining, and reclaiming black love, twenty-first-century style.

### Twenty-First-Century Barriers to Love

LOVE IS COMPLEX—and true love is hard to find, nurture, and keep alive. Hard but not impossible. Two sets of challenges come to mind when I think of key relationship barriers that accomplished black women face. First, as BlackandMarriedwithKids.com family coach Ronnie Tyler points out:

> Our mothers and aunts have taught us how to achieve, but not necessarily how to be wise, or how to encourage our men, and uplift them, be soft, or to be a wife. Our mothers wanted us to take care of ourselves, and a lot of us don't know how to switch roles, so we are confused. I agree that I would raise my daughters to recognize that if a man dogs her, she won't have to hesitate because she'll be equipped to take care of herself. Unfortunately, our men are seeing too many sisters "doing it on their own."

Ronnie's husband, Lamar, weighed in:

> Men are thinking, "Well, I saw mama do it, and my aunties do it—so I feel justified not paying child support or being around. Sisters can hold it down on their own." That is a bad mentality. The data shows that this is a big deal with single heads of households. What our young brothers are learning about being around women all the time is that they are learning to manipulate women and run a game on them— they're not learning that a man puts himself last. . .I am the head of my household, and the buck stops with me.

The second challenge we rarely discuss is the impact of today's technology on our dating and relationship-building skills. Technology offers instant access any time of day or night, yet men and women seem more out of touch with each other than ever. Oprah talked about this on a show that aired in May 2009: "It seems that we are so focused on our gadgets that we've lost our connection with each other as people." To prove this point, the families featured on the show had to live without technology for one week. "We tapped into something that more and more Americans are yearning for—less stuff and more meaning in their lives," Oprah says.[22]

So let's start by getting a grip on what modern relationships really entail these days. By taking a deeper look at the research findings, expert testimony, interviews, and focus group findings, let's uncover what we want from this thing called love and how we can develop the relationships we truly desire.

## Relationship Trends

MAYBE IT'S JUST me, but I'm really struggling with understanding and defining the different stages of relationships these days. The whole process can be confusing and cause lots of hard feelings. Men and women seem to want and need different things from one another that require more compromise and better, more honest communication.

Although we now embrace a broader definition of what a relationship is, that doesn't mean we all grasp or like the new rules of the game. I grew up thinking relationships covered dating, courting (a more committed version of dating), engagement, and marriage. Of course, there were people "shacking," "swinging," and taking part in extramarital affairs and homosexual partnerships, but people around me didn't openly discuss such arrangements.

Today dating could mean sexting, online dating, hookups, watching pornography (apparently that's the go-to place to learn "mad skills" for the bedroom), and, yes, man sharing. Although I think some of us still go out to dinner, take in a movie, or enjoy a concert together, that's not what anyone is talking about these days. Remember when your boyfriend in school asked you to "go with" him? That meant go steady, or be boyfriend-and-girlfriend. I'm thinking they don't do that anymore.

Our younger sisters are no longer girlfriends: they aspire to be a man's "main chick," "jumpoff," or "friend with benefits." Some high schoolers and college women identify themselves as "LUGs" (lesbians until graduation) or "BUGs" (bisexual until graduation). There's no doubt that young women have adapted and adopted some very interesting ways of making up for the shortage of acceptable black men in their lives.

We all know the drama surrounding the search for black men.

Introductions through friends and family are few and far between. I'm personally fascinated by the stories I hear about man-hunting treks to the clubs with the girls. (How is that working for you?) And whether we like to admit it or not, more of us every day are trolling the online matchmaking and dating services like blackpeoplemeet.com, eharmony.com, and match.com. Been there, done that—scary!

Modern relationships are much less rigidly defined, as more of our friends and family are cohabiting, having casual sex, or seeking adulterous liaisons. But some relationship experts and therapists have problems with these loose arrangements, and so do I. I don't want to be judgmental here, but as Dr. Audrey Chapman suggests, "If we continue to 'loosen or make liberal' the definitions of relationship, we may be headed for some serious emotional difficulty as black women."

This is especially problematic for those of us over forty who believe in a more old-fashioned dating and courting process. That's because so many of us are really over the dating game—both the traditional and the new no-ties kind. We're desperately looking for romance and love in a committed partnership. But, sisters, there is no magic wand; this does not come instantaneously. Like all good things, it takes time, friendship, and commitment to develop an authentic and blessed union.

## What Does a Good Relationship Really Look Like?

ACCORDING TO LOVE and relationship expert Joe Beam, who is a bestselling author and founder of LovePath International, a good relationship is based on four principles (PIES):

1. Physical attraction (people are attracted most to people who exude health, wellness, and fertility[23])
2. Intellectual attraction (understanding, connection, values)
3. Emotional attraction (this person evokes good emotions in me—he makes me laugh, smile, and feel good)
4. Spiritual attraction (connection of beliefs and values; this person makes me aspire to something greater)

"Physical [attraction] is simply not enough to build a life with someone. I wish I could get people to understand that out of the gate. It would save much heartache down the road later," says Beam.

It's fair to say things have shifted dramatically for women in the last twenty years or so. More women are independent and financially secure; they buy their own homes and expensive cars and take vacations around the world. Naturally, many of the things our grandmothers and mothers looked for in a mate we no longer hold as valuable. Men now have to step up in ways that may be uncomfortable for them. Women want something deeper: true intimacy, love, respect, romance, tenderness, friendship, and a full relationship because they can get all the other stuff on their own.

The challenge is that being perceived as "too independent" and constantly talking about how we will not "settle" is a double-edged sword that we need to handle carefully. One important thing, however, that I don't hear us discussing is the fact that many of us simply have not had positive relationships modeled for us growing up, and we have no idea what a loving partnership truly looks like. It is hard to live what you do not know or understand. We have mentors in the workplace. We have trainers in the gym. We have people who teach us how to cook, transform our homes, train our pets, and even raise our kids. But how many of us have people who have taught us how to love and be in a relationship?

As I mentioned earlier in this chapter, the Obamas represent what many sisters in my generation thought was possible but never achieved. Their modern-day love story—from dating through today—grew into that old-fashioned kind of love that we saw in our grandparents' generation. They are a team, they are best friends, they hold dear the true meaning of family, they love their children, and they are two whole human beings who admire and respect what the other brings to the table. They are partners on a journey.

Although we can learn from the Obamas at a distance, it is clear that some accomplished black women have a rough road ahead if we want to find love, not because of all of the daunting statistics and news reports but because, as I said in Chapter 1, *we have yet to conquer ourselves.* We also need some up-close, happily married role models to give us real-time hope and guidance. That's because many Gen X and Gen Y women have grown up in single-parent or divorced households, without the benefit of seeing how supportive, energized, loving marriages really work. There are plenty of successful married couples with kids who are living out their version of the American Dream. Talk to them. Talk to your married male friends. Ask them how they manage to juggle a family, home, and career.

A dear mentor of mine was telling me about an interesting experience she had while engaged to the man of her dreams. Although she and her fiancé were raised in happy two-parent homes, her former boss, Earl G. Graves, founder of *Black Enterprise* magazine, was determined to prepare them for marriage the right way. At Barbara and Earl Graves's twenty-fifth wedding anniversary gala, Earl sat my friend and her beau at a table with four older couples who had been married twenty-five years or longer. The topic of conversation for the table that evening was the secret to a long, happy marriage. Perhaps Earl's strategy paid off: the couple celebrated their own twenty-fifth anniversary in September 2010.

MSNBC journalist and *Tom Joyner Morning Show* commentator Jeff Johnson, author of *Everything I'm Not Made Me Everything I Am*, agrees that the biggest challenge facing black male and female relationships seems to be the lack of married role models growing up.

> White men have more replicable role models of families that are working and thriving, whereas many black males do not even know their dads. Many of us have not seen our fathers be loving husbands, or emotionally available for their female partners. Boys and young men need to see their fathers be hardworking, responsible, and loving. Black boys and girls need to see their parents build a partnership within a marriage. . . . [Without role models,] we are not conditioned to value each other outside of just dating and sexual gratification. As boys, we are not taught to value women as friends, as people. Instead, we teach girls to jockey for position for men's affections, and we teach boys to value women based on what they can do for them.

## Interdependence: Why We Put a Ring on It

MARRIAGE COUNSELOR AND family therapist Senovia Ross interviewed for this book believes that understanding the parameters of a healthy relationship is the best way to ensure that your dating and marriage expectations are realistic.

> I'm always telling the couples I counsel that you can't live life as a single person and continue to be in a relationship. A relationship requires you to share yourself with another person—not just physically, but spiritually, financially, with transparency, and interdependence. This

is critical for a relationship to work. Once you [form a relationship,] . . . you have to balance his needs versus your needs. If you refuse to make the adjustment, your relationship will fail.

Ms. Ross cited Mrs. Obama as a good example of a powerful, accomplished black woman who made an adjustment from the campaign trail to the White House as First Lady in part because she wanted to make sure her children adjusted well and in part because she wanted to support her husband's career. At first she was harshly criticized for this transformation, but I admired her decision. What appeared to be a move to the back seat may have strategically placed her right in the driver's seat of power and influence around the world.

Sure, a solid marriage takes work and compromise, but it also leads to happiness often not acknowledged in our community. *New York Times* columnist David Brooks discussed the benefits of marital happiness in an op-ed piece:

> Marital happiness is far more important than anything else in determining personal well-being. If you have a successful marriage, it doesn't matter how many professional setbacks you endure, you will be reasonably happy. If you have an unsuccessful marriage, it doesn't matter how many career triumphs you record, you will remain significantly unfulfilled.[24]

Our ABW research found that black married professional women *and* men are very satisfied with their relationships. Three-quarters of married women respondents report that they are content with their current spouse, and most would say "I do" all over again to the same man. Those numbers hold up for the men we surveyed: a whopping 86 percent of the men surveyed say they are happily married; 79 percent would marry their current wife if they had it to do all over again. A potential signal for a need to rejuvenate the passion in marriage is the absence of a satisfying sex life. Since marital bliss does not always translate into sexual bliss, it was encouraging to learn that almost two-thirds of the married women (62 percent) claim they are "sexually fulfilled" in their marriage. But that number dips when it comes to men: less than half (48 percent) "strongly agree" or "somewhat agree" that their marriage is sexually gratifying to them. Mature married men between fifty-five and sixty-four years old were generally happy with their sex life.

The best news is that 78 percent of the married men don't believe that cheating on their wife is an option to fulfill their sexual desires. According to researcher Dr. Silas Lee, who conducted the men's research for this book, this data should not be exclusively interpreted from a physical perspective but rather with consideration for the multiple dimensions that bond people in marriage—respect, trust, goals, and authenticity. Pollster Kellyanne Conway agrees with his analysis and adds, "I find it to be very good news that, contrary to reports that black women and men are less satisfied in marriage, our data shows the opposite and that sex is not the only glue holding these marriages together. Black couples still treasure some of the very same qualities our grandparents' generation valued."

## Twenty-First-Century Dating: New Rules with Not So Good Results

*T*he most important rule is never, ever call a man, since it takes away the challenge, and without a challenge his interest will plummet. Trust in the natural order of things the book advises. Namely, that man pursues woman.

From the authors of the *The Rules,*
Ellen Fein and Sherrie Schneider

# 5

## REAL TALK ABOUT TWENTY-FIRST-CENTURY RELATIONSHIP EXPECTATIONS AND TRENDS

"Dating should be less about matching outward circumstances
than meeting your inner necessity."

—UNKNOWN

*I* think we can all agree that modern dating is, in a word, complicated. So, if we are going to have real talk about some of the barriers to finding love and reasons so many desirable, accomplished, and wonderful sisters are still single, we have to start with the twenty-first-century dating landscape. The facts beyond the staggering numbers inequity between black men and black women is just the surface of the problem. As I touch on in Chapter 4, there is a whole new language that young men and women in their twenties speak: they text; they date via the internet on match.com, eharmony.com, or blacksingles.com; or they use more exclusive dating services like It's Just Lunch or Together. While this may be normal to you young sisters in your twenties, it is much less so for women of my generation and older, who grew up with a whole different set of rules and expectations for dating, courtship, sex, and marriage. And it is a great source of angst for many women over thirty now trying to compete for a smaller pool of available black men.

To illustrate the point, I had dinner recently with some of my younger sorority sisters at Howard University, and as I always like to do when I connect with the younger sisters, I started getting in their business, asking about dating, grades, relationships, and so forth. When one young soror showed me her cell phone, I was mortified at the text messages from a young brotha on campus asking for a date. He said: "Hey oh—you tryin to chill?" She responded, "Maybe, what's up?" He responded, "I got some food, you tryin to cook?" And it went downhill from there. When I picked my jaw up off the floor and regained my composure, I asked the young sisters if this was the norm. They assured me that it was. I asked them if they had ever gotten flowers or candy or been taken to dinner. They assured me that they had not. What disturbed me most was that they were okay with this—and the reason is because they have never known anything else. For women my age, however, we remember what it was like to date in our twenties, when men were respectful; they courted you and met your parents. Thus, many of us have opted out of dating and cover ourselves in religion (see Chapter 6) and being "busy" because we just don't like the new rules of the game. Many of this new generation of young sisters and brothers do not know their fathers. They have never seen a woman be doted on or courted. There has been a major shift in just the past twenty years in how we relate as men and women and how we act that out in the dating game. Unlike the rules that applied to court-ship when my mom and dad were dating in the early 1960s, and when I was dating as a younger woman in my twenties and thirties during the mid-1980s and 1990s, the modern dating game favors males and asks very little of them when it comes to being intimate and having sex with women. Sisters, please don't miss this because it is true, and it is at the heart of why so many of us are unhappy and feel empty when it comes to dating.

The other often unspoken challenge for the modern sister (I dare say all women) is that we are just too damned busy. When my mom was my age now, she had been married for over twenty years, she had two kids (one in law school, the other in high school), and she was a registered nurse (a career she entered when I was about twelve years old).

My life is dramatically different from hers. I just turned forty-four years old, and I am never married (albeit happily dating), I have no kids (although I wanted a house full), I own my own home, I can come and go as I please, and the world is my oyster for traveling, pursuing dreams, and whatever else I like. For better or worse, I am the norm for many professional sisters my age (according to the Yale study mentioned in Chapter 4[1] and our own study, 60 to 70 percent of professional sisters are not married). And I have come to conclude (very late in the game) that part of why I never got married is because I was just too busy achieving things and pursuing my career goals. Dating, like relationships, takes work and commitment to make it successful and fulfilling.

As life coach Valorie Burton writes in her book *How Did I Get So Busy?* "The problem with being too busy is that you lose your sense of self. In the race to get it all done, you give up the experience of being fully engaged in anything."[2] I am so there!

The man I have been dating for some time is equally busy. He travels a lot and is often away. We get along great, and we are good *when we are good* and when we can connect, but it may not be enough. One of us or both of us will have to change for this relationship to go to the next level. I bring this up because I want you to know, as I said at the outset of this book, that the things I am sharing here are as much about me as they are about you. Like many of you, I need to redefine the rules of my life, particularly in the romance department. I think in our modern-day, power-brokering, BlackBerry-driven world, it can become way too easy to live without someone in your life when you are on your own for so long, as I (and many of us) have been. It takes a lot of work to drop some of the independence and "I" for more companionship time and "we." It is something I struggle to balance every day. I know I want marriage and a family, but it has become so easy to be on my own and not have to share my life with someone, even though I want that very much. *Go figure.*

## Twenty-First-Century Dating

IT'S HARD TO build a relationship without going through the dating phase. How else do you get to know someone? In the high-speed, high-expectations sweepstakes of modern life, somehow the lines between dating and relationships have become blurred and problematic. So, as I have done throughout this book, I turned to those who can give us some guidance. I interviewed *Essence* dating and relationship guru Demetria Lucas to break it down for us. She says that "a relationship is about commitment. You date to have fun or to find a relationship. The problem is that black women really don't know how to date." Lucas believes that many young women want a committed relationship almost right from the start. "We need to be more like the guys—date around. Have more fun," she advises. The tricky part is that dating today often includes sex, especially among self-proclaimed sexually empowered young women. The unspoken protocol for modern dating suggests that couples start having sex sometime between the third and fifth date.

"The standards governing these types of relationships have shifted," says Lucas, the author of the forthcoming book *A Belle in Brooklyn*, a novel based on her blog by the same name. "For instance, just because you're sleeping with a guy doesn't mean he sees the relationship as exclusive." We used to call this cheating. Unless you explicitly discuss exclusivity and what that means, you cannot assume that your man is faithful. "Monogamy is still important to most women," adds Lucas, "but given the odds out here, some are willing to settle for being a man's 'main chick' or 'steady' among many others."

Lucas used a friend's story to illustrate her point. "Janell was dating a nice guy. Although their relationship was never defined, they enjoyed each other's company. When Janell hosted a party and her guy showed up with another girl on his arm, she threatened to hit him over the head with a champagne bottle if he didn't get out of her sight. Her male friends chastised her for getting upset because the relationship wasn't exclusive. She never had the conversation with this man. I understand that, but I confess I was appalled that her man showed up to *her* party with another woman. For me, that's just downright rude and disrespectful. Allowing a man to disrespect you like that is a deal breaker. As Steve Harvey says, 'Men respect standards. Get some.'"

Since the rules seem up for grabs, black women often feel like we are in a struggle with our men. When men say or do something we don't like, it really hurts.

High-profile ballers and celebrities dating outside their race is also a hot-button issue. Although 70 percent of black men are married to black women, the media bombards us with images of Reggie Bush, Tiger Woods, and Taye Diggs with Caucasian, Latino, or Asian women on their arms. While black men go multicultural, the media is simultaneously blasting headlines that ask, "Why can't successful black women get a man?" The whole scarcity phenomenon is making some women desperate (especially our younger, college-age sisters) and increasingly likely to do almost anything to snare a man. The idea of a woman putting her needs first seems almost revolutionary. That's very different from the attitude of many of their single older sisters, aunts, and friends, who refuse to turn somersaults to accommodate a man.

After talking to several twenty- and early thirty-something sisters, I better understand why they are so fed up with their men. Here's the 411 on the younger IBMs—highlights from our younger sisters filtered through my vantage point:

- Black men, particularly young ones, aren't interested in and don't see the value of being in a committed relationship until later in life. Sowing wild oats after the marriage leads to nothing but heartbreak. So this painful reality is probably a good thing.
- Women want to lock down exclusivity a lot earlier than men, which is scaring the hell out of these barely-out-of-college men. This is an extremely difficult situation for countless reasons. Falling in love with a man who insists on seeing and sleeping with other women while he says he's into you is disheartening and demeaning. Even more important (and this is a huge problem according to the Centers for Disease Control), his sexual activity puts you at an enormous health risk for a dangerous range of sexually transmitted diseases, including HIV/AIDS.
- White guys (and men from other cultures) seem more comfortable courting, settling down, and marrying by their late twenties or so. But that's when the brothers feel they have enough money to focus on being a "player" and living the life.
- Materialism and hanging at the clubs while ordering bottles of champagne like P. Diddy is very high on the testosterone to-do list. These guys may actually like a girl and want to date her, but marriage? They prefer to keep their honey "on hold" until they get ready
- IBMs are into only beauty queens—the super-fine, long-haired, sexy honeys (Beyoncé wannabes). Brothers have big-time problems letting go of their fantasies and finding love with real women of all sizes, shapes, and hues.

These younger sisters' impressions may be true, or they may simply be distortions fueled by media coverage and music videos. Think about it. Who in the mainstream media was reporting on black love twenty years ago? Maybe all the negative press about modern black love is pushing these sisters to overreact. On the other hand, some of their points may be valid, and since we can't change all the brothers, we must ask ourselves: What are you going to do to find the right one for you? What standards are you willing to compromise and/or change to have the kind of relationship you seek?

According to our focus groups and survey research, apparently, many sisters aren't willing to make compromises. Many of us feel that we're doing fine all by ourselves. Sixty-six percent of the ABWs surveyed say that they'd rather be alone than settle. This is an *easy way out* for us. It suggests that something is flawed in the man who might be pursuing us, or that he is somehow less than we deserve. It lets us off the hook of challenging ourselves and critically exploring who we are and what we want.

Here's what two ABW focus group participants said about settling:

> Let me explain to you why I, as a black woman, will not settle for anything less than I am worth. I have done a tremendous amount of work on myself. I am highly educated, kind, loving as a person. I have had many years of therapy to move past and heal the terrible hurts I have experienced in life and have come to a place of peace and contentment. I do desire to have a partner with whom I can share the journey. However, he must have done much work to divest himself of the shackles that this racist, sexist, classist, homophobic society— what bell hooks, my former professor and heroine often dubs "white supremacist capitalist patriarchy"—burdens us with to varying degrees. He must be someone, like me, committed to social justice, personal and spiritual growth. *I know I can go it alone.* I may be alone now, but I'm not often lonely. I know that in truth, I am never alone. That's how deep it is for me.
>
> I take "settle" to mean giving up what feeds me—accepting a space that does not encourage me to be my best, which does not challenge me to be my best. Deciding that I can progress in a space that does not recognize or appreciate who I am and what I can become.

This is an expensive order to put on any relationship's table, and it will take a very, very special man to live up to these requirements. Realistic? Perhaps. Perhaps not.

But the absolute resolve of never-married women to live alone if the package isn't perfect has Dr. Audrey Chapman, relationship expert, psychologist, best-selling author, and popular Howard University radio talk show host, extremely worried. Chapman warns that if never-married black women don't come to grips with handling the new dating scene, reconciling their conflicts with sexuality and faith, and dealing with past hurts, betrayals, and disappointments, many will live out their lifetime alone, which will have major consequences." (I address those consequences in more detail in Chapters 7 and 8.) As Chapman notes, "Black women pressured by the Christian community to marry and have a family will become depressed, resentful, and bitter. I see it all the time in my practice. That is not a formula for wellness and fulfillment."

As Jeff Johnson of the *Tom Joyner Morning Show* said to me in a one-on-one interview for this book:

> Sisters seem to be double-minded about what they want. They're looking for perfection even when they themselves are not perfect. Women want more than they're willing to give. Many men and women are selfish, plain and simple as that may be. But what sisters don't get is that men focus on how a woman looks. We want to possess a woman. We also look for what a woman can do for us.

Johnson adds that thinking like that presents a big challenge when dating because "we don't focus on the 'heart' of a good woman." On the other hand, Demetria Lucas feels that listening is a big challenge for women and suggests that we try to listen better and be more open to feedback. "I learned to listen well from my father. Now I really try to hear and understand the feedback I receive from my male friends."

Some black women also have problems acknowledging our role in what is wrong or what we need to change, adds Lucas. "Too often we fail to acknowledge our role in the dates and relationships that go wrong. That has to change. We must be willing to say, 'I messed up too. I am flawed. I need to change as well.' But sometimes it's just easier to duck and cover versus dealing with my baggage, pain, and insecurity."

Sisters, I cannot say it enough: we must get out of our own way. We seem bent on blocking our own path to true happiness, fulfillment, and joy. Trust me, I know how we got here. I do. But isn't it time to let go and start loving ourselves, and expand our vision so we can truly open our hearts to loving someone else?

One of the mantras I'm tired of hearing from sisters is "He just needs to love me like I am." Or "What you see is what you get. If you can't deal, then I will be fine on my own." *Sisters, sisters, sisters.* The law of attraction says that what you speak into the universe comes back to you. You attract what you are.[3] If you project "I am better off alone," you will be alone. We have got to stop this madness. We get angry when someone says we need to lose weight, comb our hair, or put on some lipstick. We get offended when someone says we need to stop being so angry or so overly religious that we scare people off. We are always ready to pounce, go off on someone, or reject sound wisdom and counsel, and then we wonder why we have such challenges in the dating game.

The truth is that some of us need to shed some pounds. You know if you have too much junk in your trunk. Some of us need to take our drama down several notches. Some of us need to work less, drink less, curse less (a big one for me!), and sex less. Some of us need to stop having to always have the last word (boy, do I know this one!). And some of us need to learn to be quiet and listen to another person's point of view, insight, and wisdom on how to grow into a woman who understands this truth: it's not just a matter of finding the right person; it's about *being* the right person. Long-time singles also need to do a self-check and assess how willing we are to see the world beyond that "it's all about me" perspective that I mentioned previously. I've been on my own since I was eighteen years old. Learning how to share your time, your heart, and your home isn't that easy. But the difference is I get it now, and I am in a very good place. My energy is right, and the requests for dates from quality men are overwhelming—if I weren't already taken, I would be having the time of my life dating the old-fashioned way!

## All the Single Ladies

EVEN DEMOGRAPHERS ARE concerned about the increasing number of never-marrieds. The numbers aren't in our favor: there are 1.8 million more black women than black men in America. Even if every black woman in America married a black man today, one out of twelve still wouldn't make it down the aisle. Equally disturbing, if a significant number of educated, affluent black women don't marry and have children, America may experience a decline in the number of middle-class upwardly mobile black families.

Life and relationship coach Valorie Burton talks about a power struggle, or competition, that has emerged between black women and men. She stresses the importance of trying to make a heart connection, setting aside all this measuring up, and redefining what we need. Does he like you? Love you? Respect you?

We have lost our basic communication skills with black men. The conversations related in the talk shows, books, and blogs capture people talking at each other, not with each other. Women have to ask their men what they want from life and where they want to go—and be willing to build the common ground to help each achieve their goals and desires. We've lost the concept of union. This serious conversation is not an ice-breaker for a date. It's a discussion that happens much further along in the relationship—when both parties are seriously interested in putting stakes in the ground and pouring the foundation of a life together.

With some clear thinking, prayer, and faith, there is always hope. This inspiring focus group confession warmed my heart:

> Settling meant giving up hope that I can connect with someone who fulfills my qualities, characteristics, and values that I desire for a mate—my ideal. It also meant that my future does not have as many possibilities as what is before me. But after fifty-three years of being single, I'm now engaged to the right guy and am not settling. In the past, settling may have been being with someone who wasn't necessarily on my same level professionally, intellectually, or physically. Settling to me now means sacrificing my desire to connect with my divine right life partner. This one was easy; our paths crossed one evening, and we've been together ever since—no wavering. And *he* wants to take care of *me* for a change! He has not made the kind of money in life I do because he chose a career of service, but I think that's part of the reason he is so right for me—he's a caretaker, like I've been for so many years, but *he* takes care of *me*.

## Dating a Married Man: Cheating or Surviving?

THIS PAST YEAR we all read the screaming headlines about singer Fantasia's love affair with a married man that resulted in her attempting suicide by ingesting a bottle of pills. In an interview with *People* magazine shortly after the incident, Fantasia explained her emotions: "I was tired of people doing me wrong, constantly, over and over again, dealing with my family—my father, dealing with men and their [expletive]—I was tired. My head was hurting me. I was over it."[4] How sad and how tragic. Here is a beautiful young sister with a great voice (she just released her third album), money, and the limelight, and yet she had a secret: she was having an affair with a married man named Antwaun Cook.

To make matters worse, after the affair became public, his wife, Paula Cook, threatened to sue Fantasia under the old common-law "home wrecker" statutes, which still exist in seven states and allow a party to sue her adulterous spouse's lover for "alienation of affection" and "criminal conversation."[5] What a hot mess this situation turned out to be. Like many women before her, Fantasia got caught up, and in the end, she stood alone in the court of public shame as the home-wrecking hussy. It is as old as the story of Mary Magdalene in the Bible, sisters—the "other woman" always loses; the blame is always cast on her. I would ask you to count the cost before you allow yourself to get in such a place because the cost is very high.

I know. I have been there. It is a sad day in a woman's life when she gets to a place of such loneliness, unhealed father-daughter pain, or brokenness that she either knowingly or unwittingly gets involved with a married man. The truth is, based on the experts I have consulted and some empirical research, more of us are choosing to date or have affairs with married people. Shocking, I know, but it is yet another symptom of the changing moral culture and "anything goes" world around us. Just peruse the web—there is actually a website exclusively for married people who want to have affairs (http://www.ashleymadison.com) that has been profiled on *Dr. Phil* and *Good Morning America*. I mean, how messed up is that? Another factor that feeds into this phenomenon is that approximately 56 million adults are single in the United States.[6]

Current statistics confirm that *one in five* American women cheats.[7] "I've seen an increase—as have my professional colleagues—of middle-aged, upwardly mobile black women dating married black men in the hopes that they will leave their wives," says Dr. Audrey Chapman. "But these men do not leave their wives, and so the women end up compromising themselves in very damaging ways. These women are so lonely they're willing to settle for this type of situation."

As I mentioned, I have traveled that painful dead-end road. So I know of what I speak. Many years ago, I found myself lonely, vulnerable, and starved for attention and affection—the perfect storm for making poor choices. I did not consciously seek out this type of relationship. In fact, it caught me completely off guard. I tried to pray it away. I tried to ignore the warning signs, but ultimately I succumbed to the temptation and illusion that I believe Fantasia experienced.

I was like a thirsty woman wandering in the desert looking for an oasis. I had lost my heart, my femininity, and my sensuality. I was dressed in corporate suits all the time, hard charging, battle-hardened, and suppressing my femininity and my sexuality, as so many of us do, under a heap of regret and religious dogma. I had a lot of unhealed emotional baggage from my father, from men who had hurt me, and from myself. I functioned like an efficient machine made to work and compete with men. Unbeknownst to me, I was in dire need of human connection and love. I got involved with someone I trusted and connected with on a deep emotional level, who made me feel beautiful and desirable. I was like a flower that blossomed. I became open, vulnerable, and softer. I fell in love, deeply, and in doing so, I got involved in an emotional hell zone that robbed me of years of my life. In that process, I betrayed a friend, my family, my God, and most of all, myself.

It was hard even after all these years to forgive myself—but I finally have, because I learned to talk about it and not live in secret shame anymore. In talking about it, I found that a lot of sisters have been there, and like me they needed to confess, forgive, and heal in order to move forward (see Chapter 8). The saddest part about the Fantasia saga is that everyone attacked her and vilified her. The wife wanted to sue her instead of dealing with an unfaithful husband. As Fantasia confessed in the *People* magazine interview, she was dealing with a lot of unresolved deep pain in her life that led her to make some unhealthy choices.

Sisters, if you are in this type of love affair, please get out or tell someone who can help you get out (as I did when it happened to me). Oprah recently had a show on this very topic titled "I'm the Other Woman."[8] This program featured women who date married men, and they spoke candidly about their experiences. What I have found is that many women try to fool themselves about the realities of what happens when you get involved with a married person. As one woman told me, "If you understand the rules, you can make it work for you. It's better than having no man in your life." What a fool she is!

There are no rules. Cheating with a married man or woman is wrong. And as the third wheel, I promise you you will lose, sister. Even if you get that man, what will you have? A man who violates his wedding vows, cheats on his wife, and irreparably hurts his children to be with you. Is that what you really want? *Really?*

I counsel anyone who asks my opinion on this subject from my own experience and with the words of a noted psychologist: "An affair is like a nuclear bomb that goes off in the lives of all involved in the triangle that is created by the affair; one that leaves devastation, regret, guilt, pain, and sometimes mortally wounded dead human souls and spirits, even dead physical bodies."[9]

His sentiments are dead-on. I thank God every day for the love of my good friends, my family, and my iask sisters who helped me to get past this terrible failing in my life and have the courage to face it, speak out about it, and help others never to walk down such an empty and destructive road.

## Is It Time to Bring Home a White Boy?

WHAT IS IT about the black female–white male dynamic that sends sparks flying? What keeps so many successful single sisters from exploring relationships outside our race at a time when the pool of eligible black men is at an all-time low?

Speaking at Howard University a couple of years ago, I mentioned that I was dating a white man very seriously, and loved him deeply. The jaws dropped. One young sister in her early twenties stood up and asked, "What did your family think?" My mom, who was in the room, just smiled. My answer: "Ultimately, they were fine with it." Her response: "My father made it absolutely clear—'Don't bring home a white boy.'" We all laughed, but her point was serious.

We have all heard that directive, whether from our fathers, uncles, brothers, or male cousins. Anyone who has dated a white guy has endured the "How could you, sister?" looks when walking down the street holding his hand. *Don't date a white man* is a cultural message stamped deep into every black woman's psyche. It is an enduring taboo deeply rooted in slavery (which I discuss in detail in Chapter 2).

In an ABW internet poll taken in fall of 2009, we asked 1,700 self-identified professional black women several questions concerning their dating lives, including the following: Would you as a professional black woman date/marry a white man to find the love you desire? Table 5.1 shows the results.

The most surprising finding in our survey is that 10 percent of black women would not even consider dating someone who is black. One reason for this might be the perception that black men have abandoned black women, so the ladies aren't even willing to give them a chance. As pollster Kellyanne Conway noted, more research may be required with black women to probe why they would not date a black man.[10]

No doubt this is a hot topic on the black blogs and in the mainstream media. Now at last there is an honest, eye-opening examination of this social phenomenon. I had a chance to interview Karyn Langhorne Folan, a black woman happily married to a white man, about her new, ground-breaking book, *Don't Bring Home a White Boy*, which boldly debunks the notions that can keep interracial dating off the table for many black women:

- After slavery, I could never date a white man.
- My family would never accept him, and his would never accept me.
- White men don't find black women attractive unless they look like Halle.
- Our biracial children would have no sense of identity.
- It means I'm a sellout or filled with self-hate.
- We'd just be too different.

TABLE 5.1: Would you as a professional black woman date/marry a white man to find the love you desire?

| RESPONSE | PERCENTAGE OF RESPONDENTS |
|---|---|
| Yes, and I have dated white men and have enjoyed it | 31 |
| Yes, and I married a white man | 3 |
| I am open to doing so but have never tried it | 44 |
| No, I am *only* interested in dating/marrying black men | 8 |
| No, I don't feel white men are seriously interested in black women | 8 |
| Not sure—still too many taboos for black women to date white men | 6 |

"Race is not the key factor in what will make a successful marriage. The character traits and values of the person you love are what make it work," says Folan. "People always assume that there will be a lot of drama in interracial marriage. They are wrong. More of the drama comes from other people outside of the marriage—family, friends, people in social settings. Black women need to gain cultural fluency, because the twenty-first century is going to be the century of multiculturalism. Sisters need to stop being defensive. Stop thinking in terms of inferiority and superiority. Black women have to be willing to have a back-and-forth exchange with men outside of the race."

Still, taboos and reluctance remain in the minds of both black women and white men. As we discuss in Chapter 3, black women and white men seemingly have an innate tension and inability to connect in the workplace as mentors and as friends. Yet I know from my own life that loving a white man is no different from loving any man. As Karyn Folan said in our interview:

> I did not decide not to date a black man or a white man. I wanted a relationship again, so I made a list of qualities that I wanted in a man. I didn't put anything on the list that didn't reflect who I was. I married my husband because I felt I could *be me* with him. I never felt I had to suppress my personality. He was secure with himself and very easy to be around. He [worked hard to win over] my daughter from my previous marriage to a black man. We now have a child together.

She added, "My husband and I model *cross-cultural* understanding." According to Folan, the only time they've had a conflict over race was when Harvard professor Skip Gates accused a white policeman of harassment when he questioned why Gates broke into a home in Cambridge. (Professor Gates had forgotten his keys, and the home he broke into was his own.) Folan says she saw it from Gates's point of view. Her husband sided with the policeman. "We got past it quickly," she explained with a laugh.

In another insightful interview with a beautiful twenty-six-year-old black female marketing executive in Virginia, I heard this interesting take on interracial dating:

> Maybe black men are dating outside of their race more prevalently than black women because we do not make ourselves available to men of other races. Or we don't *want* to be made available to them because we have been told all our lives that a white man and a black woman go against the grain, either by our mothers, grandparents, or even the shows we watch. Now I'm asking myself, "Why?" Why do we feel like there's no one out there that can love us like a black man can or

should? Perhaps it's because we [black people] regularly make fun of and desexualize the white man. Think about it. Stand-up comedy acts for years by black comedians have poked fun of the corny white man and their inability to dance, be "cool," and make love like a black man. Jamie Foxx and others have compared the bass and smooth beats of R&B music to the rhythm of a black man's lovemaking and then mimic some corny hillbilly song when portraying the white man's approach and performance. It's funny and harmless for the most part. Or is it? Have we been brainwashed to think we could never fit with a white man because they weren't good enough for a black woman? I think we have been conditioned to not see the white man as a possible mate from our very own black men while they have *no problem* sleeping with and marrying white women.

But what is it like to marry and have kids with a white man? I had an extensive interview with a couple in Virginia who are friends of mine. She is a forty-three-year-old black journalist, and he's a white graduate school administrator and counselor who is ten years her senior. The couple met during her senior year in college in the early 1990s. I asked them both what made it work and what they saw in each other, particularly given the age difference. She explained:

Mark and I had the same value systems, and we had fun together. He was kind and supportive of me and my personal goals, which was important. I tell young women to find a man who is proud of you. Someone who is comfortable with himself—and not intimidated by your success. Someone who will love *you* no matter what. He needs to be a strong person. Mark never stops talking to his friends and family about how proud he is of me and the kids. Black women who are successful and professional need to be looking for those qualities and not the materialistic things.

Mark said:

Being married to Jean has not made one bit of difference in how I am treated or how people see me. Sure, we get the stares sometimes at the grocery store when the cashier tries to put the grocery divider between my wife and I, and we have to say, "We are together." Or when she was with our three children, people thought she was their nanny when they were younger or that I adopted them. It's small stuff like that. But at the end of the day, living in the D.C. metro area has been easy for us in terms of acceptance.

Pausing, Mark reflected on the historic *Loving v. Virginia* case, which in 1967 legalized interracial marriage, and how much those two people called Loving—a white man and black woman—loved each other and simply wanted to be together. Yet they ended up changing the law forever in America. His conclusion: "I guess we really have come a long way."

Love knows no color. Yes, I hope and pray we as black men and women get our act together and work on returning to love. But even if we cannot do so, sister, you need to find love wherever it greets you. It just may be the blue-eyed white boy that you pass each morning on your way to work. It just may be the Latino gentleman who opens the door for you each day on your way to lunch. Or the Asian fella sitting in the cubicle across from you at work. And let's not forget the Native American Adonis who works out next to you at the gym each day. Whatever the case, like a free and gentle flower, we must open ourselves to love. You will never know love unless your surrender to it.

## Your Love Plan

Now it's time for you to reevaluate and redefine your relationship bottom line and come up with a strategic love plan. Start by answering the following questions and maybe having a sister/brother dinner at your home to discuss them, or lunch with friends who can engage in healthy relationship discussions.

- *What does a really good relationship look like?* Talk to men and women in relationships you admire and ask them to share their insights, strengths, weaknesses, ups, and downs. Most of all, find out what it really means to fight fair, forgive, and reconcile.
- *How do we date successfully and find the right mate?* It doesn't matter what the dating trends require; you have to do what's comfortable for you. Nevertheless, it's important to understand the dating landscape and the unspoken rules behind this sometimes puzzling ritual so you'll know what you're up against.
- *What really matters to you in a man, and what would make you feel*

*like you have to settle?* Remember, life isn't an all-or-nothing propo-sition. Success in life requires resilience—bouncing back and recov-ering from things gone wrong, including bad relationships. Are you punishing yourself unconsciously for some brother who broke your heart ten years ago? Consider the consequence of unrealistic expec-tations and the absence of real self-knowledge. Are life's inevitable growing pains worth a lifetime of loneliness? Don't let your inner twenty-something and her unresolved issues sabotage your life at thirty- or forty-something.

- *What do I bring to the relationship table?* There are women out there—and we all know them—who seem a little uptight, a bit rough, and not that physically attractive but still find love and get married. They found that one man who wants them just the way they are—and so can you. But each of us has to be realistic and do some self-assessment. Not all of our stuff is all that. And some of it repels the people we want in our lives.

- *What are you willing to compromise and change to have the kind of relationship that you seek?* I can't stop laughing about this ideal black man concept. What does an ideal black woman look like? I want to know because I don't know anyone who fits that bill.

- *Are black men the only game in town?* Ask yourself: Am I willing to break outdated cultural taboos and bring home the white, Latino, Asian, or Eastern European man?

PART III

# Moving Beyond the Pain to Purpose

"Happiness is the consequence of personal effort. You fight for it, strive for it, insist upon it, and sometimes even travel around the world looking for it. You have to participate relentlessly in the manifestations of your own blessings. And once you have achieved a state of happiness, you must never become lax about maintaining it. You must make a mighty effort to keep swimming upward into that happiness forever, to stay afloat on top of it."

—Elizabeth Gilbert,
*Eat Pray Love*

*S*ex is the physical dimension of intimacy.

True lovemaking is the one act in which all three aspects of intimacy come together—*emotional, spiritual, and sexual.* For us humans, sex isn't just about making babies. Far beyond our child producing years, we carry need for sexual fulfillment. For us Sex is about becoming ONE with another person.

Joe Beam,
*Becoming One*

# 6

## JESUS IS YOUR SAVIOR, NOT YOUR MAN:

### *Candid Talk about the Church, Sexuality, and the Role They Play in Our Quest to Be Loved and Fulfilled*

"We are born with four natural drives: hunger, sleep, thirst, and sex. If we suppress any of these for too long, consequences, often not good, will result. Human beings should have balance in their lives: Whatever the pursuit, moderation most frequently is the most healthful path."

—REVEREND SUSAN NEWMAN, "Oh God"

*J* am not a preacher, sisters, but let me be perfectly clear: *Jesus is your savior. He is not your man.* And there is a big difference between the two.

Under the increasingly popular "Jesus is your man" theology, women are getting confused about the role of Christ in their lives. And we need to get unconfused quickly. We need to question the motives of spiritual leaders who encourage single black women to take the vow of celibacy outside of marriage one step further and live lifelong monastic existences. We were made for love, warmth, touch, companionship, sexuality, and intimacy. Anyone who is preaching anything contrary to this message from the pulpit, sisters, is not preaching the gospel of truth, and it is time we had a candid conversation about what some have called a "culture of bondage" for black women in the black church.[1]

Do I have your attention?

These may seem like bold statements (as one of my editors said, "I don't want to be anywhere around you when the churchgoing sisters read this chapter—you are going to need a flak jacket."), but I want to dive right into an issue that is disturbing and real and affects the well-being of generations of churchgoing black women in America.

You will recall that in the summer of 2010, a national controversy erupted when black dating advice columnist Deborrah Cooper wrote an article titled "The Black Church: How Black Churches Keep African American Women Single and Lonely."[2] The article is a no-holds-barred, in-your-face, straight-up confrontation of the black church (dare I say all churches) and their teachings relative to human sexuality and twenty-first-century dating. Instead of regurgitating what Cooper said in that piece and what her critics said in response, I'll share with you some thoughts from a very insightful sister-to-sister interview I conducted with her exclusively for this book in the fall of 2010.

I want to be clear at the outset, however, that my goal is not to take sides in this fight (of course, I have an opinion). My goal in this chapter is to present you with the data we uncovered in our ABW national survey and focus groups on the issue of our sexuality and faith and to share with you some varied expert opinions of people in the clergy and in spiritual/emotional counseling, who deal with these issues daily. I want to delve into what sayeth the Lord (i.e., the Bible) and how we need to relearn to manage our spirituality, sexuality, and humanity in a way that keeps us emotionally and physically balanced and healthy. Simply put, sisters, my job here, as in the other chapters of this book, is to give you information and prescriptions that you decide how to fit into your life plan or not as you strive to lead a truly healthy and fulfilling life as a hard working black woman in America.

So let's get into it, shall we?

In the past decade or so, a very controversial religious movement called the "prosperity gospel" has emerged in the African American community. The prosperity gospel is essentially a "name it and claim it" theology: God wants His people to prosper, so those who follow God and give generously to his ministries can have anything they want. But critics of this "gospel," from Bible-quoting theologians to groups devoted to preserving the separation of church and state, abound. At best, they say, such a theology is a simplistic and misguided way of living. At worst, they say, it is dangerous. I agree. To be frank, aside from making a whole new generation of preachers, televangelists, and authors very rich (you know who they are—no need for me to call out particular folks), this gospel has done little to help anyone.

Instead, it has misdirected scores of black women (particularly single, high-earning black women) to give more of their money, and more of their time to the church in the hopes that doing so will get them the life and the mates that they seek. When they come up short—the pastors and leaders often tell them their faith *is not strong enough* or that they need to *pray harder* and be more devoted to see the desired results. This is where our discussion should begin. I believe what is being offered here is a false choice.

Now, sisters, before you throw the book and get upset, stick with me for a minute. You are all well-educated, intelligent women, so it is time for you to stop being emotional and to start thinking for yourselves. As you read this chapter, I would ask that you get your Bible, get a cup of tea, and open up to some real sister talk about an issue that is tantamount to our well-being as black women in this life and the next.

To their credit, many churches out there (mine included) have explored a number of different avenues to help black women deal with their loneliness and dashed dreams of marriage and having children, including sponsoring opportunities for singles to interact. Still, there is a highly vocal pastoral community preaching that abstinence and the single life is the way to go. Within this movement, some are determined to indoctrinate us by saying that the statistics suggest that some black women looking to marry will simply be *left out of the marriage pool*—so for our own protection, we should give up our hopes for marriage and adopt a lifestyle that allows us to focus almost exclusively on the church and service to others. The result is that we serve the church tirelessly and fellowship with other singles, mostly women, instead of with married couples (who in my opinion are the best suited to give us relationship advice). We are told to just keep praying for that man to come along, and one day he will show up at church with a neon sign.

## Who Can Compete with Jesus?

WHAT SINGLE MAN is going to come along and be able to compete with Jesus? Talk about pressure! Reverend Marcia Dyson believes that the I-don't–need-a-man philosophy is particularly challenging for black Christian women. She explained to me in an interview for this book that the notion of black women being alone for the rest of their lives is contrary to biblical promise. "The Bible teaches that we are designed to be a 'complement, helpmate, and supplement' to a man [Genesis 2:18]. And yet now we are telling black women to live without a man. This doesn't work on a number of levels, and we need to start talking about this honestly and working toward healing and resolution to the challenge black women are facing in this area."

Another female pastor I interviewed (who did not want to be identified) had this to say:

> I am aware of the position some in church leadership take related to Jesus being "the man" in a single woman's life. But this is an extremely delicate issue for a great deal of black women who are fragile around this topic. I believe that black women's consistent, reliable, and healthy support systems can be a significant challenge to secure in our lives. The church is often the only safe haven black women have. And before we dismantle these support or belief systems, we have to be mindful that an adequate replacement may not be readily available, which can result in a great deal of physical, emotional, and spiritual disruption in our sisters and ourselves.

After years of ingesting the "God has another plan for your life" and "your desires are sinful" theology, it has taken me a long time to accept that I am a living, breathing human being who is worthy of and needs love in her life—not just *agape* (friendship) love but *eros* (passionate and sexual) love.

Many single black women have been told that leading a life of celibacy is required, noble, or "what God has for us," but I respectfully disagree. *I believe that God has much more for us.* I mean no disrespect to sisters like Michelle McKinney Hammond, Cynthia Hale, Juanita Bynum, and pastors who are rightly calling black women to value their bodies and stop sleeping around. The problem is that they're sending a mixed message that kills our human spirit. Hammond admonishes sisters, "Don't pleasure yourself. A man will never be able to replicate the sensations you can give yourself." So now masturbation is also off the table? *Really?*

Juanita Bynum, whom Bishop Jakes introduced to the world in the 1990s, ripped the covers from sisters sleeping around in the church with her best seller *No More Sheets: The Truth About Sex*. However, after two failed marriages and several bad relationships in her life, Bynum has become more vocal about leaving Mr. Little (your man) and returning to Mr. Big (God). Bynum seemingly has shut down her prospects for love by performing, during her fiftieth birthday celebration, a wedding ceremony—in the wedding gown from her former marriage—in which she marries her destiny! Sisters, is this really what we want for our lives?

I asked Deborrah Cooper to talk to us about why she wrote the controversial article she did in June 2010 and to expound on why so many churchgoing sisters seem to be embracing a life of celibacy on the surface but struggling with their sexual needs inside, as the data in our ABW study clearly shows (more on these results later in the chapter).

A lot of black women are torn. I had one woman tell me that she agreed with what I am saying about the role the church is playing in keeping us single, but she asked me a very profound question: "If I don't go to church or have church in my life, where do I go as a black woman?" The church is a place of comfort and solace. I see black women as being asked to deny their womanhood in a quest for spiritual absolution and purity. They look to their pastors to tell them what to do with their money, their bodies, where to live, what kind of man to choose, etcetera. It has become a real issue of control over black women's lives versus what the Bible actually teaches. And as a result, the church is filled with a lot of lonely, sexually repressed, and frustrated black women.

Is Cooper on to something, or is she just a small voice crying out in the wilderness? One forty-six-year-old accomplished, recently divorced sister who was a pastor's wife in the Midwest for fifteen years gave me some great insights into what it is like to be on the other side of this prism for black women.

I lived it for fifteen years. The black church has become a very dysfunctional place. We all know it, but we refuse to address it. What I saw as a pastor's wife—as the First Lady of the church—was one of two extremes: In the first extreme, the pastor is revered as a king; the women in the church are his harem, or indentured servants. The married male leadership is quite often involved in sexual liaisons with single sisters, and their wives know it but turn a blind eye. That, of course, causes chaos in the church amongst the women. In the second extreme, the sisters are held to a strict set of rules and told how to dress, talk, think, and to be submissive. And if they veer from this script, they are labeled a Jezebel. There is serious bondage going on in the church against black women, and it is literally killing us! We are dying a slow emotional death of spiritual bondage that has nothing to do with the liberty and abundance that Christ wants for us all.

Powerful statements from two women at different vantage points.

According to a 2009 PEW Research Center poll, African Americans are markedly more religious than the U.S. population as a whole on a variety of measures, including affiliation with a religion, attendance at religious services, frequency of prayer, and religion's importance in life. For African American women, the numbers are more pronounced. More than eight in ten black women (84 percent) say religion is very important to them, and roughly six in ten (59 percent) say they attend religious services at least once a week. No other group exhibits such high levels of religious observance.

But what is the impact of what Cooper and others say is happening in the black church on upwardly mobile, single sisters? Cooper said in our interview:

The greatest impact of this new movement in black churches is that black women are being drained of financial resources due to tithes and offerings, they are being taught to fix "broken birds" [e.g., men who come out of prison and reintegrate into churches, men who are out of work, etc.], and most importantly, they spend so much time at church and doing church work that they are not putting energy into pursuing lives that give them what they want: love, intimacy, and fulfillment.

Others, like Reverend Adriane Blair Wise, a married Gen Xer and minister of spiritual foundations at the historic Metropolitan Baptist Church in Washington, D.C., (and a former women's chaplain at Howard University) don't think blaming the church is the answer to what ails us. Wise told me in an interview:

I think it misses the mark to fault the church *alone* for the large number of single, PhD, never-married, or divorced black women in the church. I think we need to go back to the foundations of the black family post–civil rights era and how our parents and grandparents emphasized education and achievement for our generation, and they encouraged us to delay marriage and children until we achieved educational and financial independence. They wanted their daughters to have all the opportunities they did not. This is a key driver as to why many successful sisters are still unmarried in their thirties and forties. So to blame the church alone is not going to help us address the problem.

Wise continued, "I do agree, however, with some critics who are suggesting that the church at large is not talking openly and realistically about sexuality and spirituality. We have to begin to teach women about how they maintain their sexual identity and still remain faithful Christians You cannot separate the two—they go hand in hand."

## Sexuality and Our Faith: Where the Rubber Meets the Road

OKAY, SO I think it is fair to say we have consensus that there is a problem in the way the black church deals with issues of black female spiritual identity and sexuality. This is nothing new, but it is surprising in a twenty-first-century context in which black women are now pastors, ministers, song leaders, and deacons. I think the point that all the women I interviewed are making is this: some Christian women are so full of *do's and don'ts* that we've lost touch with our own sexuality. Regardless of who is to blame—the church, our families, or society—we have to commit to redefining our sexuality in a way that is both sacred and fulfilling to us as women.

Sisters, who among us doesn't want to be loved, touched, cared for, and made love to by someone we trust and respect? Deep inside, we pray for such a loving and committed relationship. Yet we seem to be at war with the sexual and the sacred in our spirit. Somehow we've mastered the suppression of the very emotions that make us feel alive and attractive to others. The time has come for us to reconnect *passionately* with both our sensuality and sexuality in a way that honors our true nature. We need to experience our lost desire, revitalize our bodies and spirits, and reclaim the emotions that bring us joy and make us a joy to be around. We must learn *or relearn* how to marry our sexuality with our spirituality. We must truly value both if we are to ever enjoy wholeness.

The key for us, sisters, is to keep our desire in harmony with our spirituality. It has been this way since Eve made the fateful decision in the Garden of Eden to pursue her *desire* for the forbidden fruit. The Garden has powerful lessons to teach us. In the Garden, we learned that we were created to have relationships, desires, sensuality, and free will. So why do so many of us now bury and hide that God-given side of ourselves?

Yes, it is true that Christian women are swimming upstream in a modern culture that promotes sexual freedom, promiscuity, and independence. No doubt, social mores have drastically changed, and particularly so in the black community. Interviewing young women and men for this book, as well as reading some of the research findings, left me speechless in many instances, but we have to deal with reality if we are going to address this huge conflict in our lives. The fact is that we live in a fast-paced culture that reveres sex outside of marriage, sexual innuendo, sexual expression, swinging, living together, jumpoffs, having children out of wedlock, and doing whatever one pleases to fulfill the base sex drive. Given this context, it is not always easy to keep your sense of identity as a woman of faith. I have heard many sisters lament that men just don't want "good girls" anymore. I respectfully disagree. "Good girl" versus "bad girl" is a false choice.

We need permission to be human without feeling guilty. The church must become a place where we can talk openly about sex and sexuality without shame, fear of reprisal, or reprimand. When we suppress this very natural part of ourselves, said Cooper, we open ourselves up to harm. "Black women are not held and touched on a regular basis. It is a shame, and it accounts for a lot of depression, loneliness, and illness." I agree with her. It is long past time for black women to have some serious sex therapy to bring sex out of the shadows, educate us as believers, and relieve us of our guilt.

What our ABW research tells us is that black female Christians *are in fact sexually active* but act as if all they do under the sheets at night is praise the Lord. We hide and hope no one discovers we are leading a double life. But all of us are sexual beings. When we come to church, we don't leave our sexuality in the parking lot to pick up after the benediction. Sexuality is like a pink elephant sitting in the middle of the pews: everyone sees it, but no one wants to acknowledge its presence. No one talks about it. Yet, as the former pastor's wife shared with us, sex is going on in the church and all around the church in very unhealthy ways. This is why so many of us are either sexually repressed or conflicted about sex.

## So What Does God Have to Say about All This?

SISTERS, PULL OUT your Bibles and buckle up! You only need to read Proverbs 5:18–19 and Song of Solomon 1:2–4 and 6:2–3 to know that God values sex greatly. God created sex and desire. God does not command that we be walled-off nuns or eunuchs. His plan for us is that we be in relationships with one another, in love, and united in holy matrimony:

> May your fountain be blessed,
> and may you rejoice in the wife of your youth.
> A loving doe, a graceful deer—
> may her breasts satisfy you always,
> may you ever be captivated by her love.[3]

> Let him kiss me with the kisses of his mouth—
> for your love is more delightful than wine.
> Pleasing is the fragrance of your perfumes;
> your name is like perfume poured out.
> No wonder the maidens love you!
> Take me away with you—let us hurry!
> Let the king bring me into his chambers.[4]

> My lover has gone down to his garden,
> to the beds of spices,
> to browse in the gardens
> and to gather lilies.
> I am my lover's and my lover is mine[5]

Let's put this into context: God created sex, and He understands our need for love and sexual intimacy, as we can see from the Old Testament scriptures. He says in Genesis 2:18 "It is not good for the man to be alone let me make him a helper." But the Bible clearly commands in both the Old and New Testaments that sex is for marriage *only*. Yet, we know Christian people have sex outside of marriage every day.

So what to do?

The apostle Paul knew that men and women are going to have sex. They did it in the first century, and we are doing it in the twenty-first century (a lot). Thus, Paul suggests in 1 Corinthians 7:1–2, "Now for the matters you wrote about: It is good for a man not to marry. But since there is so much immorality, each man should have his own wife and each woman her own husband."[6] The immorality of which he speaks is sex outside of marriage—sex in and of itself is not dirty or immoral. Paul advocates marriage so that Christian men and women have an outlet for their natural sexual urges. This pro-marriage sentiment is echoed in Hebrews 13:4: "Marriage should be honored by all, and the marriage bed kept pure, for God will judge the adulterer and all the sexually immoral."[7]

Now some of you are shaking your head and saying, "Sophia, that is just dumb. Marriage is so outdated. I mean, look at the Gores separating after forty years of marriage. Divorce rates are very high. And unmarried people live together now, have babies, and are happy doing so." Let's explore these ideas briefly. The data suggests the opposite—that married women are happier overall than their single counterparts. Living with a man before marriage exponentially increases the chance a woman will be abused domestically, and the divorce rate of people who marry after living together is much higher. On the other hand, women who marry are physically healthier, are emotionally healthier, are less likely to be victims of domestic violence or violent crime, are less likely to contract STDs, are less likely to live in poverty, have better relationships with their kids, and are less likely to abuse drugs and alcohol, among other benefits.[8]

What am I suggesting is that *if* you are a Christian and *if* you are going to adhere to a plain reading of the scriptural texts, then you'll agree that sex outside of marriage is a violation of God's commands. But we still feel conflicted because we have sexual needs. As one sister friend explained recently, "I know it's wrong to have sex with my boyfriend outside of marriage as a Christian woman. No argument. But I like sex, and I don't want to deny myself that very important need as an adult woman. I feel more alive and human when I can share sexual intimacy with someone I love." *I hear you, sister, I hear you.*

So where do we go when our normal, healthy sexual appetite is on a starvation diet because of our spiritual beliefs?

Let's go back to what the national data tells us. According to the Barna Group, a Christian research organization, a higher percentage of African Americans believe the scripture is accurate, believe in God, and value spirituality in our lives than other racial and ethnic groups.[9] Our research for this book confirms and amplifies these findings, and that is why we need to tackle this subject: many of us are living outside of our faith tenets in order to satisfy our normal, natural, healthy sexual desires, and we must reconcile the two, sisters.

## Erasing Barriers to True Spiritual Intimacy and Sexual Fulfillment

WHETHER CHRISTIAN, BUDDHIST, Muslim, or other, all women must at some time explore the intersection of faith, sexuality, and reality. Here are some of the questions we must consider: (1) Does God, or our "higher power," want us to think about sex as dirty or a burden that we have to perform to keep a man? (2) Is sex a weapon we should use to get or keep a man? (3) Is celibacy the only option single Christian women have if they never marry? To answer these three questions, you must first be brave enough to *redefine* what you want from your emotional and intimate life and, second, be prepared to rethink what being a Christian or spiritual woman really means to you.

Psychologist and coauthor of *Prime Time: The African American Woman's Complete Guide to Midlife Health and Wellness* Dr. Gayle Porter and I had a chance to talk one-on-one, and she believes that black women must take full responsibility for their choices relating to sex and sensuality. Porter is particularly concerned with how single black women deal with the thorny issue of whether to engage in sex outside of marriage:

> If your spiritual frame of reference makes celibacy your only option as a single woman, then you must take ownership of your decision. If you choose to follow this tenet, then you have to accept that you are limiting your options and choices in terms of relationships, and be okay with that. But no matter what you decide, ultimately you must be accountable to yourself. You can't be angry with God for how you choose to live out your faith. That's not healthy.

I think what Porter is suggesting is revolutionary, sisters: she is speaking truth. Whatever we decide, we alone have to be prepared to deal with the fallout. My prayer is that we will have the courage to break out of our self-imposed emotional exile and think deeply about whether

God's words prohibit us from being both sensual and righteous women at the same time.

Unfortunately, many religious people lose focus of the tenets of their faith (such as love, compassion, connection, kindness, and service) and simply go through the motions of worship like robots. Televangelist and best-selling author Joyce Meyer hits this point hard at her women's conferences. Singing to the tune of "Here We Go 'Round the Mulberry Bush," Meyer belts: "This is the way we go to church, go to church, go to church," while walking stiffly upright. She uses this comedic parody to help women realize there is no joy in simply going through the motions of being Christian women. I agree. God didn't intend for us to get lost in empty religious routines. God wants us to live our faith as happy, authentic, powerful, loving women.

But what does that look like in our daily lives? Today we are tested to the core with what seem to be conflicting demands. Our men say we should be sweet, sexy, seductive, and submissive. Our families, our community, and our church want us to be strong, tough, chaste, giving, and supportive. Our children crave our attention, protection, and participation in their lives, and so we must be unassailable role models (which makes negotiating intimate relationships an extra tricky situation for single moms). But are these demands really at odds? Has the world become so black and white that we must choose to be either loveless career women or video vixens, trading sex for companionship in hopes of snagging a man? *I don't think so.*

So why are so many of us having problems connecting our desires and sexuality with our spirituality? Our research confirms what we already knew: successful Christian black women are having sex—*in and out of marriage.* Well over fifty percent of single churchgoing ladies polled (Catholic, Baptist, Protestant, and Pentecostal) admit to having sexual relations outside of marriage.

Let's go deeper, though. For starters, we must acknowledge the sexual history of black women in the United States, as a group and as individuals. As I explored in detail in Chapter 2, slavery shaped much of our sexual identity as black women. According to retired child and family psychiatrist Averette Mhoon Parker, the former head of the Washington, D.C., Department of Mental Health who I spoke with for this book:

> Sex has often been viewed as a taboo for black women because of our historical context of victimization, rape, incest, and forced sexuality.

This heartbreaking reality has been chronicled well by great writers like Alice Walker, Maya Angelou, Angela Davis, and Toni Morrison. No wonder so many black women have an innate fear of sex and our own sexuality, as it is rife with so many landmines and pathologies.

Gangsta rap songs and music videos certainly have not bolstered our fragile sexual self-esteem as black women. What right-minded woman doesn't feel compromised and offended by these testosterone-driven fantasies? The sex-for-sale lifestyles prevalent in the last two decades of hip-hop have encouraged the popular attitude that casual sex is okay. Our ABW research shows that over 75 percent of accomplished, well-educated, professional black women say they "were raised to think that freely expressing my sexuality outside of marriage was bad or in violation of God's commandments." That is a huge finding, sisters. Stop and process that for a minute. Yet, despite this foundational belief, when our pollsters asked ABWs if they had engaged in a friends-with-benefits or buddy-sex arrangement to fulfill their sexual needs, a staggering 56 percent said that they had. However, only 14 percent say that they *felt good about it* or that it was *acceptable.* As we dug deeper, we found that 42 percent of those who have engaged in a friends-with-benefits or buddy-sex arrangement do not think it was good or would not do it again. Of the 35 percent of women who say they are not into casual sex, one-fourth of this group say flat-out that sex outside of marriage or without intimacy is not fulfilling.

There you have it, sisters. Either out of loneliness or because of the intense competition for men, even self-defined religious women are ignoring the inner voice reminding them of the tenets of their faith that warn them to think hard before engaging in casual sex. We've traded this inner voice for something far less valuable. How many times have we listened to a friend share the pain and regret of giving her body in the hope of gaining companionship or intimacy, only to feel robbed when it's over? Too many to count.

Best-selling Christian author and sex and relationship expert Joe Beam is founder of LovePath International, an organization that helps married couples stay in love or fall in love again. The emphasis of his research is sexology. I had a chance to talk with Beam, and here is what he shared:

God values sex. The union of sex with someone is a spiritual as well as a physical act. I know this is a foreign concept in our modern times. But God is clear. If you can't control your sexual desires, get married.

This notion that sex is only something men desire is ridiculous. Read the text: Paul, in 1 Corinthians 6 as well as chapter 7, is speaking to men and women alike—Paul commanded marriage for sexual purposes. Let's take it a step further. Paul tells the husbands that it is their job to fulfill the wife. I read that very clearly to say, "Men: put a woman's sexual needs first," not your own. He likewise tells women to fulfill their husbands. God gets it. Men and women alike need sexual fulfillment, not just raw, empty sex.

As believers, we have the Holy Spirit dwelling in us. When we commit sexual acts with the body outside of marriage, we cause the spirit to commit those acts, too. Think about that for a moment—it is jarring. This is why so many women feel damaged emotionally and guilty spiritually when they have noncommittal, meaningless sex. Having sex is a deeply spiritual process. You cannot separate yourself into two parts. You are both body and soul, as Anita Baker sings so powerfully in her 1990s hit "Body and Soul."

Marriage was designed for sex; it is the safe outlet for our natural, normal, healthy desires. God gets it; He gets us. And more importantly, I think it is fair to say that God did not design us as women to have sex without meaning and connection. We are hardwired for intimacy and attachment. Consider this biological fact:  women emit the hormone oxytocin when they achieve sexual peak—the same hormone they emit when breast-feeding. The hormone is sort of a bonding agent that connects the woman emotionally as well as physiologically. Women are designed for combined emotional *and* sexual fulfillment. Ironically, though we pretend that we're liberated enough to approach sex like men do, many of us seemed stunned by the confusion, conflict, and spiritual damage that results from causal sexual encounters.

When did Christian women trade the names that God calls us by— holy, precious, adored, royal, beloved, daughter, helpmate, wife, and mother—to be called buddies, jumpoffs, LUGs, BUGs, main chicks, or friends with benefits? Who told us it was okay to engage in such insignificant sex? Sisters, listen up. This will hurt, but it needs to be said: we are engaging in a form of selling our bodies, without token or receipt, to men who view us as cheap prey, and it needs to stop. Consider what one black forty-year-old divorced, self-professed Christian man from Richmond, Virginia, had to say in one of our focus groups:

These women are like whores. I know it is wrong to use that term, but in my church, it is something like thirty-two to one, and the sisters let it all hang out. I am enjoying myself. I never knew such sexual freedom existed, but I would never marry any of these women. I know it is a double standard, but I am a man, and the world is not going to judge me as it does a woman. Worse, the pastor knows what goes on in here too, and he simply looks the other way.

*Tough words to swallow.* But sometimes we need to swallow some tough medicine. One of the issues that came up a lot in interviews and discussions about this topic is the clear double standard being pushed by church leadership. We put all the burden on women to be chaste, not the men. We tell women to grow old alone, without sex and love, and we encourage the men to sow their wild oats. One women's ministry leader in Philadelphia whom I interviewed had this to say:

Black women are being manipulated into accepting a blatant double standard when it comes to sexual behavior in the church. We all know there are many gay black male song leaders and ministers, and no one "outs" them. We all know the stories of a "love child" being fathered by a deacon, or a wife being told that even if her husband is unfaithful, she has to stay because to divorce her husband will destroy his image as a man of God. Men in the church are setting a standard for who we as women of faith should be. I mean, look at the books out there telling us to *act like women and think like men*. We get called derogatory names for being sexually free, and men get applauded for it. Things have not changed as women think they have.

## Is Sex Dirty?

HERE'S THE CONFLICT that needs dissecting sisters: the church and church leaders (not God) tell us from the time that we are young girls that sex is taboo, dirty, sinful, and bad. "Keep your legs closed" is a refrain we all know well. Then we grow up to be young women with normal sexual desires, and all of a sudden, everyone tells us how great sex is. Yet, if we stay single long enough, the church tells us that God has called us to a life of celibacy and service.

As the former pastor's wife we heard from previously laments, "Black women are being turned off by the church from the time they are children. By turned off I mean shut down, made to button up, be rigid, subdue our femininity. The cruelest bondage you can put a woman in is to tell her that spirit is enough when she resides in a fleshly body. To tell a woman that Jesus is all you need is against scripture, and it's antithetical to the example of the Proverbs 31 woman that we all love and admire."

It's not just the sisters who are upset about the church. According to the men we polled, over half of them (51 percent) believe that black women are more likely than white women to let their devotion to religion interfere with their intimate relationships. And our research shows that men might not be wrong in thinking that; as mentioned previously, 75 percent of women polled told us that they were raised to think that freely expressing sexuality outside of marriage was bad.

Best-selling author and professor of obstetrics at Columbia University Medical Center Dr. Hilda Hutcherson addressed these very real quandaries in a recent interview with Harlem Health Promotion Center, relating why black women have such a hard time with our sexuality:

I think this [conflict] is something that has been going on in our culture for as long as we've been in this country at least. We've had a lot of hang-ups about sex and sexuality. One of the main reasons why I think this happens is . . . the way we view sexuality in the church. I can give you an example from my own upbringing. I was taught that sex was something that was dirty and sinful and something to be reserved for the person that you love and marry and spend the rest of your life with. The problem was that once I entered into that marriage situation, I still thought about those negative messages that I had been given about sex being sinful. So sex was something that should have been a very beautiful and important part of marriage but wasn't for me. And I found in my practice that it's that same way for many, many other women. There's a lot of guilt and shame surrounding sex and sexuality. And when you look at the fact that most African American women are not in fact married, it's easy to understand why they might feel some guilt and shame about sex and their own sexuality.[10]

However, as I mentioned previously, black men and black women *do not* get the same messages about sexuality from the black church or their families. This has got to stop, and black women need to hold clergy and church leadership accountable, as women now make up the majority of black churches.

As Dr. Susan Newman writes in her book *Oh God!* "Contrary to what is being preached in the pulpit, black churches have long had a 'wink and a nod' attitude toward the sexual behavior of its male members, contributing to confusion and double talk that advanced no one's well-being. . . . We are doing a disservice to our daughters, and ourselves, trying to fit a 2001 peg into a 400 b.c. hole."[11]

In short, the church needs to change the dialogue about human sexuality and stop winking and nodding at bad-boy behavior on the part of rogue pastors, deacons, and other brothers in the church who prey on vulnerable sisters. The church's message to both men and women should be that sex is not an indecent act but a natural and spiritual bonding experience that God has reserved for marriage.

## Our Faith and How We Cope

FOR MANY BLACK women, faith is our main coping mechanism to shield us from the adversities of life. Our faith sustains us, gives us strength, and provides us a place of comfort and shelter in a world seemingly gone mad. In fact, there is a growing body of literature that claims African American women are the most likely people across race and gender lines to use religion, spirituality, and their faith as a means of coping with life's challenges and emotional angst.[12] More interestingly, black women are more likely to be faithful church attendees and to engage in private acts of devotion. We are also more likely than any other group to cite our love for God and the protection of our ancestors as a motivating factor in our life decisions, whether they are related to our careers, personal lives, or relationships. In our focus groups, which included participants ranging in age from twenty-five to sixty-two, the moderator asked about the effect of faith on daily decisions and relationships. Many of the older women in the group (age forty or older) responded that their religion, or spirituality, plays a major role in their lives and has a direct impact on their ability to be intimate with and/or develop potential intimate (sexual) relationships with men.

New York University professor Jacqueline Mattis explains why black women tend to rely heavily on their spirituality to cope with their life challenges in her article "Religion and Spirituality in the Meaning-Making and Coping Experience of African American Women."

> In the social sciences, the lives of African American women are represented as rife with adversity. The singularity of this image, although seriously problematic, has inspired a wealth of research on the coping behaviors and experiences of African American women. That body of research suggests that in their efforts to cope with life's challenges, African American women employ myriad strategies, including humor, revenge, and the advice of other black women in their social networks.
>
> However, the most consistent finding regarding the coping experiences of African American women is that religion and spirituality hold central places in these women's coping repertoires. African American women use formal religious involvement and private devotional practices (e.g., prayer) to negotiate a range of adversities, including race, class, and gender oppression. In fact, regardless of their level of involvement in organized religious life, African American women tend to use prayer as the primary means of coping with hardship.[13]

Professor Mattis's findings in sum suggest that religion/spirituality help women to do the following:

1. Interrogate and accept reality
2. Gain the insight and courage needed to engage in spiritual surrender
3. Confront and transcend limitations
4. Identify and grapple with existential questions and life lessons
5. Recognize purpose and destiny
6. Define character and act within subjectively meaningful moral principles
7. Achieve growth

Trust in the viability of transcendent sources of knowledge and communication[14]

Despite the benefits, however, some scholars and psychologists have suggested that black women are also using religion as a form of escapism from life's cold, harsh realities. They have even gone as far as to say that our response to faith is somewhat "illogical or even pathological."[15]

Although I don't believe that black women are pathological in their approach to faith, our qualitative and quantitative research suggests that there is some merit to the observation that black women cloak themselves in the protection of their religious faith and rely on it heavily to cope with the absence of love and sex in their lives.

Dr. Gayle Porter believes that spirituality and religion have had both a positive and negative impact on the lives of black women. According to Porter, the research clearly indicates that having a body of people who care for us is a primary reason churchgoers have lower rates of suicide, hypertension, and depression. However, Porter cautions that women who are too deeply involved in their churches may become codependent and rely on the church in an unhealthy way. Her advice is that we should focus on honoring the God in ourselves and not necessarily within the religious structure that is man-made.

We must ask ourselves, "Does our faith help us live the life that we truly desire?" Do we really know how to use the Word to help us navigate life's most complicated challenges, such as sex and relationships? Too many of us have resigned ourselves to a place of religious contentment that really doesn't leave us feeling very content at all. While trying to convince others of how godly we are or how in love we are with the Word and with our savior, many sisters reveal angry, cold, or harsh attitudes.

Dr. Hutcherson believes that the source of some of these issues for black women is the teachings of black churches. She's concerned that these lessons don't offer any guidance on how to reconcile our religious beliefs with having an active sex life:

> I think that the African American church should spearhead [a discussion of] this whole problem that we have with men and with women in regard to sex and sexuality. It's such an important part of the human experience that I think it's important for church leaders to take this on as something that is important for them to get involved in. When you look at the high rate of HIV in the African American community, it becomes very clear that it is extremely important that we start to talk about sex and sexuality in a very realistic way."[16]

## What We Really Want: Touch with a Purpose

STUDIES DATING BACK to a 1985 Ann Landers survey confirm that what women want is to be held, touched, and loved. They don't want disconnected, unemotional sex. When a man from Indiana wrote Landers explaining the advantages of his penile implant and how it changed his life, one incensed Oregon woman shot back, "This man is totally ignorant of the workings of the female mind and heart. If you were to ask 100 women how they feel about sexual intercourse, I'll bet 98 percent would say, 'Just hold me close and tender. Forget about the act.'" Landers rose to the challenge and polled her female readers: "Would you be content to be held close and treated tenderly, and forget about 'the act?'" She requested a simple yes or no response, along with an indication of whether the woman was over or under forty, on a postcard.

Almost immediately, women began bombarding Landers's office with responses, and not just on postcards. Many sent several-page letters discussing the most intimate details of their sex lives. Not since 100,000 readers sent antinuclear war protest letters to President Reagan in response to a Landers column had the reaction been so quick and the letters so numerous. "Apparently I had touched a hot button," quipped Landers. She presented the results (about 71 percent said yes) with her interpretation: "This says something very unflattering about men in this country. It says men are selfish. They want theirs." However, she said, "Some women need the message: loosen up, be sexier."[17]

In *What Women Really Want*, renowned pollsters Kellyanne Conway and Celinda Lake describe a survey in which they asked a national sample of women and men, "Which would you rather have—more sleep or more sex? And would you say definitely or probably more sleep/sex?" The resounding answer was that two-thirds (66 percent) of American women prefer more sleep over sex, whereas only 42 percent of men prefer sleep. Forty-four percent of men prefer more sex to sleep, in contrast to the 20 percent of women who do. (A small percentage of respondents were neutral or declined to answer the question.)[18] This confirms that some of us are just too tired to care. Today, women—single and married—are so busy juggling work, family, church, and community obligations that sex and sensuality have found a permanent place on the back burner of our lives. We heard it from men in our focus groups and survey alike that women are too wrapped up in our careers and working that we have forgotten to be women—and, sisters, part of being a woman is being sensual, sexy, and available for sex when you are in a marital relationship.

Regardless of how we prioritize sex in our lives, however, women are sexual beings, and what we really want, sisters, is *intimacy that matters.* We crave *touch with a purpose.* The reality, though, is that too many of us are what noted psychologist Phyllis K. Davis calls "touch deprived," and it shows. In *The Power of Touch,* Davis writes:

> Touching is a beautiful, connecting, survival-oriented, heart-opening act, and we need to do more of it. . . . Yet, fear of touch and its power bring up enormous fears and judgments, so limits and taboos are erected around the delicious and necessary skin stimulation. Touch affects every individual with whom we come into contact—our entire culture. It's stronger than verbal or emotional contact. No other sense arouses us as touch does. . . . We touch and desire touch because it is our biological key to the door called "species survival."[19]

Our culture also has a lot to do with how we view our sexual natures and our bodies. Reverend Marcia Dyson helped me to understand this context better:

> First, sisters need to get comfortable with the fact that feelings of sensuality and sexuality are natural. Part of how God designed us is as sexual and sensual beings—deal with it!
>
> In other cultures around the world, the awakening of a young woman's sensuality is through the touch of the elder women in their community. In China, young women are bathed with milk. In Africa, young women are massaged with heavy animal or vegetable fat and taught dances that simulate the sex act. In Northern Africa and in India, the sensuous and beautiful application of henna to the hands and feet are to heighten the sense of self and the body. Even the heinous act of genital mutilation, often performed by women, is a sexual overture, like foreplay to the needs of a potential husband. So, whether sensuous or sinister, like the wearing of the *burqa* to protect the man from his lust, women are taught that their body is of value, though sometimes their lives are not.

## What about Masturbation?

"I THINK BLACK women are struggling with being pushed off of [the love and sexuality] table, so to speak—and are being pushed to consider other options, including lesbianism," said Dr. Averette Mhoon Parker in response to my concerns about young women at colleges who now refer to themselves as "LUGs" (lesbian until graduation) and "BUGs" (bisexual until graduation). She continued:

> The difference between black women and white women in terms of our sexuality is that, historically, white women could and can now be open with their sexuality. You see it in the pop culture, and I saw this in my practice for years—it was viewed as positive. Moreover, we now see some of our best and brightest in colleges and otherwise turning to lesbianism. This is what I call situational occurrences that result from two factors: First is the absence of available men. We saw this in studies we did in the 80s and early 90s in D.C. and NYC. The second is the need women have to be held and stimulated sexually. Masturbation can be a good release for men and for some women, but most women are left feeling empty when they masturbate because they do not get the human contact they need and desire to feel loved and cared for.

Reverend Dyson disagrees with Dr. Parker's view on physical self-love, and so do 45 percent of the women we surveyed who engaged in masturbation.

> I feel that autoeroticism is healthy for women who have sexual feelings. A lot of folk would disagree, but this is just a conversation we will have to have with God. There are not enough available men to allow women to "marry rather than to burn,"[20] as one scripture states.
>
> Chastity has its virtues for sure, but the usage of sex toys, to the point where it does not become a vice, is a better option than being in an abusive, adulterous, or exploitative relationship, or having one-night stands. This is a dilemma I struggled with between marriages. I made some mistakes and wish that I had chosen a toy rather than someone who would play with my heart.

Joe Beam concurs with Reverend Dyson:

If someone is masturbating and having thoughts about someone with whom they're not in a "right relationship," [causing] them to think thoughts, view pornography, or look at magazines to achieve climax, yes, that is a spiritual problem. But if someone is exploring his or her body, and the sensations of his or her own body, I think that makes them more sensual and open so that when they do get married, they understand what they desire and how to touch their spouse in a gentle and loving way. It's all in the mind.

## Finding Our Sensual Self

As you can tell from the spirited debate around black female sexuality, the reality is that some of us are like pressure cookers. If you remove the lid even just a little bit, what you'll get is a lot of hot, dangerous steam. I submit that many black women are like this because we're not being touched and made love to by someone who honors us and is committed to us. We have to begin both inside and outside the church to talk openly about the elephant in the room: sex.

Sex is an inextricable part of who we are as humans, and over the past twenty-five years, numerous studies and medical experts have proven that people who have healthy sex lives are healthier, live longer, and are more emotionally fulfilled.[21] Unfortunately, African American women, particularly college-educated women, seem to be the least touched and nurtured women on the planet.

Connie, an attractive executive in her thirties and single mother of two, discussed with me last summer how she had gotten so lost in a giving-it-all-to-God kind of life that she forgot how to live the tenets of her faith: love, compassion, warmth, and openness. She had not dated since her divorce, and her whole life was children, job, and church. She'd forgotten what it was like to be kissed, touched, or made love to. She shared with us through streaming tears how a close friend approached her one day and said that although she was a devout Christian, she was simply "too hard" and that the need to control "oozed out" of her pores, which was why she was having a hard time attracting male companionship.

Deeply hurt by this observation, Connie cried out to God for understanding. She came to realize that she was using her legendary strength as a black woman as well as her celibate moral superiority to mask the pain she felt from having to do everything alone. The great news is that she listened to her friend's critique even though it was painful. She faced her loneliness and started to reconnect with her humanity—to take down the walls instead of hiding behind them. That's when Connie's life started to transform. Instead of the hardened church lady who hit people over the head with religious doctrine, she let herself become a softer, more peaceful, more approachable woman. She said, "Sometimes we subconsciously choose a lifestyle that builds barriers and creates a false 'there's only room for one' reality."

So many of us, like this good sister, have been living life alone for way too long. Many of us will live out most of our lives on our own. This comes with a high emotional price tag. We must come to grips with the fact that prolonged aloneness is not a natural or healthy state of being for women or men. "Our sexuality as women is extremely important to our overall wellness," explains Dr. Aby Washington. "Amorous activities, like touch, kissing, and sex, release a whole system of positive hormones in our body, like dopamine and endorphins that make us feel good and help our cognitive functions perform better."

Sisters, sex is not a burden; it is a gift. But like all gifts, if you don't open it and make good use of it, it sits on the shelf, collects dust, and grows useless.

One very attractive, wise fifty-something sister said to a few of us gathered at her house one cold winter Saturday: "I tell black women all the time that if you don't use it [your sensuality], you will lose it. Young women need to learn how to be more than the sum of their achievements and remember that men respond to confidence, femininity, and warmth—all very spiritual qualities." She went on to tell us a great story about how she met her husband (of over thirty years now) at a summer pool party back in the 1970s. At the time, he was with a proper young woman from a very good family, and our storyteller described herself as more of a "round the way" girl. She shared with a smile that her husband's date was "very pretty but standoffish. The girl was wearing pearls, a summer sweater, and a nice skirt to a pool party." That's when another fifty-something sister who was sitting with us at the table, who'd also attended that pool party, chimed in: "Yeah, and my girl over here was wearing some nice shorts, an off-the-shoulders top, and was working some bad heels. Her hair and makeup were flawless." We all laughed because we all connected with the visual. At the pool party, she was having a good time, laughing, dancing, engaging with other guests, and enjoying herself. And her future husband took note. Eventually, they met up again at another party, and he asked her out. The rest is history. Take note, sisters, because God knows I was once the girl in the pearls, as are many of you. Time to break out the sexier, softer, more sensual you.

One of the most constant refrains that our iask mentors have drilled into us is that sisters today need to be less businesslike in our approach to dating and loving our men. But trust me, there are many ways to get a man that don't start and stop with buck-wild sex. What happened to the art of courting and being fun and funny, flirtatious, sensitive, and sexy while wearing pretty dresses? If we are redefining the rules, sisters, then we need to stick to our principles, but we also need to learn to attract men to us in ways that will lead us to marriage and a fulfilling sex life.

I'll use one example from my own life. A couple of years ago, I dated a really nice guy whose job required him to travel overseas a lot. One day he called me from the Middle East early in the morning. He was being flirtatious and a bit frisky on the phone, and I was trying to shut it down because it was headed in the wrong direction—*or so I thought.* How I conducted myself with him needed to be consistent with my religious principles, right? We were abstaining from sex until marriage, which is a constant struggle for two mature adults who are very much attracted to each other. So in my mind, I had to shut down his interest in what seemed to me to be phone sex, so I quickly poured cold water on the call and changed the subject. After we hung up, I called one of my mentors who has been married for thirty years and is one of the godliest women I know. She has no problem telling me that sex is still a very active part of her marriage after all of these years. When I shared my story and the frustration I felt, she laughed at me and said, "Your generation just does not know how to handle men." I was like, "Uh oh, I feel a sister-in-the-know butt kicking coming." Instead, she offered me some really sweet and sexy ways that I could have handled the call better. What she said was profound and right on target. I should have said, "Yes, I am wearing something nice this morning, and thank you for remembering that I always smell nice. I am thinking of you, too. It is so good to hear your voice. And someday we will be able to share the mornings together and enjoy each other. . . ." Wow!

Her point was this: we want men to love us and be connected to us, but we often use God as a weapon to keep men from becoming intimate with us. As *Essence* magazine editor at large Mikki Taylor likes to say, these days men and women "don't know what to do with each other" before the relationship matures into a romantic sexual partnership within marriage. What Mikki is talking about is old-fashioned courting, the emotional dance of romantic, erotic love that has nothing to with having sex. Sisters, here is the thing: we have to relearn how to value our bodies as a holy temple without walling ourselves off. Although women are sexual beings and desire sex every bit as much as men, we are wired differently. God has designed us for sex with emotional intimacy. Sex alone just doesn't do it for us. One recent Kentucky University study found that men and women who are spiritual still view sex differently. In fact, when men became spiritual, the frequency of their sexual activity decreased. It was the exact opposite for women, who view spirituality as promoting closeness and emotional intimacy.

The bottom line is that if we want true sexual fulfillment, we need to educate ourselves about sex, review the tenets of our faith and/or beliefs, and come up with a customized personal plan for how we intend to satisfy our nature as sensual women. Men don't want hardened, armor-plated corporate warriors dictating the terms of a relationship. Nor do husbands want to negotiate around the pastor in the bedroom. Men are drawn to women who let them inside, who allow themselves to be romanced, courted, and won over. Sex is a very spiritual relationship, and we all know that soul imprints last long after that lover has left you for the night. Sex should make you feel happy, not abandoned.

### The Open Question: Discussion Points for Churches and for Us

IS IT REALISTIC for us to expect modern, sophisticated women not to have sex? Does it make them any less spiritual, or any less righteous, because they have chosen a different path? What about women who divorce? Are their sexual lives over? Reverend Adriane Blair Wise says that what we have to do is "educate black women about the realities of the consequences of unprotected and unsanctified sex." In her former role as Baptist chaplain at Howard University, she counseled young black women on issues like STDs, HIV, abortion, and rape. "No one is talking about the responsibility that comes with being both a spiritual and sexual being," Wise explained to me. "I am both emotional and physical; we all are. The problem is when we try to box people in and break them in two, it does not work. Your spiritual walk is one you grow into as an authentic and transparent woman of God."

We've covered a lot of ground in this chapter, so let's review some points that will help you think about yourself as a sensual and sacred woman all at once.

- Use your power to love yourself first, and allow that to radiate to a deserving man in your life.
- Find a church home that is healthy—a church that has a good mixture of marrieds and singles, and a good single ministry that pairs you with married couples who mentor and help prepare you for marriage if that is your desire.
- Beware of people who preach things contrary to what is in the Word. Do not allow yourself to be brainwashed into a way of thinking that restricts, confines, and distorts your freedom in Christ.
- Accept that men and women are not wired the same when it comes to sex. Men do not approach sex thinking about a relationship, as we do. Sex is sex to them, even when they like you.
- Understand and embrace your sexuality and sensuality as a woman. They are two different things. Men like women who are physically attractive, yes, but they're very interested in women who exude femininity and sexual confidence, not sexual looseness. No man wants an uptight sister with clothes all up around her neck who is sending "closed for business" signals. Ever watch the sisters in your life who are sexy, feminine, soft, and sensual? They may not wear a size six or flash supermodel looks, but they get the best men because they know how to "work it" with authenticity. Sisters, we have to learn how to work it by being our real selves without settling for giving it all away.
- Learn to embrace and explore your body and the power of touch. It's not physically or psychologically good (ask any medical doctor or mental health professional) for a woman to abstain from sex for years and years on end—to not be touched or loved or held. Too many of us are not experiencing those good hormones generated by loving relationships that Dr. Washington described. Research proves that connecting with your need for touch and intimacy is a key happiness indicator for all women.
- Understand the difference between sensual lovemaking and what's shown in pornography. Although preachers across the nation are railing against a growing number of parishioners who watch pornography, almost 33 percent of our survey respondents admitted to

viewing porn. Conversations with relationship gurus, like *Essence*'s Demetria Lucas, and focus group participants reveal that many women view pornography to try and improve their sex skills in hopes of pleasing their men. The reality is that pornographic sex is often degrading, and pornography does not show healthy sexual relationships.

- Don't settle for being a man's sex buddy or his friend with benefits or his mistress when you feel the calling to be a wife, mother, helper, protector, nurturer, and lover. You are more valuable than that, sisters!

- Stop using religion as a weapon, and start using your spiritual gifts to draw the men you want closer. Let's start taking our own counsel rather than listening to out-of-touch Christian leaders (mostly men) who would persuade us to suppress our sensuality and deny our sexuality.

- Know beyond a shadow of a doubt that God made you for relationships, marriage, and sex. God has a plan for your life, and it includes love, passion, desire, fulfillment, and—yes—*sex*!

- It is time for church leaders to recognize that there is a huge generational shift in our community, and we need to start talking to young women and men about their sexuality and their responsibilities. Stop hiding and acting as if you do not know that people in the church are shacking up. They are, and sisters, we have a responsibility to hold our churches accountable to address these issues as Christ would—directly and with compassion.

- Find the balance between your spiritual health and your emotional health. Your faith should not be a form of escape from reality; nor should it be a crutch. Your faith should liberate you to be the woman God created you to be in all respects.

*You* may trod me

in the very dirt

But still,

like dust,

**I'll rise.**

—Maya Angelou

# 7

## SEXUAL ABUSE:

### *The Hidden Wound That We Have to Talk About*

"Behind each human face is a hidden world that no one can see. . . .
We cannot continue to seek outside ourselves for the things we need
from within. . . . The demons will haunt us if we remain afraid. . . .
[S]ilence is one of the great victims of modern culture."

—JOHN O'DONOHUE, *Anam Cara: A Book of Celtic Wisdom*

*S*isters, our bodies are sacred places that hold within them our very souls. Too many of us, regrettably, have had our most sacred space violated. There are few greater violations that drive us deeper into pain, silence, and shame than sexual abuse or rape.

Every time high-profile sisters like Oprah, Queen Latifah, Mo'Nique, and Pam Grier acknowledge that they are victims of rape, incest, or sexual abuse, we cringe and shake our heads in disbelief, empathy, and sadness. Although not every black woman has been personally violated, many of us have experienced this devastation indirectly in our immediate or extended families or friendship circles. And we know that many brothers have experienced this trauma, too; Tyler Perry recently came forward on Oprah and shared the story of his deeply painful childhood sexual abuse. Sexual abuse is a real problem in our community, and it knows no boundaries of class or education, as the findings in our ABW study reveal.

Some of you may be wondering, since there are many helpful books that explore healing from rape, incest, and sexual abuse, why I am devoting an entire chapter to this subject. My reasons are twofold: First, almost half of the professional black women we surveyed reported having experienced some form of sexual abuse, rape, or sexual trauma in their lifetime.[1] Second, unexamined sexual violation can profoundly color and shape a survivor's life.

Since this is a book about redefinition, I think we can all agree that it is important for black women to break the silence and acknowledge that sexual violence, rape, abuse, and incest are devastating to our well-being. And for our young girls or teens, these are often life-altering tragedies. Part of what troubles me about this subject is that the language we use to talk about this very serious issue is often soft or amorphous. We use language like sex abuse, date rape, molestation to discuss criminal acts of violence. So let's be clear: Rape, sexual violence, and sexual abuse *are crimes.* Sex within families is incest, and it *is a crime.* No matter how old you are, unwanted sexual advances are traumatic, and they can cause a lifetime of confusion and pain.

National studies report that between 40 and 50 percent of black women have suffered from unwanted and forced sexual advances—most often when they were under the age of eighteen and usually by someone they knew. And that's not all. The experts I interviewed believe these acts are significantly underreported across the board, and especially in our community. According to the 2006 report *Sexual Violence in the Lives of African American Women: Risk, Response, and Resilience,* the numbers of sexually abused women can spike as high as 67 percent in community samples of low-income women.[2]

Among the ABWs we polled, 46 percent acknowledged that they had been a victim of "sexual molestation, sexual abuse, or rape." Especially troublesome, only 3 percent of the victims *did not know* their attackers. That means a stunning 97 percent were assaulted by someone they could identify—a family member, acquaintance, boyfriend/ex-boyfriend, or husband/ex-husband.

These heartbreaking statistics are only the first part of this nightmare. Despite the hurt, anger, shame, guilt, and emotional trauma, black girls and women are most likely to suppress their pain and suffer in silence. As a result, we experience terrible consequences. The Rape, Abuse and Incest National Network (http://www.rainn.org) cites World Health Organization statistics that claim victims of sexual assault are:

- Three times more likely to suffer from depression
- Six times more likely to suffer from post-traumatic stress disorder
- Thirteen times more likely to abuse alcohol
- Twenty-six times more likely to abuse drugs
- Four times more likely to contemplate suicide[3]

Unfortunately, what seems to suffer most is the victim's ability to form intimate and positive emotional bonds. Dr. Audrey Chapman confirms that a child or young woman who is sexually traumatized may constantly relive that trauma in some form unless there is early professional intervention. *Essence* relationship editor Demetria Lucas shared a story about a young woman whose boyfriend came up behind her and tried to hug and kiss her while she was cooking in the kitchen, causing the woman to freak out. Why? That was how her attacker used to touch her. I too have heard myriad stories of women reacting this way or crying out during sexual intimacy, not out of sexual fulfillment or physical discomfort but because of suppressed memories or trauma from past sexual violations.

Psychologist and sex therapist Gail Wyatt, associate director of the UCLA AIDS Institute, adds that a woman who has been abused and has not sought some kind of psychological help for it often learns to devalue her body. Consequently, she will more likely engage in riskier sexual behavior and not stand up for her sexual rights.

Fortunately, noted child psychologist Dr. Aby Washington whom I spoke with for this book reports, the prognosis for healing and living a normal life is really good when we can get abuse survivors to disclose early. She suggests that we think of sexual abuse and violence in the same way that we do a health challenge, such as breast cancer. Most breast cancer victims who receive early and aggressive intervention have a 90 percent or better survival rate. However, coming to terms with abuse later in life still greatly benefits your mind, body, and spirit. Ultimately, healing requires that you admit that this tragic event is a part of who you are but certainly *not* the sum of your experience.

## Silence Is Self-Destructive

So WHY DO black women silently endure the horror of sexual violation? And just what are the cultural taboos and social dynamics that keep black families in collusion and enable abuse to continue for generations?

As I mentioned in Chapter 2, for a long time our nation and the black community's attention has been largely focused on the troubles of the black man, which are numerous. Emasculation as a result of slavery. The lynching during the Jim Crow era. High unemployment in economic downturns. The crushing reality of poverty. The assault of drugs on our community. The violent and sexual abuse of black boys. The rise of alcoholism brought on by unrealized dreams. The stress of surviving in a racially charged America.

In our efforts to protect black men and save the black family, many of us have simply turned a blind eye to criminal sexual behavior. In a dysfunctional show of love and concern, we protect black men even at our own expense as black women. As a result, the survivor's pain becomes *invisible* to the family and loved ones she should be able to turn to for consolation and comfort. Many women are afraid to speak out in fear that no one will believe them or that they will face rejection or recriminations from family and friends.

Where is our compassion and call for protection for the female victims of sex abuse? Where is our outrage for offenders, particularly when they are in our families? "Having a sexual abuser in the family is not easy to acknowledge or accept," writes Robin D. Stone, author of *No Secrets, No Lies: How Black Families Can Heal from Sexual Abuse.* "Keeping abuse an open secret within the family not only fails the survivor and excuses the abuser's behavior, but also strains relationships within the family and without."[4]

In this groundbreaking book, Stone, the founding editor-in-chief of Essence.com, shares her own journey from childhood sexual abuse (at the hands of an uncle) to healing. Stone takes a candid look inside the abuse that happens in African American families and the ways in which those families have been uniquely socialized to keep secrets and cover and protect the abusers who violated them.

In his book *Woman Thou Art Loosed!* Bishop T. D. Jakes confronts the unspoken rule in our community that black women should not speak honestly about the evils done to them by black men because we want to love our men despite their flaws. What originally began as a small gathering of people hosted by Jakes in a Sunday school class in 1992, *Woman Thou Art Loosed* (WTAL) has become an international conference, a best-selling book, a Grammy-nominated CD, and a full-length motion picture starring Kimberly Elise.

*Woman Thou Art Loosed!* exposes how being raped by her mother's lover destroys a young teen's life. In the story, Bishop Jakes unveils how these tragedies often involve two offenses—the physical violation of rape and the emotional violation of trust when loved ones refuse to believe the victim's account of what happened. When the character Michelle tells her mother that Reggie raped her, her mother does not believe her or protect her from his advances. Feeling unworthy of even her mother's love, Michelle finds herself in and out of prison and dealing with drug addiction, anger issues, and relationship challenges.

In an interview about the release of *Woman Thou Art Loosed!* Jakes revealed that he wrote the book and helped with the subsequent movie adaption because he hoped they would "stir up conversation, bring awareness, and become a tool of the ministry." He went on to explain the reason for sexual abuse:

> [Abuse is] all about power and control. And people needing to be in control. And sometimes people who feel like they have no control find it easier to exercise control over somebody who has less control, such as a child. It has almost nothing to do with sex; it has something to do with power and the abuse of that power.[5]

Whether rape, sexual abuse, physical violence, demeaning language, or excessive cheating by our men, black women are taught from a very early age to just deal with whatever comes our way. *And to never run down a brother publicly!* This has had devastating consequences for black women. It forces us into a self-destructive silence that can be life-threatening. As I mentioned in the last chapter, in dealing with love and relationships, we must learn to communicate through our pain, forgive, release, heal, and find the love we deserve.

Although depictions in movies and pop culture suggest that sexual violence disproportionately occurs in lower-income communities, Dr. Aby Washington was very clear in our extensive interviews that sexual abuse, violence, trauma, and molestation of black girls (and all children and teens) occur in homes and communities of *all* socioeconomic, religious, ethnic, and educational backgrounds. Hence, we must honestly and openly address this issue among black women, black men, black families, black community organizations, and black churches to help our sisters break their deadly silence. Family support is critical to the healing process of an abused person. It's also important that the abuser be dealt with swiftly and severely whenever possible. Even Pope Benedict XVI is rethinking the Catholic Church's stand on sexual abuse charges against priests. In remarks to reporters in May 2010, the Pope admitted: "Forgiveness is not a substitute for justice."[6]

Unfortunately, exposing and punishing sexual abuse continues to be an uphill battle because "we have decriminalized sexual victimization in our minds," Dr. Washington lamented in our interview.

Consider this: Although there was a lot of buzz in 2009 about the controversial Academy Award–nominated movie *Precious* (based on the book *Push* by Sapphire), in the story, no one is punished for the unspeakable crimes that were central to the plot. We all winced and wept in horror at the monster abuser Mary Jones (played by Academy Award–winning actress Mo'Nique), who allowed her boyfriend to sexually assault, rape, and impregnate his own daughter, and then continued the physical and mental abuse herself. What made this movie so distressing to me was that even in a fictional account of sexual abuse and violence against a young black teen, no one—including the teachers who knew about the abuse—reported these demon parents to the police or child welfare authorities. What a missed opportunity to emphasize the importance of reporting these awful crimes!

Before announcing that she was going to play the brutal mother in *Precious*, Mo'Nique revealed that she had been sexually victimized by her older brother, Gerald Imes. He discussed his crime on *Oprah*, claiming he also had been sexually abused as a child and became addicted to drugs and alcohol by the time he was eleven years old. Oprah, an acknowledged sexual abuse survivor, recounted on that show the strange and often confusing behavior that victims of sexual abuse and rape can exhibit in the presence of their abusers. Years after her abuse, Oprah found herself frying eggs for her uncle (her abuser) at a family gathering. That's when it suddenly dawned on her how insane it was to be with her family, acting as though nothing had happened.

The Imes family drama that played out on Oprah's show was nothing short of amazing. The hostility toward Mo'Nique from her younger brother, who was in the audience with their parents, was palpable, and her parents seemed to be more interested in keeping the family business under wraps than truly dealing with this tragedy.

Interestingly, when told of the abuse, Mrs. Imes says, she believed the fifteen-year-old Mo'Nique and asked Gerald to leave their home. Mo'Nique's father also believed her but claimed he was in an absolute "state of confusion" when his younger son's attacks came to light years later. He did not think it could happen in his family. You could see the pain, struggle, and shame on their faces, but through it all, they kept insisting that this should have been handled "inside the family."[7] No, it couldn't! The reality is that no abuse can be handled and healed if the victim and family don't reveal the truth *and* seek professional counseling.

Gerald was eventually convicted of sexual molestation of another girl and sentenced to twelve years in prison. *Silence has terrible consequences.* Had the attack on his sister been reported to the authorities, or had his parents put him in counseling, this young woman would have been spared.

Robin Stone, in an interview for this book, pointed out that many black people have tremendous fear of authority figures, particularly when we are on social assistance or in some way being supervised by the government. "Black families are disproportionately in contact with social service agencies, and as such we tend to fear the backlash and repercussions on us if we report crime or abuse," explained Stone. Often, we fear that intense scrutiny of our families or friends could result in criminal charges and other repercussions that would destroy the family. As a result, when trauma or tragedy strikes, we feel paralyzed and do what comes naturally: hide our secrets and suffer in silence. Filmmaker Tyler Perry chronicled this theme in his movie *Madea's Family Reunion.* As a young woman, the character of Vanessa is repeatedly raped by her stepfather. Her mother, Victoria, tries to rationalize the situation by focusing on how well her husband provides for the family.

"So as a community, we must find better ways to address this very difficult challenge," said Stone. We must create safe harbors that take the stigma out of reporting wrongdoing.

## *Getting the Help You Need*

ALTHOUGH I CANNOT stress enough the importance of getting help as soon as possible, experts encourage abused women to give voice to their pain no matter how many years have passed. We are only as sick as our secrets.

I know, because a few years ago, after many years of silence, two members of my family revealed that they were sexually violated as children. They both suffered for decades, living in silent torment and experiencing nightmares, alcohol and substance abuse, depression, bad marriages, and low self-esteem. Sadly, but not surprisingly, when they finally broke their silence, the reaction from family members was one of shock, insensitivity, and recrimination. Even though the perpetrator had long passed away, everyone felt that the two survivors should not have come forward after such a long time. Their mother, who had been unaware of the crimes, was upset and sad to hear about the abuse, but she didn't understand why they took so long to tell her. She grew up in a time when you just dealt with the abuse and did not discuss it. The family's response was so hurtful, the victims felt violated all over again. I share this family tragedy to illustrate how important it is to embrace victims of sexual violence with love and support. We must make them feel safe and courageous for breaking their silence, no matter how long it took them to come forward. Otherwise, we run the risk of hurting them again.

Sisters, no matter how hard you may try, you can't wish the abuse away, pray it away, or pretend it doesn't exist anymore. Keeping secrets can only last so long. That's why survivors need special support when they finally face their suppressed pasts.

The repercussions from early sexual abuse last well into adulthood, no matter how high your salary or your heels. That's why it's so important to face your fears. In her paper "Sexual Abuse: Surviving the Pain," Barbara E. Bogorad, the founder and former director of the Sexual Abuse Recovery Program Unit at South Oaks Hospital in Amityville, New York, explains that the problems tend to fall into four areas:

1. *Survivors feel like damaged goods.* They often suffer from low self-esteem and depression and become self-destructive.
2. *Survivors feel a sense of betrayal.* They have trouble trusting others and controlling their anger, and they have difficulty forming relationships.
3. *Survivors feel helpless*, which leads to anxiety, fear, a tendency toward re-victimization, and panic attacks.
4. *Survivors feel isolated*, different, and stigmatized and generally don't develop a good support system.[8]

I remember when a member of the iask organization shared her heartbreaking story with a few of us at a women's conference a few years ago. She explained that during her preteen years, a much older male family friend would touch her, stroke her, and be nice to her and eventually drew her into a full-blown sexual relationship. (This type of behavior is called "grooming," a term for the period when the abuser patiently and sometimes gently walks the victim through the process of touching and fondling—almost like courting the victim.)[9] The women she confided in could feel her shame and disgust for "liking" the attention and touching at the time of the offense. Like many sexually exploited youngsters, she developed into a hypersexual teen. Although healing has not been easy, she now draws on her experience and courage to counsel others who suffer from abuse and neglect.

A history of childhood sexual abuse also overshadows all other factors that place a woman at risk for contracting HIV, suggests a new UCLA and Charles R. Drew University study. That's because "sexual abuse has its own unique effect on women's decision-making," reports Dr. Gail Wyatt, principal investigator for the study. The study found that women who experienced chronic childhood sexual abuse were seven times more likely to engage in high-risk, unprotected sexual behavior as adults. "We found that the same factors that increase a woman's risk for contracting HIV might also contribute to her risk for rape and domestic abuse. Relationships with coercive and abusive partners severely diminish a woman's ability to negotiate safer sex," says Dr. Wyatt.[10]

Giselle, a beautiful woman now in her late thirties, is married to a very successful doctor and has several children. Like many child victims of rape and abuse, she struggled with some serious emotional and psychological challenges. She suffered in silence for years, never confronted her attackers, and tried to wear a happy face. But one day she blurted out to her best friend, Samantha, that she had been abused as a child by at least two male relatives, had been raped in college by a friend of a boyfriend, and had been recently diagnosed with dissociative identity disorder, commonly known as multiple personality disorder. Ironically, her dissociative disorder was diagnosed only because she'd sought help for severe depression because of infertility issues. Giselle was determined to bury her painful past because she feared that exposing something like this would threaten her marriage, social status, and her desire for a family. When she revealed these very disturbing things to Samantha, it was a relief. Imagine the emotional hell Giselle must have endured trying to suppress her past and heal all by herself.

One thing I learned from writing this book and speaking with the experts is that sharing our hurts and pains with girlfriends is a great place to begin our healing, because the process of revealing abuse has to start somewhere. However, once you get to a place where you're ready

to "come out," you must also work with someone who is professionally trained and can help you process your emotions and deal with the
serious mental and physical illnesses that secret survivors often suffer
from. Our girlfriends are just not equipped to do this. Iyanla Vanzant
offers this, which speaks to this point, in her book *Acts of Faith*: "Have
you ever wondered why people hide their dirty laundry in the closet of
your mind? Somewhere deep inside you may feel honored when you
are entrusted with another's downside. What you fail to realize is that
knowledge creates responsibility. When you are asked to remain silent
about the secret and hidden acts of another, you are lured into collusion."[11] I agree with her 100 percent.

## Healing from Sexual Abuse and Violence

SO WHAT DO we do when abuse touches our home and family? How
do we cope and make sure that the victim is made whole and protected?
First, know that you cannot do it alone and that there are no quick
fixes. The healing and recovery process can be long and complicated, so
buckle up.

One place to start finding help and resources is the free and confi-
dential 24/7 National Sexual Assault Hotline (1-800-656-HOPE). Alter-
natively, you can log on to the website of the Rape, Abuse and Incest
National Network (www.rainn.org). Additional resources are listed at
the end of the chapter.

The following is a list of first steps for recovery that I've compiled from
talks with Dr. Audrey Chapman, Dr. Aby Washington, and Robin Stone.

- At whatever point you as a survivor decide to tell the truth and
  break the silence, you need to start with professional help. There
  is a lot of internal dysfunction when we have been assaulted.
  Churches, friends, and families can help people heal, but they are
  not licensed professionals. You need the help of an experienced
  therapist or social worker who can offer you the ongoing support
  you need.
- Once you decide to seek help, make sure that you are dealing
  with a licensed clinician who has extensive experience in sexual
  abuse. Talking about your past can be graphic and painful, so find
  someone with whom you'll be comfortable sharing intimate details

of your life. Consider whether you want a male or female therapist. Does race matter? Do you prefer a location close to you or outside your neighborhood? Check out the reputation of the practice or therapist. This can make it easy to decide how long you're willing to commit.

- Consider joining an abuse survivors program. Survivors of Incest Anonymous (www.siawso.org) offers a twelve-step program. Traditionally, twelve-step recovery programs offer you a proven framework for addressing your problem and working through your emotional turmoil.

- Prayer and spiritual support are key and should be incorporated into your overall healing plan. Research shows that prayer and spiritual interaction have produced measurable elevations in mood. Step 2 in the Survivors of Incest Anonymous program focuses on tapping a higher power to "restore hope, healing, and sanity."[12] But remember, you won't eliminate the fallout from abuse with just prayer alone. So consider working with a spiritual advisor as a good companion effort to clinical therapy.

- Be prepared to have difficult conversations about your personal life, your thoughts about sex, and your sexuality. Your goal isn't just to be a sex abuse survivor. You want to rebuild your life and develop the healthy, meaningful, and intimate relationships you deserve.

## RESOURCES

ONLINE NATIONAL RESOURCES:

- RAINN/Rape, Abuse, & Incest National Network: http://www.rainn.org/
- ASCA, Adult Survivors of Child Abuse: http://www.ascasupport.org/
- Black Sexual Abuse Survivors: http://www.blacksurvivors.org/resources.html

BLACK PSYCHOLOGISTS:

- The Association of Black Psychologists has a national list of black psychologists at  http://www.abpsi.org/.

BOOKS RESOURCES:

- *African Americans and Child Sexual Abuse,* by Veronica D. Abney
- *Boys into Men: Raising Our African American Teenage Sons,* by Nancy Boyd-Franklin, Pamela A. Toussaint, and A. J. Franklin
- *Broken Boys/Mending Men: Recovery from Childhood Sexual Abuse,* by Stephen D. Gruban-Black
- *The Courage to Heal: A Guide for Women Survivors of Child Sexual Abuse,* by Ellen Bass and Laura Davis
- *I Will Survive: The African American Guide to Healing from Sexual Assault and Abuse,* by Lori S. Robinson and Julia A. Boyd
- *Lasting Effects of Child Sexual Abuse,* by Gail Elizabeth Wyatt
- *No Secrets No Lies: How Black Families Can Heal from Sexual Abuse,* by Robin D. Stone
- *Racism & Child Protection: The Black Experience of Child Sexual Abuse,* by Valerie Jackson
- *Sexual Abuse in Nine North American Cultures: Treatment and Prevention,* by Lisa Aronson Fontes
- *Stolen Women: Reclaiming Our Sexuality, Taking Back Our Lives,* by Gail Wyatt

*Y*our past does not define your future—your actions and beliefs do. Remember that you are not your past or your mistakes. Release the mistakes of the past and carry forward only the lessons they contain. You have the power to rewrite your story at any time.

—Linda Joy

# 8

## DWELLING IN THE VALLEY OF OUR PAST:

### *Learning to Forgive, Release, and Heal from Our Hurts*

"Our unhealed wounds are invisible prisons."
—KATHERINE WOODWARD THOMAS, *Calling in "the One"*

*M*y dear sisters, of all the issues we face, none concern me more than those rooted deeply in our past and in our inability to forgive those who have hurt us. So much of the ongoing criticism of black women reflects that our collective history and personal lives have challenged and hurt us on so many fronts that we have become both *too strong and too hard*. I'd be a rich woman if I had a dollar for every brother who has told me how much he loves, respects, and desires a strong, accomplished black woman but just can't get past the wall of physical, emotional, and spiritual damage done to us. Last fall, when our national focus group moderator asked black men what challenges they felt they faced in relationships with professional or accomplished black women, the comments were striking. "There is a lot of emotional scarring that you have to deal with when it comes to some sisters." Another commented that the reason he prefers to date outside the race is because "black women have more trust issues, more emotional issues, and need more healing." *Intuitively, sisters, we know this is truth.* So how did we get so stuck?

My goal in this chapter is to walk us through some of the forgiveness issues that came up in our ABW research and focus groups and to pull back the layers of what many see as the angry black woman syndrome. Many of us are in fact angry but with good reason. At some point, however, we must recognize the need to move beyond the anger and pain and start living a life that is healthy and transformative.

## Stuck in the Valley of Our Past

MANY SUCCESSFUL BLACK women spend most of their adulthood trying to overcome the challenges of childhood—the disappointments, abuses, betrayals, and tragedies. Despite the often excruciating pain, we can't seem to release our firm grip on old wounds often inflicted by people we love. This was confirmed over and over again in our focus groups. The damage caused by a wide range of problems—from divorce and absentee fathers to alcoholism and sexual abuse—has broken our hearts and hardened our souls. And the fallout has been a history of failed relationships, sexual confusion, illness, and lonely lives.

I had a chance to interview Westina Matthews Shatteen, a fellow at the Weatherhead Center for International Affairs at Harvard University. A retired managing director for Merrill Lynch, she now serves as a trustee at the Berkeley Divinity School at Yale University and at the University of Dayton and serves on the boards of the International Women's Forum and the Shalem Institute for Spiritual Formation. Said Shatteen:

> Well-educated, single black women—particularly Gen X—bought into the dream but did not get it. Many have been hurt by some man in their lives. Hurt equals broken trust and shame. When we open up, we open up our hearts so completely and trusting and wanting to be *loved* that we love hard. Every woman wants a life mate. It is hard to be a black woman today—with all the expectations and pressure, being single heads of households and higher earners. The roles are reversed in our community. At the end of the day, a woman wants someone she can break bread with, put her feet up with, and grow old with. When you're climbing the corporate ladder, you are juggling a lot of balls, and you need a support system. Self-talking—"I can do bad all by myself"— sustains us; we can go it all alone, or so we think. It just leads to a very unhealthy cycle.

We are the embodiment of the hopes and dreams of an entire race of people, many of whom were deprived of their dreams. We are first-generation doctors, lawyers, executives, engineers, professors, and entrepreneurs. But a fat paycheck and a fancy job title don't make it any easier to live out someone else's definition of who we should be. And it is unhealthy to have so much of our self-esteem wrapped up in what someone else believes we are worth. So we pay the price daily of trying to excel and uplift our race from under the yoke of subtle discrimination and not-so-subtle negative stereotypes. Still, we ban together chanting, "We're too blessed to be stressed."

## Too Strong for Your Own Good

SO WHY IS it that some black women are perceived as too strong for our own good? Perhaps because we've wrapped ourselves in attitudinal armor that makes it extremely difficult to be open, honest, and—God forbid—vulnerable to people whom we desperately want in our lives.

For better or worse, we seem resigned to repeat the patterns that we witnessed in our own families. Our mothers, grandmothers, aunts, and older sisters were tough on us and on themselves as they tried to prepare their baby girls for the real world—often without the help of strong, supportive men in their lives. Life happened, and some of what happened deeply hurt us and our families. One of our ABW focus group participants, an attractive, divorced entrepreneur, suggested that this pain is so deep for black women that we need to have an open dialogue with our mothers so we can share with them how profoundly many of us have been affected by the pressure to educate and achieve professional success at any cost.

Another huge challenge for us is that we have not been taught to reach out and ask for help. *Oh no, no, no.* Black women do not ask for help. We even refuse to accept it when it is sincerely offered. As I mentioned in Chapter 2, we have come to depend on self over everything and everyone else because too many of us have been disappointed and hurt by life, our men, our friends, our colleagues, and mostly by our own misguided choice to try and be *all things to all people.*

Although many of us swore that we would never do things the way our parents did, or that we would never adopt their dysfunctional ways of coping, we did it anyway. Strong black women don't burden our families, ministers, teachers, or friends with our problems or pain. You all know the drill. One sister in our national focus group expressed this sentiment loud and clear: "I feel like everyone has some type of emotional issue. It's just a fact of life, so why should anyone listen to my sobbing? So I just have to get over it." Despite our prayers, hopes, and dreams, we seem to end up at the same old dead end—unable to move toward the happy life we always envisioned for ourselves.

Author James Baldwin describes this dilemma best: "Not everything that is faced can be changed. But nothing can be changed until it is faced." I agree. While there are no simple answers for why we're stuck repeating old patterns, I am convinced that we come to these dead-end roads because we continually carry the corpses of our past mistakes, regrets, and pains. Carrying baggage from our past is a surefire way to hinder our best living. It rots our potential. It keeps us locked in a prison of our own making. It cements our attachment to an unsatisfied life filled with feckless friendships, emotionally unavailable partners, and stalled careers. It is time for us to *let go*, sisters, and find a way to truly forgive. We have all heard the saying "To err is human; to forgive is divine." Forgiveness is much more than mouthing the words "I forgive you." And it doesn't work to simply recite the line in the Lord's Prayer: "Forgive us our trespasses, as we forgive those who trespass against us."[1]

The research conducted for this book confirms what many of us already know: black women have a very hard time forgiving others *and* ourselves. Our personal memory chip does not easily process *forget* or *forgive*. We hold on to our wounds as if they are a monument to what we have endured and who we have become. After all, some wrongs don't deserve to be forgiven, right? But lack of forgiveness—holding on to anger, resentment, or hatred—renders you the biggest loser. It means that you are letting the past dictate your present. Past people, places, and things that you can't release are holding you hostage and robbing you of your peace of mind and potential for joy. Sometimes forgiveness is the only way you can release your pain and move on with your life. Remember that scene in *The Diary of a Mad Black Woman* when Cicely Tyson's character gives words of wisdom to her daughter, Helen (played by Kimberly Elise): "When somebody hurts you, they take power over you. If you don't forgive them, then they keep the power. Forgive him, baby, and after you forgive him, forgive yourself."

Senovia Ross spoke with me for this book and wholeheartedly agrees:

Forgiveness requires that you tap the God-spirit that resides in you. It requires us to do more than just talk about what's happened. You have to work though the issues and the pain. Once you do that, forgiveness is a decision you must make. The point is not to let someone off the hook but to free yourself of the [bad] experience that you are holding on to. Not forgiving keeps you stuck.

*There it is, sisters.* Postponed personal healing is the consequence of not dealing with the inevitable conflict, hurt, pain, and adversity that we all experience in our life journey. For many of us, conquering ourselves means calling on the healing power of forgiveness *before* we can claim the fabulous lives, love, and purpose we all seek.

## Forgiving the First Man Who Hurt You: Black Girls and Our Fathers

NO MATTER HOW successful we may become, dealing with and over-coming the wounds of our childhood can take a lifetime of work. The bitter reality is that many black women do not overcome; they simply suffer. They wither on the vine and refuse to accept what life has to offer. We don't always see ourselves as worthy of life's simple pleasures, like love and companionship. Intimacy can be elusive when childhood memories don't include healthy, loving relationships with our fathers, brothers, uncles, and other men in our lives. Recently, Academy Award winner Halle Berry sat down with CNN and discussed growing up in a household plagued by domestic violence. She witnessed her father abusing her mother and had this to say about how it affected her:

I think I've spent my adult life dealing with the sense of low self-esteem that sort of implanted in me. Somehow I felt not worthy. Before I'm Halle Berry, I'm little Halle, who was a little girl growing in this environment that damaged me in some ways. I've spent my adult life trying to really heal from that. I have a spot in my soul that understands the devastation that this causes a family and how hard it is to rebuild your self-esteem when you've suffered.[2]

I also understand these feelings, as I have struggled over the years to successfully rebuild my relationship with my own father. And I'm not alone. While researching for this book, I came across a powerful story on Essence. com titled "Balancing Act: Why Forgiveness Isn't Always Divine," written by a young sister named S. Tia Brown. The posting discusses her challenges in developing healthy relationships with guys after being abandoned by her father: "I have a confession. I'm used to coming in second—well, with men," she writes.[3] I think many of us feel this way. I know I did for years.

As a young woman, I seemingly excelled at everything I touched. School was a slam dunk, and I even managed to date the All-American high school quarterback. In college, I dated and fell in love very early with the most wonderful man in the world. When he died of a sudden illness just a year later, I was devastated. I buried myself in the pain by drinking and driving myself even harder. I truly adored him. But the truth is, even with him (and he adored me and treated me like a princess), I never felt quite good enough.

The source of my pain was my broken relationship with my father. My dad and his side of the family drank a lot and often sparred verbally and at times physically during my formative years. Although we never said the words, they were alcoholics. My father, unlike many men, did not abandon us, and he never failed to pay the bills. In fact, he was a devoted father in that he never missed our sporting events or award ceremonies. But his drinking and anger were a familiar part of our lives. The rages and angry outbursts left me (and my younger brother) and, of course, my mother traumatized—something we all still wrestle with to this day. I learned very early to cover up and just go to school and smile as if no altercations had occurred the night before in our home. Some of my teachers could tell there was a problem starting in the first grade. They sensed that an incident had occurred when my work was not in on time or when I just sat quietly behind my desk.

The fact that I am talking about this publicly in this book some thirty years later is a testament to my desire to help others heal from past pain. The truth about my upbringing is embarrassing to me and to members of my family. I love my family despite their flaws, so please know that it is not my intent to embarrass or hurt anyone. Some of my family members and close family friends may attack me or be upset with me for telling our secret. But that is their issue, not mine. Thank God I am no longer stuck in a place of hiding or covering up.

I share these deeply personal parts of my life because I know there are young sisters out there now who are exactly where I was in my twenties and thirties: still hurting. My hope is that they will learn the lessons of forgiveness and release much faster than I have. Part of truly forgiving those who hurt us is "coming clean," telling the truth, and letting the wound hit the air with the bandage ripped off so it can heal properly. I have grown and moved to a place of accountability to myself. I have to honor my boundaries and my needs as well as balance that with the needs of others. Loving our family means that we make allowances for the fact that they may not be where we are in their own healing and growth. That is okay. But when we cover up generational pain, and act as if all is well, we rob ourselves and our families of truly getting to know us on a much deeper and meaningful level. The fact is as long as we lie, cover, and protect, we are not being our authentic, transparent selves. I am a woman now. I try to be a good woman every day. I don't want to be that scared little girl anymore who cries herself to sleep at night trying to figure out what I did wrong. I am finished with keeping the family secrets in order to be considered a loyal member of the family. I am finished with fearing rejection if I don't play by the unwritten rules of silence when inappropriate or hurtful actions take place. The personal price is simply too high.

Love, like forgiveness, cannot be conditional. You have to be all in or all out. Like Tia (the Essence.com writer), I was not emotionally, sexually, or spiritually available for a relationship for many years of my life because I was always dancing with the remnants of a disappointed, hurt little girl who wanted her father's love, approval, and protection. More than that I longed to see in action how a man truly loves a woman and his children beyond taking care of his economic duties. I didn't realize till I was in my mid-thirties how deeply this all affected me. Still, I looked to my father to define what love from a man should feel and look like.

What I have learned after many years of therapy and in researching and writing this book is that my response and my ache for my father's love and attention is very normal. The father-daughter bond is critical for girls growing up. Your dad is the first man you love. I am very thankful that my brother is a good father to his two young daughters. They adore him. They even have a sign that hangs in their bedroom that reads: "I met my Prince and his name is Daddy." Just as many young black boys feel unresolved rage and anger toward their mothers (as Janks Morton discusses in Chapter 2), many sisters feel hurt and abandonment at not knowing or connecting with their fathers in a positive and healthy way.

One of my good friends, Marci[4] (who is the same age as I am), fed up from feeling abandoned and unworthy of love, finally had a "come to Jesus" meeting with her father over how he had treated her and her siblings when he walked out on their mother and family for his long-time mistress. Talking to her dad opened up old wounds, and he cried when she described the hurt and pain he caused. He left, so he confessed, because he was angry with his wife. She seemed to have lost her zest for life, preferring to have more children than focusing on his needs as her husband. He also explained that he had been disconnected from his daughter in particular because she reminded him most of his ex-wife, her mother. After listening to his side of the story, Marci explained how his abandonment sent her spiraling downward, causing her to suffer from depression, illness, and extreme issues in dating men. They say children repeat what they see. So, following her father's example, she too would abruptly walk out of a relationship without bothering to inform her lover. But her purpose in confronting her father was not to simply lay on a guilt trip. Instead, she took ownership of her behavior, worked through forgiving him, and began the long process of self-forgiveness and healing. During that time, she learned to trust and love again. One year later, the right man showed up in her life, and she is now on the road to marriage. *Forgiveness introduces us to love.*

It's interesting how early you learn to compartmentalize pain and focus on excelling in other things in life. While my father was disrupting our home, I busied myself becoming captain of the track team, being a good student, becoming class president, playing in the band—you name it. I did it and did it well. I learned to hide with my achievements, but God knows I had no clue I was doing it at the expense of my personal fulfillment.

The good news, though, is that Marci and I are living proof that you can heal damaged relationships with those who have hurt you in the past by committing to your own self-healing. Remember that you alone are responsible for what you think, feel, and do. You can choose to hold on to painful events from your past, putting a weight on your shoulders, or you can choose to remove that burden by releasing it—that is, giving it no more emotional energy and therefore no more power. In other words, let the past exist in the past, and live in the present. You can't change what happened back then, but you have choice about how you live now.

Although my father sacrificed his wife and children on the altar of divorce in 1990, today, to his credit, he is clean and sober. He is retired now and a very different man from the one I grew up with; he is a great pop pop to his two granddaughters. Although our relationship is still not in a healthy place, I can support the fact that he is a good grandfather. Perhaps it was the letters that my brother and I wrote to him years ago expressing our hurt over things that had happened in our home. Or the fact that we ourselves are now adults and have made our own mistakes and can more easily understand that my father grew up with two generations of alcoholism in his immediate family. He and his siblings endured distress too, as did my beloved paternal grandmother before them. These problems run in cycles in families, and somebody somewhere has to forgive, release, heal, and break the cycle. I give my brother credit, because he has done that better than I have in some respects. He is a good husband and father. He is a man of God. He does not drink, curse, or cavort around on his wife. He made a decision to be a good father and husband, despite what he saw growing up, and that takes courage. I am proud of him for that and have told him so.

## I Love You, I Forgive You, but I Have to Let You Go

ONE OF THE things that I have come to learn with great difficulty is that forgiveness is not instantaneous. True forgiveness is a journey that restores, releases, and renews our souls. Furthermore, forgiveness, contrary to some popular but distorted theology, does not mean we have to allow the forgiven person to remain a part of our lives or continue to be a part of his or hers. Sometimes the trust is so irrevocably broken that no matter how much we may want to make things work, it is best to just let it go.

As a dear friend said to me recently, "Cutting off a colleague from work who stole your intellectual property or severing a relationship with a good friend who has hurt you is tough enough, but when you have to cut yourself off from family members who are emotionally abusive or unhealthy, it is not an easy process." I agree with my friend, and as Oprah demonstrated when she shared the story of how she found herself in the kitchen making eggs for a family member who had molested her (see Chapter 7), there is a part of us that believes we owe it to people to keep their secrets, even though they have wounded us and not made any attempt to apologize or make amends. Sisters, this is simply not true, and do not let any theologian, pastor, or friend tell you otherwise.

For more perspective on the issue of what is forgiveness and what it is not, I turned again to Westina Shatteen, who has spent years helping young women deal with their spiritual journeys and with forgiveness. Shatteen initiated and still chairs the highly acclaimed annual Black Women's Leadership Summit, sponsored by the Executive Leadership Council, which the top one hundred black women executives in corporate American attend to hear from CEOs of Fortune 500 companies. I asked her to walk us through her definition of forgiveness and how we move forward from past hurts in a way that makes us whole.

> Forgiveness is simply not being able to hold on and nurture the resentment of a past justice or hurt. You decide not to take the hurt into your life. The challenge with forgiveness, however, is that we don't understand there are consequences to the action. Even if you absolve the person. Forgiveness is not making the offender whole and clean; it is about making you whole and clean.

She continued, explaining that forgiveness is not a quick process and that it can take years to heal. A dear friend of hers who had been nursing a wound for years and had been working through the process of forgiveness told her that she knew she was healed when, "one day I went to reach for the resentment, but it was not there."

I also asked Shatteen if forgiving someone meant you had to keep that person in your life. She replied, "Forgiveness *does not* mean I have to be around that person if they can harm me still or if something is not working. You can forgive but walk out with your back to the wall. *Trust is key. Trust is earned*, and once you violate someone's trust, you have to earn it back. It takes a long time to earn trust back; it could be years." She makes a good point: there is a big difference between forgiveness and restoration. Restoration of a broken or injured relationship means rebuilding of trust between the parties. And it requires one other critical element that Shatteen pointed out: "When someone has injured us, we desire an apology; it is very human. But there is a big difference between a formal amends and changing our actions. Repentance is changing your mind and your actions. It is how we treat people. We have an accountability." She shared a brief story of how she had hurt a dear friend and decided to write her a letter asking for forgiveness. At the bottom of the letter, she put "cc: God" to let her friend know that she knew God was watching and that she was holding herself accountable for her future actions in a much higher court. I like that "cc: God." That's powerful.

## Forgiveness and Sexual Abuse

TAKING THAT FIRST step toward forgiveness isn't easy. For those suffering from the devastating pain of sexual abuse, rape, or incest, the road to forgiveness can be long and rocky. According to researchers such as University of Washington associate professor Carolyn M. West, sexual trauma and assaults are seriously underreported crimes in the black community and extremely difficult experiences to recover from.[5]

As mentioned in Chapter 4, more than half of the professional and working black men we surveyed (55 percent) ground black women's relationship challenges in being hurt "at the hands of other black men." More than one-third (37 percent) claim that our "psychological and emotional baggage from disastrous past relationships" is a big factor in why they have a hard time dating and marrying successful black women. I'll never forget how moved I was when my friend, a handsome forty-eight-year-old divorced military officer, explained how much he loves black women because he was raised with strong black sisters and an even stronger black mother. However, he lamented the emotional trauma he encounters when it comes to sexual intimacy with black women because so many of us have been abused or hurt by male relatives, boyfriends, or someone we once trusted. Sitting with us were five other men who all nodded in agreement. One brother gave voice to their sentiment: "Yeah, it's a damn shame how the sisters have been messed over, mostly by us."

Although the formula of forgiving, releasing, and healing has helped thousands of victims of the most heinous sex crimes move on with their lives, the process isn't pretty or easy. It often requires the support of a trained professional. But taking this time to invest in your emotional and spiritual well-being is worth it. Fortunately, black women, particularly educated black women, are starting to talk about their deep emotional and sexual traumas and learning how to process their emotions in a constructive way. Noted psychologist and relationship expert Dr. Audrey Chapman commented during our interview:

> Some are going into therapy and support groups to address our pain and share it, while others are working inside the support systems of their churches. Many congregations are developing programs that go

beyond the Bible as a prescription and instead taking a holistic mind-body-spirit approach. This is a significant step, as many churches had been traditionally very resistant to such programs.

## Forgiving Our Families and Communities

TIPTOEING THROUGH THE minefields of the past is challenging on so many fronts—even when life is filled with success. High-achieving black women dressed in beautiful St. John knit suits and accessorized with Gucci handbags and Jimmy Choo shoes are *the* poster girls for over-stressed lives. Much of this stress comes from well-meaning loved ones who only want the best for us as they push, prod, and sometimes shove us up the success ladder.

Rhonda Joy McLean, coauthor of *The Little Black Book of Success* and deputy general counsel at Time Inc., one of the largest media companies in the world, knows this turf well. McLean shared with me how all eyes were on her as a young girl growing up in her small hometown of Smithfield, North Carolina. She was one of only three African Americans in a high school of five hundred students. In fact, she and her two friends integrated the school. McLean was accustomed to being in the spotlight as a gifted mezzo-soprano and an excellent student. But one semester she didn't make the honor roll. When her name didn't appear in the local newspapers, her parents were bombarded with calls from neighbors wondering what was wrong with Rhonda Joy.

Although McLean is a hard-core advocate for aiming high—"after all," she says, "that's how we moved from slavery to the corner office"—she pointed out that "some black women have taken achievement to an extreme. We've become afraid to fail. Some of us will not admit when we need help or when we don't know something, so we cover up out of fear. Success can be a very isolating place if we don't address unhealthy expectations." This is especially true if the expectations aren't in line with our own wants and needs and if we're not battle-ready for the corporate games played out in workplaces across the nation.

Take my friend Anna, who was so overwhelmed with her family's determination that she become a physician that she never bothered to consider whether this career made sense for her. So she did what was *expected* of her, instead of what was *important* to her, and suffered the consequences of working in a demanding profession that she did not enjoy. She felt it was her duty to sacrifice her happiness to meet the expectations of those around her. After picking up the pieces of a life shattered by severe depression, resentment, chronic ailments, and divorce, Anna made the tough decision to leave medicine to pursue a profession of her choice. She did this without the support of her family. But to move on, she had to forgive her family *and* herself for not making choices that reflected the life she wanted. *Forgiveness also can introduce us to self-love.*

## Never Let Them See You Act Human

SISTERS, WE NEED to rethink our unhealthy eagerness to please others, to represent others, and to care for others. We can't become so bound to our history as a people that we don't make time to take care of ourselves. If we don't take care of ourselves first, we won't be any good for anyone else.

We need to give ourselves and each other permission for some self-care and understand that everyone needs to lean on someone sometime. Truth be told, sisters, many of us have "superwoman syndrome." Or, as *Essence* editor-at-large and beauty lifestyle coach Mikki Taylor puts it, "We are caught up in that old 'go on, girl' syndrome where we encourage each other to do damage to ourselves. We see a girlfriend is tired, weary, and broken, and we will tell her, 'You know how we do, girl, just keep going—you can handle it.' This is how we reinforce each other that it is okay to keep pushing ourselves to the brink, and it needs to stop."

Taylor surely hit the hot button with that observation. When the moderator broached this topic in our focus groups, the room lit up. Black mothers believe a survivalist approach is paramount to preparing their daughters to navigate the real world's myriad challenges, disappointments, opportunities, and setbacks. No wonder black families teach their daughters that lamenting our losses and hurts is a sign of weakness. "Seeking help can be interpreted as weakness or being inept," explained one focus group participant. They all agreed that black women are not encouraged to "tell our business" but instead "keep it in the family." That's because "knowing what pushes your buttons can be used as ammunition against you," explained another woman. "Once you put it out there, it's hard to retract." Being vulnerable also leaves you open to more painful relationships or may derail your chances for advancement at work. "I never want anyone to see me as being vulnerable," said one very buttoned-up sister. "I'm afraid that if I let people see the emotional, sensitive side of me, then [they] will perceive me as being weak."

Think about what these women are saying. Have we come to a point in life where wearing our superwoman mask 24/7 is the only way to go, for if we dare to take it off, we will be punished or harmed?

## Numb to the Pain

OUR EMOTIONS LIVE, SISTERS. They live in us no matter how hard we try to cover them. They are alive, and they affect every decision we make, whether we understand that or not. To be sure, humans are a complicated lot, but black women are an even deeper well of complexities—a mixture of feeling uniquely blessed and uniquely cursed all at once.

The irony for many of us is that we hide pain so well that we don't even know we're in pain ourselves. With every disappointment or hurt that comes our way, we just suck it up and keep pressing onward. But in reality, we are not moving forward at all. On more than one occasion, when I asked older women in my family or in my social networks why they didn't share some tragic event or painful experience in their lives, they'd reply, "I didn't want to inconvenience anyone with my problems." Imagine feeling that if you shared your pain with someone, it would be an inconvenience to that person. *The truth is that many of us feel this way.* The time has come for us to stop this utter nonsense. *Keeping quiet is destroying us emotionally and physically, sisters.*

One of the mantras of truth that I learned in my many years of attending Al-Anon meetings (a spin-off of Alcoholics Anonymous that offers strength and hope for friends and families of problem drinkers) is that "you are only as sick as your secrets."[6] What does this mean? It's a reminder to children and family members of alcoholics to process the pain before it makes us sick. One of the hardest lessons I've learned is that suppressing emotional pain, conflict, and hurt is a surefire formula for physical illness. For most of my life since I was a teenager, I have dealt with physical ailments, such as ulcers, ovarian cysts, migraines, hernias, chronic strep throat, a weakened immune system, and finally a full-blown endocrine disease that appeared in my mid-thirties. I am now absolutely clear about what's triggering all this mess: years of stress, pain, broken relationships, and unresolved conflicts in my life—much of it, unfortunately, a result of my conflicted feelings about my father, because of his drinking and temper, and my mother, because she stayed and kept us in harm's way. The good news is that my mother and I are very close, and I understand how her past hurts shaped her life choices. I have had a chance to heal these past issues with her, and my father and I are a work in progress. *Forgiveness really does reintroduce us to love.*

When I realized that my physical ailments were linked to my emotional well-being, I started devouring books and information on what the medical community thinks about the connection between forgiveness, unresolved issues from the past, and health concerns. In my quest, I came across Dr. Don Colbert, who has done some groundbreaking work in this area. In his book *Deadly Emotions: Understand the Mind-Body-Spirit Connection That Can Heal or Destroy You*, Dr. Colbert writes:

> The mind and body are linked. . . . Certain emotions release hormones into the physical body that, in turn, can trigger the development of a host of diseases. Researchers have directly and scientifically linked emotions to hypertension, cardiovascular disease, and diseases related to the immune system. Studies have also highly correlated emotions with infections, allergies, and autoimmune diseases. Specifically, research has linked emotions such as depression to an increased risk of developing cancer and heart disease.[7]

Interestingly, the physical ailments and diseases Dr. Colbert lists in his book can result from suppressed emotional pain, depression, and what he calls "deadly emotions." Almost all of them (such as hypertension, heart disease, lupus, fibromyalgia, breast cancer, etc.) are rampant in the lives of black American women, according the Centers for Disease Control in Atlanta.[8] These medical statistics were overwhelmingly confirmed in our national sample of successful black women.

Dr. Aby Washington, a well-known clinical child psychologist in Washington, D.C., concurs that emotional stress can cause physical problems. She was not surprised to hear that I developed onset adrenal disease (also known as Addison's disease) in my mid-thirties because as a child I lived in what she called a "cortisol rich" environment as a response to the constant stress in my home. When we are traumatized emotionally and for sustained periods of time, the body washes itself with cortisol to prepare for a "fight or flight" response. However, our bodies are not good at self-regulation and can go into overdrive. After a while, the adrenal glands stop producing enough of certain hormones. More disturbing is that people like me will usually continue to seek out high-stress environments (such as unhealthy relationships or high-drama friendships) that feed the stress hormones—it's like a drug addiction. We crave it. And I now realize that, sadly, I have routinely invested myself in emotionally unhealthy, stress-inducing people and situations to get my fix.

## Facing the Demons That Haunt Us

A WISE PERSON once said, "If you always watch the demons behind you, then you will never see the angels ahead." Whether we are willing to admit it or not, strong black women wrangling with their past need nurturing and support. Face it—our friends, family, and prayer circle may not be enough to help us on our journey to forgive, release, and heal. Sometimes the wounds are so deep that we need professional counseling in conjunction with our spiritual tools.

As I mentioned previously, forgiveness goes deeper than the surface level. Faux forgiveness does not work. I know way too many "church sisters" in my circle who are fooling themselves that they have completed the necessary work to forgive. Some of these sisters are the meanest, angriest, most verbally abusive come-knock-you-out sisters I know. I have been one of these women at times. Too many of us rationalize that as long as we have a Bible in hand and we can recite chapter and verse, or because we shine on the board of trustees or in ministry leadership, we are forgiving, nice people. *No.* A truly forgiving and forgiven person is one who radiates light, laughter, tolerance, compassion, and empathy consistently. You are not working toward forgiveness, dear sister, by holding a Bible in your hand and using it as a lethal weapon. If you walk around with a chip on your shoulder, or if you go around psychoanalyzing everyone else while failing to take your own inventory, you are neither forgiving nor healed.

One of my friends really hurt me last summer with some intentionally cruel words and an overall combative spirit. My first thought was to retaliate—give her back what she gave out. But I tried something new. I decided to love her more and to actively forgive her instead of matching the ugliness. Of course, this sister will tell you in a minute that she is a devoted Christian and a master of forgiveness. *She is not.* (None of us is.) I decided to proceed with love and refused to gossip with other friends about what happened. Eventually, my friend reached out and invited me to talk and have tea. I think our relationship is stronger now because she knows that I didn't bad-mouth her or just throw her away when I was hurt. Today, we can both remind each other how truly walking in humility, love, and forgiveness—as opposed to just pretending—requires daily effort, honesty, and God's grace.

In our interview, relationship therapist Senovia Ross said that when you don't forgive, your past will continue to follow you until you address it. She elaborated:

> Lack of forgiveness prohibits our spiritual growth and personal evolution. So many of us go into survival mode and convince ourselves that we're too busy to address our issues. However, when we don't deal with our past, we inhibit our ability to be creative and free-spirited. Holding on to hurt takes up a lot of mental space. So we "store" our pain and pretend it doesn't affect us. But it does and often manifests as illnesses and disorders such as back pain, headaches, ovarian cysts, fibroids, stomachaches, and sleeplessness.

In our national online survey, we presented respondents with a series of hypothetical situations and asked whether they would forgive the person in question. The scenarios were based on real-life dilemmas discussed in focus groups and brought up in other research conducted for this book. The cross-section of situations gave us a good indication of how we feel about forgiveness. Overall, the data revealed that we are slow to forgive and that there are some situations that are tougher to swallow than others.

Interestingly, a majority of black female respondents deemed a workplace transgression to be the least forgivable of the four situations presented. A solid 74 percent of the women polled were not likely to pardon a colleague who lied about them to get a promotion they were slated to receive. Why such an overwhelming response? The experts I tapped were quick to respond. For a high achiever who has sacrificed so much to reach her goals, a backstabbing colleague thwarting her advancement would be too much to bear.

About two-thirds (68 percent) of the respondents were not likely to absolve a family member who had physically or sexually harmed them, 65 percent were not likely to forgive a husband or boyfriend who abandoned them because of health issues, and 64 percent were not likely to excuse a woman who had an illicit relationship with her boyfriend or husband. *Interesting.* Whether respondents were Catholic, Protestant, or Pentecostal, or whether they went to church regularly, had little effect on their responses. In fact, if anything, the religious respondents were *less likely* to forgive in all four scenarios. This is a fascinating commentary on how our faith convictions are often not reflected in our daily lives.

What are the research findings really telling us? What we see is a pattern of professional black women being hurt, not forgiving, and in many cases being vehement about not forgiving or releasing the transgressions, even when these women are self-defined Christians or women of faith.

The good news is that we don't have to struggle under such a heavy yoke anymore. Contemporary culture encourages us to deal with our wounds, talk about them, get counseling, and seek healing. Just turn on your television or radio. America is filled with the possibility of healing and transformation if we are ready to work to change our lives.

Dr. Audrey Chapman explains that to understand the power of forgiveness and harness that power to rebuild your life, you must steady yourself to ask some tough questions. She offers the following insights to help you truly forgive, release, and heal.

1. **Forgive yourself.** We blame ourselves and feel shame for things that have happened in our past. That's not fair to you, and makes it tough to move on. So start the forgiveness process by giving yourself a clean slate.
2. **Accept that forgiveness is done to release you.** You may not be able to truly forgive someone else, but you can release him or her from the hurt or offense for your own good. Forgiveness is a self-healing process and mechanism. Cleaning out the cobwebs from your mind is an empowering experience. Completing a ritual of forgiveness and release can help (e.g., write letters that you never intend to send).
3. **Forgiveness allows us to understand our own weaknesses and frailties.** Forgiving others helps us understand and empathize with others, and this is a good way for us to heal. It's humbling when we recognize that we need forgiveness from others, too. It makes us capable of apologizing for our wrongs and offenses. It allows us to better understand, for instance, that an alcoholic is often living and fighting with his or her own demons. This makes that person unable to function as a loving family member or friend. And as they say, "hurt people hurt other people." Forgiveness helps us come to terms with human frailty and weakness.

4. **The forgiving process is both powerful and painful,** so it's best to get professional help when in emotional distress. A professional therapist will help you understand that at some point we all inflict pain. Making this connection can help us become more empathetic to others. I do an exercise with my patients called "the empty chair." My patient will sit across from an empty chair and visualize the person who has hurt her or whom she needs to forgive. She actually talks to this person. Although this can be a powerful and therapeutic exercise, it's wise to do with a professional nearby because it can easily evolve into a very emotional and volatile experience.

5. **Working toward the benefits of healing is critical to the process.** When you are healed, you will have humility, empathy, and compassion. If you are a Christian, it is only when you actually live out the Word that it affects others. An unhealed person is angry and bitter, has a broken spirit, and walks around with a cold, broken heart. Many physical and emotional illnesses are fueled by this type of stress, which can result in a weak immune system, high blood pressure, obesity (a lot of people eat when frustrated), anxiety, and the inability to accept comfort when offered.

Senovia Ross has provided a forgiveness self-checklist. Consider these questions for sincere reflection.

1. Is there anything from my past (immediate past or long ago) that I truly need to forgive someone for?
2. Is there anything from my past (immediate past or long ago) that I truly need to forgive myself for?
3. How is it serving me to hold on to mental and emotional clutter and pain?
4. Once I recognize that it isn't serving me well, what am I going to do with it? Tuck it back in my off-limits box, or release it? (Hint: the longer you hold on, the longer you remain a victim.)
5. What will I choose—forgiveness or unforgiveness?
6. When is the last time I cried or released my hurt feelings or emotions?

Finally, I want to share some strategies from my iask sisters that will help you build a community of support around you as you leave "unforgiveness" behind.

1. **Get physically, mentally, and spiritually strong enough** to take on the hard work of forgiveness. Dredging up old hurts and wounds that you have spent years burying takes a lot out of you emotionally. So start taking really good care of yourself by exercising, resting, and eating well.

2. **Find a good psychotherapist.** If you are dealing with old wounds, sexual abuse, unforgiveness, and emotional pain, praying or meditating it away *will not* work, sisters. Dumping your issues on your closest friends will not work well either. Picking a therapist is like choosing a friend. You will spend lots of time with this person, so it should be someone you like. Interview potential therapists, or seek recommendations from friends you trust. It is also very important to find someone who has a good bedside manner and who will respond to your needs in the sanctity and peace of a safe, reputable, clinical setting that does not interfere with your work or personal environment.

   Many health care plans and companies cover such visits. Most employers have an employee assistance plan that will help cover the costs. Take advantage of these services, since they are paid for by your employer. Therapy is an investment in *you*. If you can spend hundreds of dollars on clothes, shoes, and cellular devices, then you can spend that money on your emotional health and wellness.

3. **Let it go!** Sisters, learn to forgive. Polish off your conflict resolution skills, and learn how to confront without being confrontational. Facing up to people who hurt you can help you reconnect and repair damaged relationships.

4. **Bury the past.** Literally. Write out your thoughts, and give them a ceremonial burial, burn them, shred them, or throw them in the trash. You can even lay them at the altar on your church. Some churches offer that ritual during Sunday services. I cannot stress enough how important it is to *release* what you have been holding on to. We can learn from even life's greatest tragedies and setbacks. It is all a matter of how we decide to deal with what life has handed to us.

5. **Seek out support** from your trusted sister network or spiritual circle, as well as your family, in your healing process. Make sure that those you invite in will be a source of comfort, strength, and support.

6. **Reengage in all life has to offer.** Start making choices that lead you to feel good, happy, challenged (in a good way), and confident. I took up acoustic guitar and other hobbies that brought me joy. Social

connections with friends are also essential to our well-being. It is not good for us to be alone as we attempt to heal from old hurts.

You may ask, "How do I forgive?" First, say the following words out loud to yourself daily.

*I want to want to want to forgive*
*I want to want to forgive*
*I want to forgive*

Then, consider the following.

1. **Look at yourself first.** Take your own inventory, and be honest with yourself about any role you may have played in the injury or wrong.
2. **Know that forgiveness is a process**, and time is a great healer. Forgiveness is something we all struggle with. Recognize that all things end; that is a part of living.
3. **Take action** if you seek forgiveness. Initiate the process of making amends.
4. **Take action** if you are seeking to forgive. Allow some space for the other party to make amends and rebuild your trust, but be clear that there are consequences for the bad actions.

# PART IV

# Redefining Ourselves—
# What Really Matters

"When we focus on what is in that small rear view mirror behind us versus the vast clear windshield in front of us—we can get stuck. It is easy to feel defeated when life is not seemingly going the way we imagined it would. Delayed does not mean denied—what you may think is "finished" is in fact just the beginning."

—Anonymous

Sophia and her two nieces

# 9

# EMPTY WOMB, BROKEN HEART:

## *Redefining Motherhood in Today's World*

"The English Language lacks the words to mourn an absence. For the loss of a parent, grandparent, spouse, child, or friend, we have all manner of words and phrases, some helpful, some not. Still, we are conditioned to say something, even if it is only 'I am sorry for your loss.' But for an absence, for someone who was never there at all, we are wordless to capture that particular emptiness. For those who deeply want children and are denied them, those missing babies hover like silent, ephemeral shadows over their lives. Who can describe the feel of a tiny hand that is never held?"

—FORMER FIRST LADY LAURA BUSH, *Spoken from the Heart*

Of all my achievements in life, none has brought me greater joy than being the only aunt to two little girls who stole my heart from the moment they came into this world. Alexandra and Mikaela, now thirteen and eight, are the light for me. Plain and simple, I love them like I never knew I could experience love before. They make me laugh, they bring me joy, they keep me young, and they fill that void in my heart that I had reserved specifically for my own children. Many of my fellow sisters out there know the joy of which I speak because, like me, you love your nieces and nephews, and they are a big part of your life. They feel like your children too, and you thank God for their presence.

Facing the fact that I am now entering my mid-forties and may not bear my own children has been the most difficult experience of my life.

The hardest part of this journey as a single woman is that as you come to grips with this challenge, you must deal with the loss alone. When I read the part of former First Lady Laura Bush's memoir on her trials with infertility in her thirties, I was deeply touched because she nailed it; the desire to have children (for most women) is a profound and instinctual one that is like an ache when it is left unfulfilled.[1]

This is a tough topic for many childless accomplished women to discuss publicly, just as it is for many of you to read about. This issue knows *no color lines* when it comes to professional women, because as we know, professional women in general (white, Latino, Asian, Native American) are having a harder time finding suitable husbands. For many of us, this can delay motherhood until we're well into our forties or eliminate it as an option altogether.

Nowhere is this dilemma more acute than for professional, upwardly mobile black women. However, as we've learned from other discussions in this book about black women, letting people see beyond the veil that we have carefully constructed around our hearts isn't our strong suit, particularly when our hearts are broken. I've spent many a sleepless night walking the floor weeping, asking God, "Why? Why me?" But then I remind myself: *Why not me?* I have learned to be thankful that I am alive, and who knows what can happen? There is love and motherhood after forty-four (as you will read in NPR host Michel Martin's touching feature essay on the topic in the bonus section of this book). The important thing I remind myself of is that I have lost sister friends who were well under the age of forty when they passed away from breast cancer, serious illness, or an accident and never got the chance to experience motherhood in any form.

I recall a conversation I had with a black woman in her thirties who'd been married at age nineteen to a noncommissioned military officer who cheated on her and physically abused her. She developed cervical cancer as a result of being infected by him with HPV. Now she cannot bear children. We were talking about our nieces and nephews, and how much they mean to us, when she started to sob uncontrollably. I asked her what was wrong, because she had always worn such a brave face with everyone, saying that having children was not a big deal to her. She used to brag about taking holidays away from her extended family so that she could have some "me" time. She tearfully confessed that having children meant the world to her and that she only pretended it wasn't a big deal. That was the only way she knew how to manage her hurt and grief.

She was raised to be a wife and mother but had been so consumed with fending for herself that she hadn't had time to focus on this unacknowledged, deep need. Thinking about not being a mom was more than she could handle. Acting like kids didn't matter enabled her to move forward in her life. I understand.

For those of you who are now in your forties or older, facing midlife can be hard enough, as perimenopause begins and your body starts to change. But facing midlife without having met one of your most precious goals—the goal of motherhood—is even harder for such driven, successful planners like us. A *USA Today* article about this new generation of so-called working non-mothers is on the mark:

> They are women who have birthed successful careers, accumulated status, and achieved comfortable incomes. But they have never gotten around to having the one thing they always intended: a child. New research, some of it controversial and already creating a stir, indicates there are legions of these women from Wall Street to Hollywood Boulevard. And their message to their younger sisters is: Get a plan. Envision your life at 45, and if you want that life to include a child, think now about how you will make it happen.[2]

I've talked with many black women on college campuses across the nation about motherhood, and I could see the fear in their eyes as they struggled to ask me how not to end up in my shoes: well-educated, successful, and childless. They shouldn't feel bad for asking. It's a fair question to any woman who offers to mentor young women. Every woman has the right to want to be an accomplished career girl and a mom, too. You *can* have it all, sweet sisters, but maybe not all at once.

The issue of motherhood and the accomplished twenty-first-century woman is an emerging topic of interest across race and gender lines. Unfortunately, as I mentioned earlier, black women with four-year college degrees and higher are disproportionately childless. Some of us are in denial because we cannot bear to face the pain, and others have become proactive and opted for adoption or artificial insemination, asked a male friend to be a sperm donor the old-fashioned way, or raised nieces and nephews as their own kids in the absence of the biological parents.

As I traveled, held focus groups, taught workshops, and conducted listening sessions with thousands of professional black women ranging from age twenty to sixty over the past six years, I was touched by their stories about this deeply personal subject. So I decided to give voice to their experiences. For many, this was the first time they had talked about their feelings about not having children. "If you had asked me at twenty-five years old if I thought I would never marry and have kids, I would have laughed at you," said one beautiful sixty-three-year-old sister who holds a PhD. "My advice to young women is do not involve yourself in relationships with men that are not headed toward marriage. Remove yourself quickly from an abusive situation, and make motherhood a priority earlier in your life."

## How Do You Deal with the Loss of a Dream?

YES, IT IS a deep ache, a longing unfulfilled, and one that I've had to mourn and learn to live with. Not surprisingly, our ABW survey results confirm that over 20 percent of professional sisters experience bouts of the blues and depression because of the fear that they will grow old and never have children and families of their own.[3]

My goal in this chapter is to shine light on this sensitive issue so that childless women can stop suffering in silence. Let's walk this leg of the journey together, exploring our feelings of loss that are complicated by a lack of support from loved ones. I want to move this challenge to the forefront of discussion with compassion, understanding, and viable solutions that do not conflict with our faith, values, or desire to have children in our lives. It is also important to highlight some of the real emotional, spiritual, and workplace stigmas that childless women endure.

I'm determined to address the question on every young woman's mind: How do you build a successful career without abandoning your desire to have a family of your own? As professional women age, the pressure becomes enormous, from families and friends alike, to "hurry up and do something" or lose your fertility forever. The pressure from society is equally challenging in the workplace, the church, and the community because American culture reveres the family and mothers. There's something about a woman who has children of her own that humanizes her in the minds of others—it makes her seem more approachable, warm, nurturing, and open. What makes childlessness so traumatic for a single, unmarried woman is that she doesn't get the support or empathy from friends and family that married women suffering from infertility problems do. But the pain is the same. There are numerous avenues of encouragement out there for infertile couples, from support groups to books on how to cope with infertility, stillbirth, and miscarriage. However, there are no books that I could find that speak to the women who are what I call the "involuntary childless." So I decided to start this dialogue. I want to encourage those of us who want children, and who have yet to find our life partner, to redefine the meaning of motherhood in a way that will allow us to experience what all my friends who are mothers have told me is an "ecstatic love that knows no bounds."

I challenge our churches to find meaningful ways to reach out, support, comfort, and encourage childless women in their quests to understand their loss, adopt a child, or volunteer their time to girls in need instead of throwing a Bible at them and telling them to just pray it away. And I ask everyone else (including us) to stop making mean, uncaring, or just plain incorrect assumptions about women who don't have children. You wouldn't believe the nonsense I've heard. Childless women have not been cursed by God. We aren't selfish, career-driven snobs who brought this on ourselves. We didn't choose career over marriage and family (funny nobody ever says this to men). And we are not lesbians because we haven't married yet and don't have kids. In our focus groups, two accomplished, attractive, single sisters in their early forties lamented that they'd been asked on numerous occasions if they were gay simply because they had no kids. What an unnerving and inappropriate question to ask to a woman just because she's childless!

There are no quick answers or easy fixes to this very complex problem. I don't have answers to lots of the questions women who want children might ask. My hope is that discussing the challenges and sharing stories of healing will open new doors of love, life, and family. I want to help us move from a place of loss, fear, and sadness to one of action, courage, and faith, in which we explore other options for becoming a mom. The good news is that in researching for this chapter, I uncovered some encouraging stories of women who redefined their path to motherhood in the quest to bring the joy of children into their lives.

## Redefining Motherhood

LIKE MOST LITTLE girls growing up, I dreamed of becoming a mom someday. In my dreams, I married in my late twenties, had babies in my early thirties after graduate school, raised them to be good people, and then grew old with my husband. Part of my American Dream included an all-American family.

My daughter's name would be Catherine. She'd be my princess and everything I'm not. She'd have an easier path than I did, with more choices, attend an Ivy League college, and perhaps become a successful musician or artist. I'd indulge her and lavish her with love and kisses. She'd be safe and protected. Her world would be peaceful, something I never really experienced as a child because of constant turmoil in my home. I would encourage her to find her own way, her own path to happiness and success.

And, of course, I also dreamed of having a son, Samuel, who would be my gift from God. And after my medical diagnosis in my mid-thirties, I prayed for him and fought mightily against the odds for him. Maybe he'd be a track athlete (like his mom) or a football and baseball player (like his dad), or maybe he'd be a great physician or missionary and help to make the world a better place.

It simply never occurred to me when I was younger that I would never marry and have children. Now that I'm forty-four years old, my hopes of having biological children of my own grow dimmer every day. I have not totally given up, but at this stage of my life, I am willing to *redefine* what my American Dream family looks like. I realize that technological advances mean that I could easily go to a sperm bank, hire a surrogate mom, and try in vitro fertilization, but who wants to endure that process alone? Not to mention that in many corners—from church to workplace—it is still frowned on for professional black women to go it alone and "manufacture" their own offspring in a lab. Trust me, I have been considering it for years.

As one article aptly explains, when white single professional women have children, the world views this as "a kind of liberal empowerment." That's not the case for their black counterparts. This conclusion is strongly supported by the research of Yale University's Averil Clarke. Our concern, says Clarke, is that black single moms may be perceived as stereotypical ghetto baby mamas.[4] Fair or not, the data reinforces that perception: according to the National Center for Health Statistics, 28 percent of white women gave birth out of wedlock in 2008, but 72 percent of black women and more than 52 percent of Latinas did.[5]

Clarke explains in the article, "When it comes to the issue of black women and should or should they not make a choice to have a child alone, these women are very much aware that the decision to do it makes people question their class status. We associate single unwed child bearing with poor African American women."[6]

There is a real stigma attached to a black woman having a baby on her own. It's one thing for a woman to be a single mom as the result of abandonment, divorce, or the death of a spouse. We offer these women encouragement and support. But it's quite another for a modern, professional woman to venture into solo motherhood. If she goes down that road and runs into problems, she may not find the help she needs from friends and family.

As Toni Oliver, founder and CEO of Roots Adoption Agency in Atlanta, Georgia, says, "The unfulfilled desire to be a mother can damage a woman emotionally." Oliver's agency, in addition to providing adoption services, offers counseling to prospective mothers who have invested much of their self-worth into becoming mothers.[7] While we know that women of all races and ages experience infertility for various reasons, that is not the issue millions of aspiring and professional black women face. We face the reality of not ever having had the opportunity to try and become mothers because of the social and religious pressures we face to be married first.

I know firsthand the struggles of looking into single motherhood because of the life-changing medical condition I was suddenly facing in the summer of 2003. This condition caused sudden and devastating reproductive consequences. After bravely fighting for my fertility for five years (seeing specialists, naturopaths, and healers), my prayers helped me decide to adopt a baby. I found an agency in California that specialized in the adoption of biracial infants (my two nieces are biracial) and completed the paperwork. I was excited about my decision. At the time, I was working in a big law firm, was on partner track, was making good money, and felt I had to choose between my career and my need to be a mother of my own children. *I chose to be a mom.* I went to my section leadership and asked to go part time, which is eight hours less a week. Scaling back my hours would result in a pretty significant pay cut, so I decided not to go part time and instead hire some help. I shared my news discreetly with some colleagues and friends, and everyone was happy for me, at least on the surface. I think it's fair to say, however, that from my employer's point of view, this decision signaled that my career was no longer going to be the primary driver of my life. We all know the drill.

The sixty-, seventy-, or eighty-hour work week is hell on married professionals with kids. The same demands on a single woman are even more daunting.

Despite my enthusiasm, I started to feel the stress of being responsible financially, emotionally, and otherwise for this new little person I wanted to bring into my life. I was not going to have the luxury of staying home for the first two years of my child's life. I would have to wake up nights alone, change diapers alone, and foot all the bills alone. It was all very sobering, but I was still ready to go through it. The craving for children had been with me for years. The bittersweet emotions I felt each time I went to a friend's baby shower, or visited that friend in the hospital after the birth of her new son or daughter, were overwhelming. Yet I smiled through it all as my heart was breaking. As fate would have it, I lost my job later that year to downsizing and had to put my adoption plans on hold. So once again, my dreams were crushed. But I suffered in silence and just kept going.

## The Challenge of an Empty Womb

YEARS AGO, A pair of married friends of mine were having problems conceiving. We were all in our late twenties at the time. Sadly, whenever my friend would conceive, she would have a miscarriage. I remember it like it was yesterday—the hell that she endured each time her cycle would come, each time she got her hopes up, and each time the fertility treatments failed. Her husband, a medical resident, withdrew into his work. She withdrew from her friends and social network, unable to hold down a job, as she faced their life without the desired children, playdates, and family outings expected in such social circles.

She became deeply depressed, and I was unable to comfort her with prayer, cards, flowers, and even gift baskets on Mother's Day with notes of encouragement that one day she would be a mom. Finally, she followed the advice of many of us and adopted a baby. Within a month or so after the adopted baby arrived, she was pregnant. It was a very happy time for everyone involved. Not surprisingly, she was quickly welcomed into the mommy fold that had been denied her. And, as Proverbs 13:12 says, "Hope deferred makes the heart sick, but a longing fulfilled is a tree of life."[8] She was like a new person—full of life and joy. I was very happy for her.

Years later, I was diagnosed with a chronic autoimmune illness that had caused my ovaries to go through premature ovarian failure.[9] Unlike with my friend, no one really rallied around me to share my enormous grief and anger when the doctors told me that I probably would never be able to bear children. Besides my mother, only one dear friend, Janet—who'd lost a teenage son in a car accident a few years earlier—acknowledged my loss. I still have the letter she wrote, in which she compassionately told me that my loss was every bit as valid and important as the loss of someone whose child had just died—and that I needed to mourn my loss and learn, as she had, to live without a child. Coming from her, that meant the world to me.

Regrettably, the friend that I stood by was not as supportive of me. After she was blessed with her family, she didn't have much time for me and my issues. I know many stories of childless women who lost friends when motherhood came knocking for their friends. *Is it that they just don't care? Or does our barrenness bring back too many unhappy moments?* In hindsight, I get it. I don't like it, but I get it—sometimes people are just not where we are, and often people who have just endured a traumatic experience don't want to be reminded of it. Sisters, hear me on this: true sisterhood, friendship, and family require us to be there for those we care about—in good times and bad. It is not what we say but what we do that matters most in life. We all need to get better at comforting, supporting, and loving people with our actions when they need us most.

## High-Achieving Black Women Can Reach Motherhood

WHAT WE KNOW from recent national and international data trends is that the number of single women has more than doubled in the last three decades.[10] And as we discussed in Chapters five and six in detail, the modern sexual revolution continues to redefine roles for both women and men; unfortunately, the roles that are emerging are not so good for women who are seeking the husbands and kids they desire.

One study published by the authors of a new book, *Premarital Sex in America: How Young Americans Meet, Mate, and Think About Marrying,* paints a fascinating picture of how the explosion of educated, successful women in America over the past twenty years has come at a great cost to women's sexual bargaining power. The fact is that women outnumber men in college and they are out-earning their male peers when they first enter the work world—to such a degree that many consider it evidence of a "boy crisis." Translated: when it comes to relationships, women are now competing for men—and men are calling all the shots—which means men are giving *less commitment* and yet getting more sex.

As I have addressed in previous chapters, black women often face a somewhat unique series of challenges in charting a course through education, career, sexuality, marriage, and childbearing that often leaves us single and childless even when we'd prefer marriage and family. We know from the Yale study mentioned earlier in the chapter that 70 percent or so of professional black women are unmarried, and we know that another 44 percent of black women will never marry.[11] Our study confirms these numbers to be true—67 percent of the women in our survey were unmarried, high-achieving professionals. What we don't discuss, however, is the impact these dangerously low marriage rates may have on the desires and hopes of a new generation of educated, professional black women who are coming behind us. Why does this matter? It means that our best and brightest are not producing offspring. That speaks for itself.

Somewhere along the way, we (career girls) lost sight of the working married moms in our lives who may not have been professionals but took pride in the fact they were able to juggle a family and work outside the home. We don't focus on role models in the church, in our communities, or in our sororities who have managed to climb the career ladder with children and husband in tow. I am asking this new generation of sisters to consider returning to this value.

One of the things I love most about First Lady Michelle Obama is that she helps the world to see strong, accomplished black women in a multidimensional role. She makes clear to everyone that her role as mom is second to none. As she likes to say, first and foremost, I am "Malia and Sasha's mom."[12] Alarmingly, too many young women these days assume the "Obama standard" just isn't possible for them. Our mothers often underplayed the joy that motherhood brought them as they emphasized the importance of their daughters becoming independent, making a good living, and taking care of themselves. Some went further and told their daughters that "men are no good" because they themselves had endured difficult relationships. Many Gen X and Gen Y women were raised by single mothers (or divorced ones), and their struggles often sent a very firm message to young girls: delay having children until you can provide for yourself.

As I mentioned in Chapter 8, one dear friend of mine (who is an age cohort, professional sister, and single with no kids) suggested to me that one of the things we as career-driven black women need to do to help our healing is to have a conversation with our mothers to let them know that we love them and appreciate their strength, *but* that some of what they told us and steered us toward has had serious consequences. What she is suggesting is that we open up an honest dialogue that allows us to talk through some of the challenges we now face in ways that restore, renew, and heal us so that we do not feel bitterness or anger toward our mothers, who thought they were guiding us properly away from more traditional roles. As one forty-nine-year-old single, never married, fabulously accomplished sister friend lamented over drinks with the sisterhood one night, "Our mothers raised us to be independent and successful. But they forgot to teach us how to balance and become successful wives, mothers, and human beings, too."

Every career woman I know who has been on a panel or made a speech in the past five years where there were young women in the audience got bombarded with work-family balance questions. A twenty-year-old black female premed student at Howard University asked a question at the National Black Women's Town Hall Meeting in the fall of 2009 that stuck with me for days: "Sometimes I feel as if I attend an all-girl's school here at Howard because the campus has so many more women than men. I want to be a successful professional black woman, but I also want a family and husband. I fear that if I am too strong and independent, I will scare potential mates off. How do I avoid being that stereotypical successful black woman?" This is an important question, but the problem is that many speakers and panelists are not prepared to answer these questions with a dose of compassionate love combined with common sense. We must offer these young ladies viable options—and stop focusing on the media speculations on whether successful black women will ever find a man. The statistics are scary, yes. But the reality is ours to mold the best way we can. While we want to encourage young black professionals to excel at their careers, we must emphasize what it takes to make that happen when marriage and having a family are important to you.

There are genuine consequences when you let life move on its own timetable. As psychologist Dr. Gayle Porter commented in our interview, "Life balance can't happen by accident." One ob-gyn I interviewed was even more direct: "There are 520 weekends in a decade—the time when most people date. A woman really needs to be focused on marriage during her late twenties and mid-thirties."

If you are a mentor to a younger sister, this is the conversation you need to have with her: The reality is that building a lifestyle that suits all our needs is hard. And our needs change over time. Living the good life takes enormous planning. And it may mean that you have to make some tough choices—about your career, about where you live in terms of support from your family, about the man you choose, and about whether you're looking for a man who wants a working wife and is willing to be a good father to your kids. Above all, remember that your decisions have consequences.

As mentioned previously, our ABW research tells us that it's not the degrees or the high-ranking jobs that keep the men away. It's who we are as women and what we have to offer the men in our lives in terms of warmth, friendliness, openness, and sensuality that fuel a love connection. Unfortunately, too many of our professional sisters never remove their corporate game face—which is a big turnoff to our men. Reread Chapters 4, 5, and 6 if you didn't get that message loud and clear—and give them to your younger protégés to study. In the name of honesty, let's also admit that some of us ambitious single ladies are having too much fun making money, building our careers, and making our own way in the world to think about settling down until we're in our mid-thirties or later. That's fine until it's not working for you anymore. Then what? By the time you find a husband, if you do at all, you may be facing your forties, when conception becomes more difficult. I'm also talking to the young women whose work is totally consuming—those extreme careerists struggling to keep their heads above water as they try to make partner in a law firm, or those MBA holders in the running for a high-profile department director's slot. If the job requires their attention 24/7, combining a family with that job may not be in the cards until they hit their late thirties. And then they may be racing the fertility clock. It's a tough personal decision to make, but one each young woman must make for herself. It may be time to reevaluate your priorities and make some tough decisions to help you combine your career and family ambitions.

Real life has a way of interrupting our plans. So think about setbacks, relationship challenges, an unexpected health crisis, divorce before you have children, personal loss, caring for a sick parent, or professional challenges that might require you to reboot and set a new course. These are all things that young people generally don't factor into their future plans.

We might all do well to take a cue from CNN correspondent Soledad O'Brien. The award-winning journalist in her essay for this book (see the bonus section) shares that she was very strategic about whom she dated and planned what she wanted while still in college. If the men she dated didn't envision themselves with a working wife and children and a timeline that worked for her, she moved on quickly. Today she is happily married to a man who supports her career. Together they're raising their four children. The message here is don't let life pass you by while you focus only on your career. If you want children, they must be factored into your life plans earlier than you think.

## Barriers to Motherhood That We Can Work On

KEEPING OUR BODIES healthy is the best way to guard against the myriad of fertility challenges. We're seeing fertility problems occur at alarming rates in black women—problems that make having babies trickier as we age.

I conducted an interview with Dr. Fred Steinberg, ob-gyn and chief of residency at Cooper University Hospital in Camden, New Jersey, to discuss the dilemma facing young black professional women's reproductive health. Having mentored many young female medical students, Dr. Steinberg encourages women to have frank discussions with their daughters, nieces, and younger sisters about their reproductive health early in their lives if they intend to pursue a professional career.

> What I see now is a two-tiered black community. By that I mean . . . the highly educated, fabulous, black female residents at the hospital who want to date and marry someone *in their league* and have a family of their own, but their options are not very good. The black male residents are scarce, and when they do exist, they know they are a commodity and can be selective. Then I see my patients, who are mostly lower-income inner-city residents, unmarried with multiple children. There is a widening gap in the black community with regard to childbearing that I have never seen before in my forty-plus years of being a doctor.
>
> The other challenge that I see is that during their prime reproductive years, black professional women are busy becoming someone—making something out of their lives. Those are critical reproductive years that you can't get back. Women have it tough because they have to be committed to childbearing during the same years that they have to be committed to their careers.

In our ABW national online survey of 540 professional black women, 31 percent say they suffer from fibroids, and about 25 percent cite obesity and high blood pressure as health concerns. As we've discussed, stress-induced problems like these can also affect the well-being of your mind and soul and cause reproductive problems such as infertility, miscarriage, or early onset of labor during pregnancy. Our ABW focus group discussions also showed a clear connection between physical conditions and unresolved emotional issues and unhealthy relationships. This finding supports theories by spiritual wellness and health gurus like Louise Hay and Dr. Christiane Northrup, who have long suggested that the key to health for women lies in our ability to release and heal from old hurts. Louise Hay[13] is the author of the international best seller *You Can Heal Your Life*. Her courses and workshops are based on practical methods that are highly effective and have helped me to heal my own body. All her techniques are designed to identify and clear out long-held emotions that may be creating health, relationship, or other problems in our lives but that we may be unaware of.

For one focus group participant, a diagnosis of fibroids at age twenty-three (she was married at the time) was followed by a hysterectomy and then deep depression. To combat these feelings, she turned to alcohol and drugs and eventually sought out medical help. Being unable to bear children, among other issues, ultimately led to her divorce. She explained:

> At the time, I was married and had no children. It was a very, very emotional time for me, making the decision to get pregnant or not, because the doctors said if I wanted to have children, I needed to do it then. But I chose not to. I'm thankful that I didn't. Having all that happen to me so young impacts the mentoring work that I do today. Figuring out who I am and finding peace within my life has enabled me to reach out to girls and help them realize that *they are enough* just the way they are.

Another woman in the session had been diagnosed with late-onset fibroids. This drove her to conduct a long-term introspection and eventual lifestyle change. As I listened to these women share their stories, I felt a tremendous sense of sorrow and relief—relief in that I saw they'd come out okay on the other side of the very pain that I and many others have endured. It broke my heart and gave me hope all at once.

Fortunately, there is good news on managing fibroids. Dr. Carolyn

DeMarco, who specializes in women's health and alternative medicine, advises her patients to break down the proper care and management of fibroids into five steps:

1. Decrease the estrogen overload.
2. Support liver function.
3. Increase pelvic and general circulation.
4. Do a cleansing and detox, especially for the liver.
5. Deal with emotional conflicts that might be relevant.

Other things to check for are low thyroid and adrenal function.[14] Women's health expert Dr. Christiane Northrup says that fibroids represent creativity that was never birthed. She talks about dead-end jobs and relationships as well as conflicts about reproduction and motherhood. This connection is something worth exploring, since you'll recall that our surveys show that black women have a very difficult time letting go of past hurts and managing emotional wounds.

Like fibroids, other illnesses threatening your reproductive health can be managed if you start early enough. Be diligent about tending to your reproductive health if you're still in your childbearing years, and you may be able to prevent or turn around problems before they threaten your ability to conceive and carry a child.

## Loving a Child—Biological or Not—Is What Really Matters

NO ONE WHO wants children should be deprived of them. Whether you choose adoption, in vitro fertilization, a surrogate mother, or volunteering, the key is to find the right solution and support you'll need to turn your dream into reality.

I was a bit dismayed by how unsympathetic some of the women in our ABW focus groups were when the discussion turned to childlessness. Married or not, no woman should be told to "just get over it" when dealing with an empty womb. One of our participants flippantly remarked, "Have a child if you want one. Don't burden others with your desires." Another participant chimed in right after her: "*Tough*. If single professional black women want kids so badly, why not adopt? It's almost as if they want the birth experience more than anything else. I'm not judging . . . but there are tons of kids who need homes." Of course, adoption is a viable option, but sisters, please cultivate a little compassion. The desire to be a mother, conceive, carry, and give birth to a baby is a natural and normal desire, and deeply personal. Believe me when I say that when a woman has to confront the possibility that she may never have children of her own, it can be very traumatic.

Although adoption is the most obvious option that people who want kids turn to, it's not the only one. As I mentioned previously, technology has allowed many women past the age of forty to conceive children on their own. In vitro fertilization and other insemination procedures are expensive and may take years to be successful, but if you have the resources, the commitment, and the good health to try, go for it. This is your personal decision. There are also other options, such as becoming a mentor or a big sister, volunteering as a coach at the elementary and high school levels, volunteering at a women and children's shelter, teaching a Sunday school class, or helping out at the day-care center in your community. Children always need more people to love and care for them.

My point, sisters, is that you can get involved in the life of a child in a way that will be rewarding for that child and for you on a deep emotional level. One of my best girlfriends just got married at age fifty-one to a great guy who has a young daughter from a previous marriage. She has always wanted to be a mom, and now she is one. I had the privilege of mailing her a Mother's Day card this year, and she was moved. She never thought motherhood could happen to her, but now it has!

In our national ABW survey, women were asked, "Which of the following would you consider if you realized that, due to your age or health, you were less likely to have a family of your own?" The respondents could select as many of the six choices as they wanted. The good news is that 56 percent of the women we surveyed saw adoption as a viable option for professional black women—married or not. Forty percent felt it would be a good thing to invest more time with nieces and nephews. Thirty-five percent supported volunteer work with children. These numbers are encouraging, especially the adoption numbers, since the idea of single women adopting has been met with some resistance in certain circles in the black community. But the success stories are so compelling. The experiences of two women I know who adopted sons come immediately to mind. One is an attorney in Arizona and the other a social worker in Virginia. Both hold advanced degrees, are unmarried, and simply grew tired of waiting for Mr. Right to come along, so they chose to be moms on their own. Although it's not easy to juggle a career and a little one solo, they both recommend adoption as a way to bring love to a child's life while bringing joy and fulfillment to your own.

A colleague once related a story about a couple, John and Barbara, whose attempts at parenthood were met with miscarriage after miscarriage and then a stillborn baby after an eight-month pregnancy. Heartbroken, fragile, defeated, and discouraged, Barbara took time off by herself to get healthy and think about her options. Although her husband was adamant about not adopting, she didn't see any other solution that would work for her. In vitro fertilization was not an option. When she returned home, looking good and feeling strong, she convinced her husband to give adoption a go. A few months later, they were taking baby Malik home. Soon after, my colleague witnessed John pushing his son's carriage around town. She couldn't help laughing with tears in her eyes. John seemed to be floating on air with the biggest smile on his face that she'd ever seen. Now Malik is in his second year of college.

To gain more insight on adoption, I spoke with therapist A. Njideka Wiggins, who is clinical coordinator for Family Advocacy Services of Virginia, a treatment foster care agency in Newington, Virginia. She also serves on the board of directors for African American Adoptions, Inc., a nonprofit organization whose mission is to raise awareness of the critical need for "forever homes" for black children in foster care. According to Wiggins, one reason that more black professionals don't choose to adopt is because so few are aware of the tremendous need to give kids stuck in the system a safe, loving home, especially those over five years old. "Everyone starts out wanting a baby, but there are usually not a lot of black infants available," says Wiggins. "That's largely because we often waste time trying reuniting kids with their parents [some are able to care for them, but many are not]. So by the time they hit foster care, they are five years or older." Wiggins also covered some of the other stigmas and concerns that women must consider before they adopt:

> I think every woman has been conditioned to expect and desire that they will have babies of their own. Women are ingrained with this stuff from the time we are little girls, with dolls and a baby carriage. Some women want to feel the baby growing inside of them and need that birth experience. If that is something you desire, but it's no longer an option, you need to feel that, mourn that loss, and then be ready to accept what you can have. Black women are masters at taking nothing and making it do what we want it to do, so why can't that be the same

with kids? These kids need love; they deserve love. You have the ability to look beyond what you thought you wanted to see what you can have. We get stuck with the ideal—the 2.5 kids, the husband with a big job. I am not saying you have to live plan B—this is *not* a less-than proposition; it just means it is a different one.

Keeping these points in mind, I put together a list of questions (with answers from Wiggins and others) that singles and couples considering adoption should ask themselves, ask the adoption agencies they're working with, research online, and of course, ask adoptive parents—probably your best source of all.

- **Can I do this alone?** If you're single, your main concerns are probably the resources you need—financial, emotional, and caretaking. You may also worry about having male role models around to replace the father that your adopted children won't have. But sometimes you need to go by faith. If we spend our whole life waiting until we can afford children, family life may simply pass us by.
- **Are there support systems for people who adopt?** Yes. Your adoption or foster care agency is there to help you and will offer lists of organizations to tap for support and information. Employee assistance programs at work also can be very helpful. Some companies even provide financial support for adoption. Talk to your friends who are adoptive parents about your desires, concerns, and fears. They will provide you with the best insight and often the most encouraging words of support.
- **How will it affect my life?** Kids change everything, whether you adopt or have kids biologically. Like any parents, your life will change, and often your needs will be second to your children's. Your personal time will diminish, but your home will be filled with the love and laughter of a child.
- **Is it difficult bonding with older children?** Older adopted kids may have issues with being abandoned, abused, or unloved. These children may have problems communicating with you and will need counseling, support, and lots of love and patience. They need you to open up and be willing to share yourself with them. You'll need to win them over with love, trust, loyalty, respect, and warmth.

Sisters, I promised you at the outset of this chapter to raise this very sensitive issue so that we could work together to move beyond it while at the same time considering how to offer our love to kids who so desperately need it. I hope that you've found value in our putting this subject on the table. My impassioned plea is for our families, churches, and friends to become more aware, loving, and compassionate about the special dilemma that many black women face. For younger sisters, please don't be afraid to pursue your dreams or be who God made you to be. If you want to be a doctor, be one. If you want to be a lawyer, be one. If you want to be president of the United States, be that too, *but* if you also dream of having children, don't forget that as a woman you're biologically engineered to have babies and to do so when you're young.

One woman in a focus group shared a story about their family reunion in Alabama. She, her cousins, and her sisters (all now in their forties) lamented to their elders that they were encouraged to achieve, make money, and have success but not to be moms and wives. Instead of showing pictures of their kids and grandkids like other female cousins (who were not as educated), they were showing pictures of their dogs, new cars, new homes, and travel destinations. Her sister, who was forty-five at the time, started to cry because she felt she'd played by the rules and still come up short.

Many of us may feel this way, but today we can move forward to pursue exciting new options with the support of family and friends. As some of the essays in the bonus chapter at the end of this book attest, love can happen at any time, and so can the joy of children. You will also see from some of our famous sisters that they had a strategy for love, success, and career fulfillment, and it worked. Keep the faith, sisters—you can have it all.

*O*ur greatest glory is not in never falling, but in rising every time we fall.

—Confucius

*Y*our willingness to look at your darkness is what empowers you to change.

—Iyanla Vanzant

# 10

## IT'S THE CLIMB:

### *Facing Life's Storms and Remaining Resilient*

"I believe we have two lives: the one we learn with and the life
we live with after that."

—GLENN CLOSE, *The Natural*

Whatever path you choose in life, my dear sisters, know this:
life is a *storm*. I have always held fast to this metaphor. It comes from
one of my favorite books, *The Count of Monte Cristo*, written by Alexandre Dumas, a French author whose mother was an Afro-Caribbean
Creole woman. The hero of the story is Edmond Dantès, who has
been wrongly imprisoned for fourteen years and robbed of his life by
three jealous friends. After escaping from prison, Dantès finds a great
treasure, becomes the Count of Monte Cristo, and seeks revenge. In an
impromptu speech to a young man on his sixteenth birthday, Dantès, in
the movie adaptation of the book, shares these profound words: "Life is
a storm, my young friend. You will bask in the sunlight one moment, be
shattered on the rocks the next. What makes you a man is what you do
when that storm comes. You must look into that storm and shout . . . Do
your worst, for I will do mine!"

And so it is with us, sisters. Many of us know how to endure and be strong in the face of life's storms. We yell, "Do your worst!" and then stiffen our resolve and handle our business. As strong black women, we have all been there—time and time again, we have stood in the midst of the storm and been tattered by its winds. But have we learned how to thrive in the storms of life or just survive them?

If we identify with the black female characters in movies like *For Colored Girls*, *Waiting to Exhale*, and *Precious*, then too many of us are emerging from life's storms battered, bruised, walled off, and isolated, even from ourselves. That's because we need to adopt better ways of coping. The truth is, sisters, some of us are so far submerged in what I call the *interruptions* and *darkness* of our lives that we don't know how to bask in the sunlight when it finally reappears. And the worst part is we refuse to admit it when everyone else can see we're shipwrecked.

*I know because I've been there.* The past four years of my life have shown a perfect example of someone who was one minute basking in the sunlight and the next shattered on the rocks. I started this book journey in 2006 as a successful attorney in a big law firm. I began dating a wonderful man, but I lost my job in 2007. I then got a better job but was laid off after only four weeks. I parted ways with my man, and then abruptly my beloved dog Nelson died. But then I got to cover the historic 2008 campaign as a pundit and paid journalist, and I started to thrive, selling my first nonfiction book idea to a New York publisher. Unfortunately, though, I had a serious bicycle accident that resulted in a skull fracture and neurological damage, and I had to write the book with a head injury and severe pain. On the upside, iask at that time celebrated five years of success as an organization. However, I was sued twice while writing this book by the lawyer I hired to help me review my firm separation contract back in 2007. Thankfully, he lost both times and ended up getting publicly sanctioned by the bar for his conduct. All of this while managing a chronic endocrine disease.

Since then, I have continued to be successful as a TV commentator and journalist, the man I adored came back, I got a new book publisher, I've watched my business grow, and I've saved my home from foreclosure and started to dig out of debt. I've never felt or looked better and am now very excited about my future. Here is my point: people only see what we want them to see. While all this hell was breaking out on me, I had to keep living. People would see me on TV looking great, or writing a cover feature story on the First Lady or president for *Jet*, or contributing op-eds to the *Washington Post*, and think that my life was great. Only those closest to me knew the nightmare I was going through. Here I had founded this fabulous sister network designed to help women just like me in tough times, and I could not bring myself to let the sisterhood know exactly what was going on for fear nobody would really care.

The difference between those who use life's storms to thrive and those who succumb to them is a matter of perspective. My belief is that we have only two options when faced with difficult circumstances: wither and die *or* rage against the storm and shout, "Do your worst, for I will do mine!" The latter has been the course I've chosen my entire life. But know this: constantly engaging in battle—at home, at work, at church, in relationships, or wherever—takes a mighty toll on your mind, body, and spirit. My goal in this chapter is to encourage us to *stop* and focus on self-care for just a moment, which is something we as black women are simply not comfortable doing, as we discuss later in this chapter. If we consider all that has been covered in the first nine chapters of this book, it is clear that we as black women are under a great deal of career, familial, relational, spiritual, and financial stress. There is no way we can be resilient and have the fulfilling lives we want if we don't assess carefully and critically where we are and what steps we need to take to build healthier, happier, fuller lives. Our First Lady, Michelle Obama, teaches us lessons daily about what good health, marriage, spirituality, and family look like when they are in balance. She is an important role model for the present and next generation of black women because she proves that we can in fact have it all and that we can be purposeful about living a fulfilled and happy life despite the barbs and jolts that may come our way.

## *Moving beyond Survival to Thriving*

MAYA ANGELOU, OUR wise elder sister, offers a great perspective on how we might frame this discussion: "Surviving is important, but thriving is elegant." This quotation hangs in my office. That's where we need to get to, sisters. Let's put down the bravado and take off the armor once in a while. We need a new mantra. Let's ban the old, clichéd "I will survive" philosophy and focus on thriving and soaring above the storms, no matter how bad they may be.

Remember, there are always lessons to be learned from adversity. The bald eagle illustrates this message. This majestic bird has been hard-wired by God with a strategy to navigate bad weather. When a storm approaches, it finds a high perch on which to sit and wait. It is peaceful, not harried or worried; it anticipates the storm and acts with grace and majesty. Its navigation system is already in gear when the threatening weather approaches. When the wind and rain finally hit, the eagle sets its course into the wind, which lifts the bird high enough to soar above it all. The eagle *waits* for the storm and then rides it out—with no struggle, little wing-flapping, and no push back. It does *not* escape the storm or try to evade it. The eagle simply uses the storm to *lift it higher*. It rises on the wind that brings the storm and flies high to safety.[1] Like the eagle, we must prepare to ride out the storms of our lives. As women of faith, we must believe in God's power to lift us above every challenge. But prayer alone is not enough. We must learn how to *thrive* in the storms of life, not just *survive* them. When inclement weather comes upon us, we can rise above by setting our minds and belief toward the outcome we wish. The inevitable does not have to overcome us.

A great case in point is a sister we all know, former White House social secretary Desiree Rogers, who served in the Obama administration as the first African American woman to hold this position. Some say Rogers was a target from the moment she arrived in Washington—fashionable, confident, independent, smart (she holds a Harvard MBA), and loyal to the Obamas. Couple this with the fact that she is a very attractive fifty-one-year-old black woman, who assumed a nontraditional position and was brought in to spice up the White House social calendar, and you can understand why some might have felt threatened by her. Her appearance on fashion magazine covers and in *Vogue* caused a stir in stuffy buttoned-down Washington. A major security breach at a 2009 state dinner and the ensuing national rancor caused Rogers to abruptly resign her position in the West Wing in 2010. Though many were to blame, Rogers took the high road and simply moved on. After leaving Washington, D.C., she told *Bloomberg Businessweek*, "I will be fine. I'm not crying for me." She continued, "If the worst thing that happened to me is, you know, someone said I was beautiful and I had on the wrong dress, and I should have had a clipboard, you know, okay. I'm comfort-able with the work we did." She believes she will thrive no matter what her next project. "I think I'm going to blossom. The whole experience [as social secretary] in many respects is going to make me feel more com-fortable about who I am."[2]

And blossom she did. She is now CEO of Johnson Publishing Company, the parent company of *Ebony* and *Jet* magazines and Fashion Fair Cosmetics. In an interview with the *New York Times* that she did along with her close friend Linda Johnson Rice (heir to the Johnson Publishing legacy), she reflected on what happened at the White House. "I took time to try to analyze and understand what happened," she said. "Try," she reiterated, laughing. She explained that despite all her soul searching, she never did fully understand what happened. "I never did. I never did. I can't even—I can't give you an answer on that one." She continued, "I think it's fair to say I feel much more comfortable in business than in politics. I'm much more comfortable in a meritocracy and in reward for good work as opposed to a political environment, where I feel like all of that can be confused."[3]

Sisters, remember: it's not the challenges of life that weigh us down; it's how we handle them. You can survive, you can be resilient, and you can thrive.

## An Invitation to Explore Our Best Life

I STARTED THIS book out by offering us an invitation to explore five core goals that successful black women must achieve if we want to live our best life. For many of us, this means redefining our lives to work toward:

1. **Positive, multidimensional relationships**—strong, happy, supportive, and meaningful bonds with men, women, friends, family members, and colleagues
2. **Satisfying, successful, and flexible careers** that we truly enjoy
3. **Balanced and emotionally rewarding lives** that nourish us and allow us to forgive, grow, and dream
4. **Good health** that's grounded in conscious choices and a low-stress lifestyle
5. **Spirituality that embraces us as sexual and sensual human beings** who desire love, intimacy, marriage, and family

As we go through the last two chapters of our journey—having now addressed many issues of the often turbulent lives of accomplished black women—I hope you realize just how important it is to *reassess* and *redefine* our priorities and take control of our lives.

Together we've examined how much our past affects our present perspective on life and how we cope with life's challenges, big and small. We've dissected the myths that make up the modern-day stereotypical strong black woman and redefined what it really means to be black, female, and accomplished. I've asked you to embrace the power of forgiveness and learn how to release the pain and hurt life has dealt you, so that you can heal and become whole again. The experts interviewed for this book have stressed the importance of speaking out, of breaking the code of silence that holds many of us captive, and having the courage to seek therapy to work through the emotional, physical, and sexual abuse and trauma many of us have faced. Life may be unfair, but for far too many of us, life has included horrific incidents that are seared into our psyche and have burned holes in our hearts. We've reviewed groundbreaking research on how we're faring in the workplace and developed strategies to build strong support systems to achieve new heights in our careers. We've explored the intersection between spirituality and sexuality and now accept that God made us sensual beings capable and worthy of love and affection. You are now challenged to start living your faith in a way that brings joy and happiness to your life and the lives of others.

Now that we've discussed these issues and dissected what it means to be an accomplished black woman, we should all grasp that success comes with a huge toll to pay—physically, emotionally, mentally, and spiritually. What we do not seem to grasp, however, is that to stay successful and to build successful, satisfying, and fulfilled lives beyond our career requires a game plan for living a balanced life—a life that reflects our values and priorities; respects our needs and desires; leaves room for love, passion, and touch; inspires us and the people around us; keeps us fully integrated into our world and doesn't leave us alone, isolated, and unable to make meaningful connections with our family, friends, and colleagues; and helps us to experience the simple yet meaningful joys of living.

### Balance, Anyone?

NOW IT'S TIME to talk about good health and building a balanced and emotionally rewarding life. As we have established, you can't always control the circumstances that are thrown your way, but you *can* control how well you take care of yourself. Taking proper care of your body, soul, and mind will keep you in optimum shape for handling stress of all kinds. Sisters, we all know how to do this—we just don't do it. It starts by putting yourself first and *not* running yourself ragged for others. I have bought numerous spa cards for girlfriends who are super-busy, only to ask them a year later, "Did you enjoy your spa gift card?" and learn it was never opened. Based on all I know about myself, and black women, I think our issue with self-care runs too deep to fix by our simply adhering to some checklists.

I'll give you a perfect snapshot of how hard it is for us as black women to even grasp the concept of self-love and self-care. Each year, members of the iask organization choose a theme for the year so that our sister-buddy groups can read books and build activities around that theme. The theme for 2010 was "Restore Your Glow" by taking care of self. Before we decided on the theme, I interviewed black women of all ages to find out how they felt about dedicating an entire year to self-care. Here are a few representative comments:

- Black women are taught at an early age to share and share alike and to care for everyone else above ourselves! (G.B., Georgia, 27)
- Initially, it would be difficult to get over the guilt I would feel devoting time caring for myself. I would like to redevote myself to things that bring me personal joy—just not sure I know how. (A.D., Texas, 32)
- Have been trying to do this for a few months; the guilt is definitely the hardest part of the change. My health is what caused me to finally say, "Enough!" and focus on me. I am forty years old and I have never taken care of me. (D.W., Pennsylvania, 40)

If we just reflect for a moment on what these women in their twenties, thirties, and forties are saying here, we see an obvious common denominator: *I want to take care of me, but if I do, I'll feel guilty.* Wow! I lived in that guilty place for many years and still work through it daily, trying to balance my own needs and the needs of the many people who want a piece of Sophia.

Women feeling guilty about taking time out for themselves, however, is only part of the story. It's also important to understand what's going on in our minds and hearts that allows us to give such short shrift to ourselves. Here's what one iask member said after she was finally ready to commit herself to restoring her glow:

I admit that I neglect myself. Perhaps because, as a woman, I like to feel needed. As a professional woman, I am often called upon for my expertise, and that helps me to feel needed in so many ways. But when it comes to my personal interactions, I don't feel as needed. I don't feel needed by my doctor, by my finances, by my home, by myself. I know this is a problem. So unfortunately, a great number of people will be sorely disappointed in my decision to focus on me this year, but it's imperative that I take care of my health, my finances, guard my heart and my spirit. Because, unfortunately, if I do not learn to *love* me more, I will *not* be of use to anyone who does need me in the future.

*Amen.* You know this sister speaks the truth. Sometimes we make poor choices trying to fill a void in our undernurtured soul or lonely heart. We overextend ourselves because we want to feel needed, loved, and special. I could share hundreds of stories about black women who belong to ten organizations at a time to keep themselves perpetually busy. These experiences came out loud and clear among unmarried focus group participants, who also tended to suffer (usually in silence) from a variety of stress-induced illness more than the married women we interviewed.

Another reason we do more than our fair share is that many of us still cling tightly to what our grandmothers and mothers taught us: "You know you have to be twice as good and work twice as hard just to be treated the same." Although that advice remains true in some respects, neglecting your health and well-being is just plain senseless. Remember what Time Inc.'s deputy general counsel Rhonda McLean says in *The Little Black Book of Success*: "Some black women are taking striving for success to the extreme." Dr. Aby Washington, in our interview, concurred:

Black women, sadly, are preserving and protecting our professionalism at the expense of our well-being. Yes, it is true that we have prioritized our professional persona as paramount to who we are—we have allowed it to define us. We have taken way too much comfort in our accomplishments as black women. You hit the nail on the head, Sophia. It is time to *redefine*. This is a *self*-care and *self*-priority thing. Men do that better than we do—black women are extremely undisciplined at focusing on our own self-care. This has to change now because what we are modeling to younger women is what was modeled to us. Someone has to break the cycle.

This incredible determination to get ahead was a major concern to black professional women, according to the ABW national survey conducted for this book. More than two-thirds of the respondents claim black women are more likely to have a problem "getting ahead at work" than their white colleagues. Over half (54 percent) believed even "being viewed as capable at work" was a bigger challenge for black women. It comes as no surprise, then, that this unrelenting drive to succeed against all odds came up over and over again in our interviews and focus groups. This disturbing trend was discussed at length in our Mid-Atlantic regional focus groups. We asked women to share with us the intersection between workplace stress and their emotional and physical health, and share they did. One forty-six-year-old executive admitted that she'd pushed herself so hard to perform that she developed hypertension and contracted shingles, which left her face badly scarred and looking like she had suffered a stroke. She said:

> I used to ask myself that same question and push it to the absolute limit, to the point where I crashed my immune system and sparked up shingles in the absolute most dangerous place you could have it, right in my optic nerve. It took me down every road of depression and confusion, and I was home for three weeks with a massive headache thinking, *What is happening to me?* It's a constant sense of a contraction along your nerve. And then it stops and you think, *That was deep.* And then it comes back higher and then subsides. I pushed it from a career perspective, trying to be more than enough. I wound up trying to be more than the more than enough. It pushed me into stage one of hypertension.
>
> At my resting state, I said, "What is wrong with me?" I could not get my blood pressure under control, about to hit stage two hypertension. It opened up so many other health issues, like fibroids that began to grow. I thought, *Okay, I'm not pregnant, but I sure look like I am.* My hair was falling out, my nails, my skin looked darker. I really had to go introspective, and I had a serious conversation with myself. This year, I've regained my personal health.

Another woman, a thirty-nine-year-old mental health professional, continued to work through a very difficult professional situation until her hypertension and depression landed her in the emergency room (where she continued working on her BlackBerry). It wasn't until after she changed jobs and started working at a women's health organization that she regained control of her own health. She explained:

> When I went through my period of depression, I wasn't living near my family and friends. I was working in a very toxic environment, and although I excelled, [the job] was killing me on the inside. That's when my blood pressure spiked. I never thought I could be in such a dark place. I was always known as strong, the survivor, the trailblazer. This depression literally knocked me off my feet. This experience helped me realize how fragile and vulnerable I really was.

Since this focus group, which took place in 2009, at least one other high-achieving woman in the group contracted shingles and had to take time off work. These stories illustrate how much our need to prove ourselves in the workplace and to demonstrate our skills—*more often, better, and faster* than our colleagues—can take a serious toll on our health and well-being. We're not only concerned about our careers; we're worried about how our mistakes may badly affect the careers of black women coming up behind us. Sisters, this burden is a lot to carry. It's time to let it go. The need to prove how exceptional we are is difficult to maintain. But something's got to give. Like it or not, unmanaged stress combined with the heavy baggage we're already carrying up the career ladder or around the church sanctuary is a toxic combination. This lethal combo is fueling much of the bad attitude everyone's talking about.

Like the unmarried mental health professional profiled above, singles can find balancing career, needs of family, community groups, and church especially difficult. Very few of us hesitate to ask more of women who aren't married or don't have children because we think they have more free time than the rest of us. I spoke with three seasoned veterans— two white women in the corporate sector and one black man in the federal defense sector—who have mentored and advanced the careers of black women. They confirmed that single black professional women often have a harder road to walk on all fronts.

Debbie Smith, a Xerox pioneer in the 1970s who was elevated to senior vice president of HR before she moved on to work with companies like Kodak, Bausch & Lomb, and Merck, told me in an extensive interview that, with regard to discrimination or gender bias in the workplace, black women often face unique challenges in "relatability" to their peers, which is very stressful. Smith explained:

I found that most of the time, when incidents of race or gender discrimination were alleged, it was not necessarily outright bigotry. Sometimes it was. Most of the time, it was a case of poor management. It wasn't that the manager was treating minority or female employees poorly; he was treating everyone poorly. But, for minorities and women, there was a much greater impact. They often had nowhere else to turn and no mentor to help with the situation or to provide advice. The disparate impact of poor management practices on minorities and women often made problems worse and created issues resulting in charges of discrimination.

Few managers really understood what minorities and women faced on a day-to-day basis in the workplace. Managers were much more comfortable with people who looked, acted, and thought like they did—people who shared the same experiences. On some levels, males of different races could relate, and on some levels, white men and women could relate. For women of color, this was an even greater issue. There was no shared experience and often little sensitivity to differences. The ability of women of color to overcome the isolation and the insensitivity was a challenge that many were unable or unwilling to take on. It was a challenge which demanded exceptional interpersonal skills and a very strong sense of self.

One of my mentors, Garnett Stowe, one of the highest-ranking African American men at Raytheon Company and head of their National Intelligence Programs, talked to me about the broader knowledge base that he feels is lacking among young African American women (and men):

One of the biggest challenges young black women face is that they make the assumption that we are on equal footing in the workplace because they see all of the successes of the twenty-first century around them—they see a black president and First Lady, Oprah, and others, and they don't understand the critical need for mentoring and support to help them succeed and properly manage their workplace stresses.

As for black women, the most successful black women I have seen do not try to be what they are not. They are comfortable in their own skin. They don't let it get to them. They have what I call the "three S's"—substance, savvy, and style—which, in short, means they have high ethical standards and integrity, they have a unique style of what they bring to the table, and they understand who the power players are and how to build relationships with them. If sisters can learn to do this well, it will cut down a lot of stress in their lives that often leads to illness or other challenges.

Last, Martha Barnett, former ABA president, who gives us great mentoring insights in Chapter 3, offered this perspective:

> First, we no longer train, grow, and retain talent as we once did in the legal profession, and I daresay in many companies. It is now about the bottom line—producing and making a profit. I get that, but for women of color, what I have seen is that they often do not have that extra layer of support that many white women and others have at home. I will tell you straight, Sophia, I never could have made it without my mentors and my family at home. My husband was a support and sounding board. I have seen some of the best and brightest women of color not make it because they lacked the proper support networks outside of the workplace, not just in the workplace. Everyone needs love, a support network, and a place where they can recharge. Many black women I see just do not have this, and it takes a toll.

All three of these wise people confirm that black women have a unique set of complex issues to manage that often cause them to overextend and overwork themselves into a black hole. Work is also one way to combat loneliness and fulfill the desire to be needed, which helps suck us into this endless cycle of strain. We must break out of the thought patterns that keep us in this position if we want to restore balance to our lives.

## Giving Yourself Permission

A VITAL FIRST step to self-care is to give ourselves *permission* to love ourselves and prioritize our needs. This is something that just about every woman I know struggles with, and so do I. But this type of martyrdom has to go away. We must rewire the years of self-sacrifice programming that puts our needs last. This is the same programming that caused way too many early deaths of our grandmothers, aunts, sisters, and friends—loving, selfless women who refused to tend to their health and well-being in order to make do for others.

I asked Dr. Gayle Porter, "How important is being healthy in our lives?" She responded:

> This is key: I think that again our ability to bounce back from anything is first to define life as this wonderful place of opportunities and not one of drudgery. Secondly, get healthy and stay healthy—physically, emotionally, spiritually. If you are not exercising, eating properly, [and] getting adequate sleep, your ability to bounce back from a major illness or life trauma is significantly lessened. You need good spiritual health, good people who pray with and support you. You must be emotionally healthy by showing the full range of your feelings—can you say the words "I love you" and mean them? People that are resilient are healthier and have a more balanced life, and their ability to work through things is also better.

Still not convinced? Consider this sobering fact: of all minority groups, African Americans have the most, and many times the largest differences in, health risks when compared to other minority groups. African Americans have more disease, disability, and early death as well.[4] The following are the top five leading causes of death for African American women:

1. Heart disease
2. Cancer
3. Stroke
4. Diabetes
5. Kidney disease[5]

Now name the women you know who are suffering from these deadly diseases or have died from them within the past decade. Not a pleasant task, is it? Here's an even tougher question: Are you suffering from any of these illnesses that stop even the strongest of black women? Regardless of the answer, now is the time to put your bad habits in check and get on the road to healthy living. I'm talking about creating a balanced life by getting regular checkups from your doctor and dentist, eating well, exercising, getting enough sleep, quitting smoking, minimizing drinking alcohol, and making sure your everyday life is filled with a bit of joy. Does addressing these issues make you feel guilty? It shouldn't.

Let's try this same exercise but focus on your mental health. The following are some of the most prevalent psychological challenges that black women face, according to mental health professionals.

- Stress
- Depression
- Anxiety
- Tension
- Fear (finances, relationships, being alone)

Now name the women you know who are suffering from these emotional pitfalls—the same ones we try to brush off as reactions to life's ups and downs. Are you suffering from any of these conditions?

According to the Black Women's Health website, "The rates of mental health problems are higher than average for Black women because of psychological factors that result directly from their experience as Black Americans. These experiences include racism, cultural alienation, and violence and sexual exploitation"[6]—all issues we discuss throughout this book.

If we're reluctant to take time out of our busy lives for routine physical checkups and to attend to symptoms of dizziness, racing heartbeats, stomach pain, and chronic fatigue, what do you think the odds are that we'll seek help for feelings that many of us simply attribute to "the blues"? Although 42 percent of our ABW survey respondents cite mental and emotional stability as the most important factors in our personal health and well-being, the stigma of seeking psychological or psychiatric help in the black community prevents many of us from getting the care we desperately need. As a result, the amount of unchecked stress, depression, anxiety, tension, and fear among black women is frightening.

Sixty-four percent of the women surveyed think we're more likely to suffer from stress-related disease than white women, and the experts back them up. According to Black Women's Health, the depression rate among African American women is estimated to be almost 50 percent higher than that of Caucasian women.[7] Many ABW survey respondents have experienced depression because of relationship disappointment or failure, including "lack of intimacy/love" (29 percent), "relationship obstacles or problems" (27 percent), "inability to meet 'datable' black men" (23 percent), "fear of growing old alone" (22 percent), and "marital stress." Other respondents believe their depression resulted from physical health issues, including "chronic tiredness/fatigue" (23 percent) and "diagnosis of health issue/medical condition" (20 percent).

We all read the shocking revelation by sister powerhouse Susan L. Taylor, the beloved former editor of *Essence*, who in February 2010 disclosed that she had suffered with serious depression for years, even as she was penning some of the most inspirational and powerful words we'd ever read.[8] Her revelation caused many of us to take a hard look within to make sure that we're not just stumbling through difficulty but are in a constant process of self-evaluation and healing.

Even our eating habits are affected by how we feel. In a speech for the American Psychiatric Association (APA) in San Diego, Dr. Annelle Primm pointed out that "there is a negative association between obesity and mental well-being." Primm, an associate professor of psychiatry at the Johns Hopkins School of Medicine and director of Minority and National Affairs for the APA, confirms that African American women have a greater prevalence of obesity (37.7 percent) when compared with white women (23.5 percent) and may begin overeating as a strategy to cope with sexual abuse, racism, classism, and poverty.[9]

Again, it is crucial that we overcome the guilt and other factors that are preventing us from seeking the help we need to take care of our bodies and minds. We must learn to give ourselves permission to take care of our own needs, or we may not be around to take care of others anyway.

## How Our Finances Affect Our Well-Being

INTERESTINGLY, OF ALL the obstacles that affect the emotional health of the women we surveyed, financial pressure and debt top the list by a wide margin—60 percent of respondents identified with this problem. Initially, I was shocked by this finding, but upon reflection, discussion with economists and sociologists, and thinking about my own life as a single professional black woman, it actually makes sense. As a single professional woman, I worry about my finances all the time. There is no more helpless feeling than being on your own and not having the financial means to meet your obligations, especially when an unexpected health crisis pops up or you find yourself suddenly unemployed.

How we feel about and handle money has a lot to do with our family background (and self-esteem), explains financial coach and author of *Girl, Get Your Money Straight!* Glinda Bridgforth in an interview for this book:

Many black women grew up with a lack of financial resources or wealth, and as a result, we carry a lot of financial baggage. For starters, we are often the first in our families to attend college or be professionals, and sometimes that means our relatives often ask for and expect financial support. Since many of us feel a sense of responsibility to care for others, we do so even with our finances—and that makes us feel good. However, the fact that we are nurturers and compassionate sometimes works against us, especially when we cannot afford to pay for the things our family expects. To help make up the shortfall, we'll dip into savings or 401(k)s to help support family members, at peril to our own well-being and retirement down the road.

This sentiment was also expressed by one ABW participant in our Washington, D.C., focus group:

I think all professional black women have to live a certain type of double life. We can walk into a corporate office building every day, but we might still need to send or wire money to someone in jail, someone who is on drugs, a single parent, or a family member who is losing their house. Who doesn't know somebody who is struggling or in a challenged position?

A big part of our money challenges are tied to our self-esteem—how we look to others is very important to us. It's a major problem with black women, according to Bridgforth:

Now that we have good educations, jobs, and positions, many of us feel entitled to buy that Gucci bag, St. John's Knit, or Mercedes Benz, whether we can afford it or not. I know I have been there myself. We look successful, but we are stressed. We live in a sort of "virtual prosperity" that is based on image versus reality. Shopping also gives us a temporary high or fix that relieves stress or boosts our self-esteem.

I asked Bridgforth how we could change this unhealthy relationship with our money and finances, and she recommended that black women try "a holistic approach to our finances because a lot of our money challenges are tied to self-esteem. We have an emotional link to our finances." By that, she means we need to align how we spend money with our true priorities. Identifying your priorities isn't always easy, which is probably why Bridgforth refers many of her clients to therapists who help people face their emotional issues related to money. In return, she's building her clientele with referrals from therapists who realize that better financial management might ease some of the burdens of their patients.

The spring 2010 report *Lifting as We Climb: Women of Color, Wealth, and America's Future*, by the Insight Center for Community Economic Development, found a vast discrepancy in "wealth gap" between black women and white women, especially among single women.[10] In a new book, *Shortchanged: Why Women Have Less Wealth and What Can Be Done About It*, the gender wealth gap is shown to be alarmingly wide.[11] And because of the compounding of race and gender disadvantages, women of color experience an even greater wealth disadvantage than men of color and white women. The Insight Center for Economic Development study finds that single black women have one penny of wealth for every dollar of wealth owned by black men and only a tiny fraction of a penny for every dollar of wealth owned by white women.[12]

Nationally, five out of ten African American women have had trouble paying bills on time, and one-third of black women are worried about their debt-to-income ratio. In tough economic times, this news is particularly devastating, as it means black women who lose their jobs or have a financial emergency will have very few reserves to draw upon to get them through. Over the last few decades, black women have made tremendous strides in terms of entering careers with high-income potential. However, these gains have met with rollbacks and have not necessarily translated to wealth or assets. In fact, in the case of homeownership, black women were 256 percent more likely than white men to receive subprime loans.[13] And upper-income black women were nearly five times more likely than white men to be saddled with high-cost mortgages.[14]

In the great American recession that started in late 2007, and which will apparently continue through 2011, black Americans experienced a mass exodus of financial wealth because of foreclosures (due in large part to underhanded subprime lending schemes), sudden job loss, and market fluctuations that zapped 401(k) and money market–based savings accounts. No groups were hit harder than the black middle class and black professional women.[15]

More important for us to grasp is that black women, regardless of education or financial circumstance, are more likely to end up living alone and in poverty as they age. Although it's a fact that women in general are more likely, even in better economic times, to face poverty than men, unmarried women have higher poverty rates than married women. The marital disparity has worsened since early in the decade. The poverty rate of unmarried women was 13.4 percent higher than that of married women in 2000 and grew to 14.6 percent higher in 2008. The risk of poverty for women of color is even greater, especially for those who are unmarried. Thirty percent of unmarried black women and 29.5 percent of unmarried Hispanic women were poor in 2008, compared with 18.5 percent of unmarried white women.[16]

Thus, it is critical for Gen X and Gen Y women to understand the monumental importance of wealth creation in their lifetime. Professional sisters must focus on wealth creation and wealth building in their twenties, thirties, and forties. Not only will we need this wealth for our own survival and retirement, but we must plan for the fact that we're likely to end up as caregivers for family members for extended periods of time and will have to take time off from work.

I'm starting to see this challenge played out for myself and my friends. As we age past forty, we may find ourselves phased out of corporate jobs and struggling to find work paying salaries comparable to our educational and professional résumés. We must deal with this issue, because it represents a serious problem for current and future generations of black women who will likely not have Social Security to rely on as a means of retirement support. Trillion-dollar deficits are projected for many years to come. This means cuts in social safety-net programs, like Social Security and Medicare, and based on what we already know about the wealth and marriage gaps, it's inevitable that black women will suffer most when that happens.

Several of the women interviewed for this book had prominent positions in their respective industries as of the spring of 2009 and were laid off from their jobs several months later or well into 2010. All in their forties and fifties, unmarried, and not living close to their families, these women have watched savings and retirement accounts dwindle. Single black women are at the greatest risk of being impoverished as they age past sixty-five years. So how do we prepare at middle age and at the beginning of our careers to weather the financial hurricanes we may face? Glinda Bridgforth offered key steps to help move us in the right direction:

1. Work to be debt free. (For example, I own everything in my home. Either I pay cash for most big purchases or I don't buy them.)

2. Save something every month—10 percent off your gross income is a minimum. (Pay God, but don't forget to pay yourself, too.)

3. Try to save six months' salary in case of a personal emergency or job loss. This happened to me, and I had to live off my savings for almost nine months before I generated income. Thank God I had the money put away.

4. Keep your credit clean. Lenders now look for credit scores in the 700 to 800 range. Find out your credit score at http://www.myfico.com. (Bad scores can also now affect your employment options.)

5. Think twice before you lend money to friends and family. It depletes your savings, and if they can't pay you back, it causes hard feelings, which can lead to further stress.

6. Start saving for your retirement as soon as you land your first job. Whether you're starting out or switching jobs, be sure to join the company's retirement plan, and check to see if your company matches any part of your savings. Don't tap your retirement savings unless you have an extreme financial emergency. The tax penalties and fees will be brutal.

7. Buy your home instead of renting, and resist borrowing against the equity in your home with loans and lines of credit.

8. Create multiple streams of income so that you're never without money coming in. Consider starting a home-based business, freelance your skills or services, or buy a rental property.

## Resilience

MY DEAR SISTERS, I am living proof that life is indeed all about the climb up the various mountains we face. Some of my greatest lessons have come from the storms that I survived. No matter how good our lives may be at any given time, there will always be another mountain to scale. The point is not to focus exclusively on getting to the mountaintop but to *enjoy the climb*—and learn from it.

When I think of sisters like Jennifer Hudson, who endured the unthinkable when she lost her mother, brother, and nephew to senseless violence, I know that we are truly exceptional. That young sister went through what can only be described as hell and came out on the other side married, with a beautiful son and a thriving career. And she looks incredible in her new weight-loss campaign commercials, in which she sings the classic Nina Simone song "Feeling Good." If she can endure such a deep and tragic loss and yet still smile, still give off such warmth and kindness, the rest of us have no excuse.

I had occasion recently to go back and read my journals from my twenties and thirties, and it was fascinating to see how much I've changed and how my life's course has changed, and discover how much I still long for some things that have yet to come to pass. Forty was a big transition point for me, as I've described all throughout this book: I was looking to become a partner in my law firm, marry a man I was seriously dating, and adopt children. But things did not work out as planned. I lost my job abruptly, did not become a partner, did not get married, and could not adopt the children I wanted so much. That was a lot to handle all at once. But it is now three years later, and I'm very much looking forward to the rest of my life. At forty, I reawakened and became so much more like the brave, adventurous twenty-year-old I once was. I am so over the old suited-up, wound-up, wounded, overworked, stressed-out, walled-off, somewhat damaged person I used to be. I'm still a work in progress, as are we all, but today I am committed to becoming better and living the life of my dreams. I hope you will too!

*Pain is a great teacher. Loss is a great teacher.* Learning to wait for what we diligently "ask and seek" is a great faith builder. I believe in the power of resilience, the power of reinvention, and the awesome power of redefinition because I know that all three are possible. Sisters, *your dreams have no expiration date!* Remember that, if you remember nothing else I say.

## Practical Steps for Living a Happy Life

SISTERS, AS I mentioned at the outset, there are no canned answers to the problems so many of us face each day. Each of us is unique, and we need to feel our own individual rhythm. We each need to find our own way. I spoke with a number of psychologists, family therapists, and women who work in the field of black women's health and wellness. As we have established, you can't always control the circumstances thrown in your path, but you *can* control how well you take care of yourself. Taking proper care of your body, soul, and mind can keep you in optimum shape for handling stress. The following are some important, basic self-care habits that can keep you functioning well and ready for any challenge.

- **Get enough sleep.** There thousands of articles on the crucial importance of sleep for us as women. Sleep is essential for your emotional and physical well-being. For women, critical hormones are made between 10:00 p.m. and 2:00 a.m. Lack of sleep can seriously compromise your ability to handle stress, be productive, and function properly. Unfortunately, busy schedules and stress can make sleep elusive. If you really aren't able to get enough sleep, don't underestimate the value of a power nap![17]

- **Maintain proper nutrition.** Many people aren't aware of this, but a poor diet can actually make you more vulnerable to stress.[18] While a hectic schedule can make it hard to always get proper nutrition, a poor diet is not inevitable—it's optional. So make the time to eat right.

- **Exercise regularly.** Exercise can be great for you physically and mentally. It provides a stress release and keeps your body healthy. It also helps your body release endorphins, which increase your feelings of overall well-being.[19]

- **Maintain social support.** Social support contributes significantly to being healthy and happy by creating a buffer against stress. Friends can pick you up when you're sad, provide insight when you're confused, and help you have fun when you need to blow off steam. Learn how to cultivate supportive friendships and expand your social circle so you'll have someone to lean on when pressured. Don't forget: it's important to provide a supportive ear when your friends need it, too! Master effective listening skills.

- **Keep your mind sharp.** If you have the attitude that stress is a challenge rather than a threat, you're better able to handle it. And by keeping your mind sharp, you're more equipped to solve the problems and take on the challenges that confront you.

- **Have the right attitude.** Much of what you experience can feel more or less stressful, depending on your point of view. Looking at things with an optimistic frame of mind can not only decrease your stress level but also keep you open to success. You can even change ingrained negative thought patterns to more positive ones by using positive affirmations.

- **Process your emotions.** Keeping emotions bottled up usually leads to an emotional explosion. It's generally healthier to listen to your feelings, process them, and try to understand them. Consider them "messengers" that tell you when something is not right with your world. A great way to process emotions is through journaling. When you write about your feelings and potential solutions to problems, you can reduce stress and may even see some health benefits.

- **Maintain a spiritual practice.** Research shows that a lifestyle that includes religion or spirituality is generally a healthy lifestyle. Many people, especially seniors, use prayer as major stress relief and a strategy for emotional health. You can use prayer to enhance your spiritual side, or use meditation if you don't feel comfortable with prayer. Spiritual practice is deeply personal. Whatever your practice, it should nurture your soul.[20]
- **Date and fall in love.** This is a big one. If sisters like actress Vivica Fox and *The View*'s Sherri Shepherd can get married for the second time in their mid-forties to younger men, and find happiness, you can too, sister. I am having the time of my life now dating because I finally realize I am beautiful, sensual, worthy, and sacred all at once. We talked about the healing power of touch. The power of connection is just as potent. Sisters, stop sitting in your house on Friday nights alone watching movies and eating takeout; you've got to get out and mingle, travel, and socialize. You never know when lightning will strike.

## REDEFINING LOVE AND SUPPORT BETWEEN BLACK WOMEN

*S*ometimes our girlfriends are the ones who become our spiritual families—people to whom, for whatever reason, we feel more comfortable going to with our confessions, problems and achievements.

From *Girlfriends: Invisible Bonds, Enduring Ties*, a book by Carmen Renee Berry and Tamara Traeder

# 11

## I AM MY SISTER'S KEEPER:

### *Why We Need One Another Now More than Ever*

"You know, it's not the world that was my oppressor, because what the world does to you, if the world does it to you long enough and effectively enough, you begin to do to yourself."

—JAMES BALDWIN

*I* hate that bitch." "I can't stand her ass." "Who does she think she is?" "She thinks she's cute." "Somebody needs to take her down a notch." "As a friend, I'm just giving you the 411 on her: she is not a team player." "I warned you about her, girl." "I don't have time to be a mentor. Who mentored me?" "I'll pray for her, but I'm not getting involved in her drama." "That's just how she is." "She'll get hers—and I want a front row seat when she does." "I am so over and done with her." "I had to cut her loose." "Don't call me your sister—I ain't your sister."

Hard to believe that the same women we love and admire, and who regularly join forces to support our churches, schools, sororities, communities, and charities, would say or think such vicious things about each other. Sadly, these brutal words punctuate the everyday conversations of sophisticated, smart, dynamic, professional women—sisters who have no problem telling you (seemingly with pride) that this is how they talk about other black women.

Let me ask you a few hard questions:

- Have you ever made any of these comments?
- Ever thought them?
- Ever sit passively by as another sister was being savaged behind her back by another black woman?
- Ever been the victim of these kinds of attacks?

In the past, I am ashamed to admit, I too have made some of these remarks. I've listened to this type of talk without shutting it down. And yes, I have certainly been the victim of such blistering attacks, as have many of you. Clearly, sisters, there is something very wrong in the *sisterhood*. You see it in the blogs, on social networking sites, in the sororities, and even in church organizations: beautiful, smart, accomplished sisters feeling angered and burned by other sisters. Recently, Oprah caught the ire of sisters everywhere when she started her television network, OWN, and there were no shows being hosted by black women. Unforgiving and sometimes verbally abusive, some sisters just don't have boundaries. They are neglectful to friends who have been with them through the worst life has to offer, and they don't understand that karma is, as the saying goes, "a bitch."

I could tell you stories all day of sisters who brought other sisters into their business or homes only to have those sisters steal from them (literally), or of the harshness with which we speak to each other when one of us is deeply hurt. One twenty-five-year-old paralegal recently shared with me and a few others in the iask network that she had been date raped at a party over the Christmas holidays. She reported it to the police. She became depressed and despondent, and when she told her mom of her ordeal, she was rebuked and told to "man up" because if she had not been in the wrong place at the wrong time, none of it would have happened. The young woman was devastated and wrote to me, "This is exactly why we never share our feelings or hurts as black women because when we do, we get crushed, mostly by one another."

As noted in Chapter 1, a very recent example of black women behaving badly was on national display when author Helena Andrews in her 2010 memoir *Bitch Is the New Black* launched a sister attack on her former employer, interior designer Sheila Bridges. Andrews writes in a chapter titled "A Bridge to Nowhere" that Bridges, who admitted to firing Andrews in 2003, is a "sociopath," "emotionally detached," "sexually frustrated," and "fucking psycho." Further, Andrews seems gleeful about the fact that the once curly-haired Bridges went bald because of a skin condition called alopecia. Andrews relishes it as a form of perverse revenge.[1] Sadly for Andrews and her publisher, her attacks led to a formal apology and an out-of-court settlement with Bridges in December 2010.[2]

What is troubling about this public exchange is that these two black women, both smart and accomplished, but at very different stages of their lives, had a chance to learn from one another but did not. Instead, the younger sister (Andrews) lashed out at some of the very behavior that older black women who are worn and weary often display in the workplace (which I address further later in the chapter), and the older sister (Bridges) felt she had to seek legal redress from Andrews instead of calling the sister one on one or mediating the situation so that Andrews might come to understand why the way she handled it was neither appropriate nor very helpful to her own professional reputation.

This incident reminds me of a story involving one of my dear friends, a high-powered black woman who was a director at a major corporation in the Midwest. She is a good woman, and everyone likes her. A year ago, the company hired a new CEO, a sister. This sister had a reputation before she got to this new job as being tough and difficult to work for. A year later, staff has quit the company en masse, and my friend, the director, lost her job. This type of sister CEO was portrayed brilliantly by Janet Jackson in the movie *For Colored Girls*—she is hard, she is self-focused, and to quote the brother from the focus group that I mentioned in Chapter 4, she is a "hammer seeking to drive a nail."

## This Is Not Who We Are

MY GOAL IN this chapter is twofold: I want to help us confront and be accountable for how we treat one another. And I want to help us move forward by making us conscious of the fact that much of the lashing out at each other we do is a result of everything we have discussed in this book: the myths about who we are, how we have been defined, and how we have internalized centuries of mischaracterizations, abuse, and stereotyping. As James Baldwin says, "[I]f the world does it to you long enough and effectively enough, you begin to do it to yourself."

The good news is that many of us are now becoming acutely aware of this type of behavior, and we are alarmed. And we're quickly losing some of our best role models for sisterly behavior—Dorothy Height, Shirley Chisholm, Rosa Parks, Coretta King. I've heard many of us asking out loud, "Who will be the next leader of our people? Each of these women had one thing in common that allowed them to achieve the praise and admiration of all who knew them: they understood the value of sister-hood. These women and the everyday sister heroes of generations past understood the virtues of respect, loyalty, and sacrifice. They understood how to peacefully resolve their conflicts. They raised other women's children when those women were sick or had to work. They helped care for their neighbors through thick and thin. They gladly worked extra shifts cleaning floors to send their children or that beloved niece or nephew to college, or to care for an elderly family member. My mom often tells me that when she was a little girl, if a woman who lived down the road didn't have any food, they took her some. If she needed help with the light bill, people took up a collection to help her pay it. If push came to shove, and these women had no family to care for them or no place to live, someone would open up her home and gladly welcome them in. These women understood that pettiness had too high a price and that bitterness, envy, strife, and jealousy are the natural enemies of love, peace, joy, and lasting friendship. These women understood that sisterhood was about a loving "village" of women who cared for and supported each other with words *and* deeds. In respect to our sister heroes—famous or not—we must reexamine our commitment to the sisterhood. Their supportive and loving approach is one my generation and the next needs to embrace and re-create in our communities.

First Lady Michelle Obama leads us by example in her commitment to sisterhood. She makes time to spend with her sister girls: they have ladies' nights out, they travel, and they go to Broadway plays together. The First Lady even hosted a special screening of the film *For Colored Girls* at the White House in fall of 2010. Sister Obama makes time to nur-ture, support, and laugh with her sisters (of all hues). She is teaching us how to live with balance, class, and supportiveness. I hope we will learn to emulate her ease and her value of family and friendships.

Last year, I was struck by a headline that blared: "First Black Woman Elected to South Carolina Legislature Freezes to Death Alone." Juanita Goggins, who had been elected to the South Carolina legislature in 1974, was seventy-five when she died. Authorities said Goggins had been dead for about two weeks when her body was discovered. She had frozen to death in her apartment.[3] This tragic story both alarmed and saddened me because it speaks about our collective sisterhood. As I wept for Juanita Goggins (and I did weep), I thought, *Where was her village? Where were the sisters at church or in her community?* And it hit me: in our modern world, we are all so *busy* and so *disconnected* (ironic, in a world where everyone has iPads, smartphones, and other wireless communication devices) that we don't value our families the way we used to or connect with our neighbors in a way that is meaningful. The hard truth is that we don't want to get involved in "other people's business"; nor do we want to feel a sense of responsibility for one another anymore. But, as Christian women (and we have already established that black women are the most self-identified Christian, churchgoing, praying women on the planet), we have a responsibility to care for our sisters (regardless of their color).

I can't imagine not relying on a caring community of women like the ones my mother, grandmother, and great-grandmother had. Just knowing that the black women who came before us had such a powerful legacy of making things happen against all odds—having virtually no resources but standing on the shoulders of one another to make it work—fills my heart with pride and admiration. That's why it puzzles me that some of us react in such a visceral and angry way when we're upset with or offended by other black women. *Sisters, it is not that serious.* It took me a long time to grasp this truth. How many times have I tried to write that letter, or make that phone call after both sides have had a cooling-off period, only to be rebuffed or cursed out or hung up on? Or another sister thug move—the person I've had a disagreement with goes to ten of our mutual friends and trashes me so that they take sides against me. And for what? Because we disagreed? Because we had different perspectives? Because one or both of us made a mistake? I mean, really! My favorite nasty sister move of all is what I call the total cutoff—the complete cold-shoulder silent treatment. It happens with no warning. I'm sure you know exactly what I'm talking about because it has probably happened to you. The most basic explanation as to why we behave like this is that too many of us lack humility, forgiveness, and basic conflict-resolution skills. As Dr. Gayle Porter said in our interview, "We love to go off on people instead of working through our feelings. Part of this is due to how we as black women have uniquely been denied the right to express the full spectrum of human emotions." Or as life and women's empowerment coach Valorie Burton said when we spoke about this subject:

> Conflict resolution isn't a skill that most of us have learned. If conflicts at home were settled by beatings, acquiescing, or being the most aggressive person in the room, we'll use these as solutions to resolve our differences later in life. We must learn that talking things out and addressing conflict in a civil way is not a weakness but strength. Being humble, admitting fault, and looking to grow and develop is a positive thing. Very liberating.

Dr. Aby Washington said in our interview that she believes that it's critical to observe how women resolve conflict if we're going to incorporate this into a new way of being. She points to Michelle Obama as a perfect role model:

> If you consider the way she handles her inner circle of women and staff, or if you consider how she handled all of the criticisms during the 2008 campaign, she handled it with poise, grace, and laughter in many instances. Even with all of the rumors about what happened with Desiree Rogers's departure, you never heard Michelle speak a negative word in public or private. She is always surrounded by other strong black women, including her own mother, who she has a very close relationship with. She clearly values her sister friends.

I agree with Washington completely. Perhaps it's because I've faced my mortality several times because of various health challenges and have come out alive that I feel so strongly about the value of sister friends. Perhaps it's because I've had the good fortune to have sister friends who loved me enough to tell me the truth *with love* when I was wrong. Or maybe it's because I've freely given and freely received forgiveness without fear that we'd walk out on one another in anger at a later time.

Sisters, many of us profess to believe in God or some form of a higher power, so why can't we do as the Bible instructs and turn the other cheek or simply follow the Golden Rule? What harm would it do to just give each other a pass once in a while? I need a pass every now and then, don't you? We can be relentless with our hunger for control, power, or vengeance. We want folks to know we're in charge at all costs. What a waste of precious energy and what a shame that we feel we have to destroy other women who look like us to advance.

To my older, wiser sisters let me be respectfully direct: we watch what you do, not just what you say. You cannot profess to be a mentor, give us guidance, and then break the very rules and virtues you ask us to embrace. I cannot begin to recount the stories I've heard of mentors gone rogue in the workplace—or worse, in the church—on their protégés. There is something dangerous about wanting to put a younger black woman in her place or to take her down a notch so badly that you resort to threats, blow a business deal, take her to court, ruin her future, or damage her reputation simply because you disagree or don't like something she did. *Woman up!* Put your faith into practice and talk to her like a person. Correct her, and in doing so, you both will grow as human beings. We are not disposable Dixie cups, sisters!

The bottom line is this: we all need to understand that it is at times of strife when we truly need to honor what we claim to value most: our sisterhood.

## *Things We Need to Work On*

CONCERNED ABOUT AND confused by the countless stories I've heard (and witnessed up close and personal in iask, in my sorority, on college campuses, in church, in the workplace, etc.) about the overt hostility between sisters, I decided that this was an important subject to raise in our ABW research and an appropriate way to close this book. I surfed the blogs and spoke with several well-respected black women leaders, executive life coaches, college presidents, and mentors who work daily with professional black women of all ages to help me better understand what's driving this *mean girl* behavior.

I came across one young sister, Kelly Suzanne Saulsberry, who tackled this issue head-on in her blog. Her January 2010 post, titled "Are You Your Sister's Keeper or Overseer?" had this to say:

> Why are some Black females so hard on other Black females? Why are we so eager to take each other down a notch? Where is this determination when it's time to face people who really mean us no good? Why do some of us make excuses for the inexcusable actions of our sons, nephews, husbands, boyfriends, male co-workers, etc., but burn Black women

at the cross who haven't done us any wrong? . . . Clearly, there are a lot of unresolved issues from our historical and personal pasts that we are not addressing. Unhealed wounds that are further infected breed more infection and deeper wounds that take longer to heal. It is time for us to acknowledge that we are in dire need of a wake-up call and to take responsibility for our own healing. This should be no one else's job but ours. We Black women—and Black men, I might add—need a good long look in the mirror.[4]

Dr. Averette Parker offered insight on some of Kelly's questions: "How we treat each other all gets back to how we feel about ourselves. We don't know how to process our emotions well, and as a result, we become angry and frustrated. And we turn on one another." Ain't that the truth! These personal limitations are deeply rooted, explained Dr. Gayle Porter. "Women who are challenged in this area are generally having difficulty with themselves. It's easier for us to go off than to talk about how much we love each other. We need to learn how to say, 'I love you' freely. We need to get more comfortable expressing positive emotions."

Dr. Aby Washington concurred:

We are angry because we feel vulnerable. Anger becomes our go-to emotion because we do not know how else to respond. Not only are black men experiencing us this way, as they noted in research for this book, we are coming off this way to other black women. We are quick to dis one another because we don't value ourselves. So when I look at a sister, I'm seeing a mirror image of myself and thinking, "She ain't worth it." What's sad is that we accept all kinds of behavior from our men, white men, white women, and others, but not from us. We know better. You don't break the sister code. And if you do, we will punish you. This needs to change fast.

Like Drs. Parker, Porter, and Washington, most of the experts and wise women I interviewed felt that too many of us are carrying around a spirit of despondency, anger, and oppression in our hearts. We rant about Don Imus calling our young collegiate sisters at Rutgers "nappy-headed hos."[5] We get angry at Tiger for not only marrying a white woman but for sleeping with twelve (or more) others behind her back.[6] We lash out at Nelly and other rap artists for demeaning black women, and we protest against BET for showing rap videos that debase and exploit black women. Yet, we don't think twice about how we act out in the same way toward one another. If we don't *change* and *redefine* the way we feel, love, care about, speak about, and treat one another, how can we expect others to honor us?

Author Audre Lorde's stirring essay "Eye to Eye: Black Women, Hatred, and Anger" powerfully presents the paradox of black women and our long struggle with anger:

> Every Black woman in America lives her life somewhere along a wide curve of ancient and unexpressed angers.
>
> My Black woman's anger is a molten pond at the core of me, my most fiercely guarded secret. I know how much of my life as a powerful feeling woman is laced through with this net of rage. It is an electric thread woven into every emotional tapestry upon which I set the essentials of my life—a boiling hot spring likely to erupt at any point, leaping out of my consciousness like a fire on the landscape. How to train that anger with accuracy rather than deny it has been one of the major tasks of my life.
>
> Other Black women are not the root cause nor the source of that pool of anger. I know this, no matter what the particular situation may be between me and another Black woman at the moment. Then why does that anger unleash itself most tellingly against another Black woman at the least excuse? Why do I judge her in a more critical light than any other, becoming enraged when she does not measure up?
>
> And if behind the object of my attack should lie the face of my own self, unaccepted, then what could possibly quench a fire fueled by such reciprocating passions?[7]

I think that Lorde nails it. But why do we turn into these angry hammers looking for nails? I asked life coach Valorie Burton if she could help me understand why so many sisters seem to struggle with their anger. What she said was very insightful:

> Female relationships and conflict starts early on in grade school. We develop a negativity bias, which is a cumulative effect. For every five good black women we meet, we hold on to the one bad black woman. We need to also look at *self* and our role in whatever conflict that

develops—sometimes we don't contribute, but often we do. Emotions are driven by your thoughts, so it is very important to explore, when we are in the moment, what are the thoughts that are in my head? Am I bringing in my past ten bad sister relationships?

I have a girlfriend whom I love dearly, but she can be a piece of work. Hypersensitive, she'll go off on you at the drop of a hat for the smallest things. There's this wall of hurt around her that you can't get past. But if confronted about it, she will deny that she does any of these things. It's exhausting. I asked Burton why we run into women who are so impenetrable. She responded:

> Sometimes you hit an iceberg, something submerged below the surface, a deeply held belief about how someone feels they should be treated that has nothing to do with you at all. They are protecting themselves at all costs, which does the opposite of what they want: people to come closer.
>
> All of us should be respected at all times, but when you run into people who are quick to become angry over little things—watch out. Anger always traces back to people feeling like there was a violation of their rights. As a child, we have no power; when we get older, we make a choice that no one will ever again violate my rights. It is a self-fulfilling prophecy, and it stems from trust issues that loom large.

She suggested that when people walk out of our lives or react in certain ways, we need to ask why. *Empathy is key.* She suggested that one way to deal with someone with such anger issues who erupts on you is to be honest with her and have a conversation that begins with something like this: "I really value our friendship, and I really value you, but we need to talk. Your response is not in line with the offense." Again, sisters, don't be a hypocrite if you once struggled with anger or similar challenges as a younger woman. Don't judge the sister; try to help her. Don't sister bash; reach out. If the challenges persist, then we know you are dealing with something deeper. Interestingly, Burton echoed what Dr. Washington stated—that this type of conflict is a serious problem that cannot be managed with steps and that these are mental health issues that need to be clearly understood as such.

We have a responsibility to deal directly with others who offend us, but there are two things we should keep in mind as we do:

1. Be self-aware. In other words, be aware of what's going on in your own head—what are your triggers that no one else knows about?
2. Make a distinction between the enemy in front of you and the enemies behind you.

Burton explained further:

Anger is a form of control, particularly in the black community, and it has worked well. The stereotype of us being angry pushes people away, white people in particular. Anger is powerful; we view it as a form of protection. If I get angry, I control the conversation, and you back down. Anger is a response to a boundary being crossed and a violation of rights.

Look at our history. Look at all the rights we have had violated—sexual, emotional, professional, relational. Black women have had a lot of rights violated, and it has been pushed off. What happens is we operate in that context. It's all about context. What did I see? What responses was I taught as a child? Modeling is key to how we interact with and react to others. A standard for handling your relationships is controlling what you'll allow into your life. Response is critical.

## We Need Each Other

"I'M TALKING RIGHT. You're not listening right." We have all heard this.

Long before I wrote this book, black women like bell hooks, Alice Walker, Toni Morrison, Audre Lorde, and Nikki Giovanni wrote about, analyzed, and struggled with how our history and our relationships have shaped us as black women. But the question on the table today is how do we deal with this seething anger we inflict on each other?

Like all of you, I've seen too many relationships and long-term friendships between black women decimated in a moment of anger, arrogance, or unrelenting pride. *It's a shame.* I've done it and had it done to me. We would rather be "right" and destroy the sister in front of us than compromise. Control is everything to us. Doing it "my way or the highway," as opposed to learning to do things a new way, is where many of us love to stay stuck. Sad, but true, and we all know it!

When I had my first company, ALN Consulting, Inc., in the late 1990s, I was offered a deal with a highly regarded black-owned IT firm that was run by an older black woman. I was thrilled to be working with her. In fact, I had turned down more lucrative offers with majority-owned companies because I thought being under this sister's tutelage would be a great learning experience. Boy, was I wrong. The admiration I had for this woman began to fade once we started to work together and I saw that she could not meet deadlines she set, she was never available to discuss project plans, and she would disappear for months on end. And, simply put, she was a bully. I felt abused. My health deteriorated, I developed a bleeding ulcer, and I knew I had to get out of this project. But like most of us, I needed the money, so I took the abuse and made excuses for her. She was overworked, she was alone in life, and she had a lot on her plate. When I found out from others who had worked with her that their experience was the same, I breathed a sigh of relief because I knew it was not me. But our relationship had to be severed abruptly after I had performed well on the contractual obligations and did not get paid. It caused great financial hardship and emotional distress that I will never forget. But I had to forgive that sister, or the hatred I felt for her would have eaten me alive. I saw her recently, and I had no problem walking up to her, saying hello, and wishing her well.

*Success is always the best revenge, sisters.* I did not sue this woman or her company, and I could have. I did not slander her; nor will I ever. God has a way of working it all out. Part of my success came in the form of my mentors, who steered me the right way when it all went down, and I landed very well.

Sisters, what I need to impress upon you is that *we need each other now*, perhaps more than ever. A full 92 percent of professional black women in our ABW survey for this book said that it was "important" to their overall happiness and well-being to spend time with other black women, including family members and friends. Fifty-nine percent said it was "extremely important" to their general contentment. Half of professional black women (50 percent) of all ages, marital statuses, religions, and income brackets gave this particular connection the highest rating in terms of their personal well-being.

But the painful truth is that we're conflicted over how we feel about each other. Black women have a deep and abiding emotional affection and connection to their elders and to each other, but our behavior doesn't always reflect this reality. All of us have walked into a room of unknown sisters and felt instant kinship. It's like going to church. Even among strangers, we embrace and kiss each other on the cheek. But the moment a sister disagrees with us, we turn on her. We need to learn not to be so quick to anger. As blogger Kelly Suzanne Saulsberry commented:

> I am not calling for us to be one big happy family that agrees or gets along all the time. We are human beings with enormous diversity and difference. We come from different walks of life, just like any other group. We should, however, be capable of respecting each other and not inflicting unnecessary pain onto each other. We need to take personal, historical, and community inventory of our lives and get to the root of our pain and anger so that we don't recycle it to our children, families, friends, and others in our communities.[8]

Saulsberry is right. Rather than inflicting pain on each other, we should help each other. We need to reconnect with that instinctual affection we have for one another and recognize that ultimately, we need our sisters to get through life's adversities. We buried a sorority sister two years ago who never married and never had children of her own. She had a biological sister and some work colleagues, but outside of the sorority, she had no one. During her battle with cancer, when she knew she would not live much longer, she told her sister that she did not want a funeral service because she did not think anyone would come. How wrong she was. I was so humbled on that day when we got to the church and saw that the sorority sisters had come out in great numbers to honor her. Her family was deeply touched. I think many of us who were single thought, *There, but for the grace of God, go I*, and it moved us to love soror Shirley, support her, and be there for her till the very end.

## Cross-Generational Talk:
### Why We Need It Now More than Ever

OF ALL THAT I value in my life, nothing matters more than the relationships I have with the older, wise women in my life. The closest of those relationships is, of course, with my mother. The other women in this circle may be as little as five or ten or as much as twenty years older than I, but they are my *sanctum sanctorum*.[9] These women are my closest council of advisors. These elder sisters hold a reserved place in my life. I can go to them for anything and know that they'll be there. And there is no discrimination—members of this personal council hail from different races, colors, and religions. But they are all women who affirm, teach, nurture, and guide me. These women love me enough to "wound me with truth," if need be, to save me when it's necessary. They have permission to do so. They don't walk on eggshells because they know me, and I know they would never intentionally harm me. I know they love me even when I err. I trust them with my life.

What I love most about these women, however, is that they also will not hesitate to take me lovingly in their arms and hug me, kiss me, tell me that they love me, take me to lunch, send a word of encouragement or a bouquet of flowers, and breathe life back into me when the cruel world has broken my heart. These sisters are there, *always*, to give an answer to a question, help me work through my challenges, or pray with me. I consider these sisters my "war council." I smile when recalling a recent conversation with Dr. Porter about how my "war council" has worked miracles in my life. Her response to my term stopped me mid-sentence: "First, Sophia, let's redefine the language of how we speak of our elders— I like that you have a 'war council,' but let's call it a 'life-affirming council' and a 'love council.'" I concur.

The scripture refers to these sisters as "Titus 2" women—women of honor who are not "slanderers" but "teach what is good."[10] These women are commanded by scripture through the apostle Paul to train younger women to be model wives and mothers and to be self-controlled, pure, and kind. The scriptural command tells us how important modeling and mentoring from the older women we know and admire is. And we pay this back by being a mentor and model of good character for the younger women in our lives.

So what do I mean by *cross-generational* talk? We need to learn to communicate effectively across different age groups and treat all women— younger, older, and peers—with respect. I may be old-fashioned, but I'm shocked by the way young black women often treat elders in our community. I recall an incident in my church when one sister quietly questioned whether a young woman's revealing red dress was appropriate for Sunday worship. Instead of accepting the advice with a polite thank you, this red-hot mamma raised her voice and lit into the older sister, who was thirty years her senior. All I could think of is how my mother would have slapped me into yesterday if I'd shown this type of disrespect—whatever my age. Sisters, we need to watch our tone, tempers, and attitude, especially when dealing with the women who've come before us and who've paid a hefty price for us to have all that we have.

I realize that this isn't always easy. At a time when we're finally building a cadre of experienced older women in our workplaces, industries, sororities, and churches, I'm starting to hear more stories about the old "queen bee" scenario. That's when high-ranking women refuse to share their insights with younger colleagues because no one was there to mentor them when they were starting out. This is what I think was the source of conflict between Helena Andrews and her first employer, an older black woman. That's why it's important to understand that mentoring is a *two-way street*. My mentors, my "love council," learn a lot from me, too. They humble me when they let me know that something I've said or done taught them to step up or think differently. Writing this book for the past two years has been one of the most challenging and incredible journeys of my life, and I wouldn't have been able to do it if not for the love, cross-generational talk, and support of women older and wiser than I. *But,* if I'd not been willing to submit, listen, and learn (and trust me, I did not always want to do so), I wouldn't have made it this far.

There are women we meet, and in an instant, and we know they'll be our friends for life. It was this way the day I met my best friend. I was weeping at my church altar when a stranger reached out. In a rare strong-black-woman moment of weakness, I took her counsel. It was the best decision I ever made. What made our meeting so powerful is that *she took a risk* and shared something very private from her own life that, she correctly guessed, was going on in mine at the time. She allowed me to cry, share, talk, mourn, and heal (I reference what was going on with me at the time in Chapter 5). She never judged me and was very clear about what I needed to do. Surprisingly, I found myself open to her wisdom and correction, and not at all interested in arguing or dismissing her tough love.

To move beyond viewing the world through our own narrow lens, we must seek out women who can help us to be better and live deeper, more meaningful lives. Be they older, younger, or within our own peer group, we have to lighten up and allow black women in our lives, as friends, colleagues, or sisters in prayer.

## Mean Girls, Tough Women

ONE OF THE most surprising observations I've made over the past few years is that our younger sisters are treating each other with more disdain than ever. We all know that words alone can be devastating weapons. But for younger women, intense altercations may turn physical. One highly regarded HBCU college president says she is deeply concerned about the uncontrolled and eruptive anger she sees among young black women on her campus: "These young sisters are angry, and they won't think twice about getting into a physical altercation with another black woman when they have disagreements. [They don't know how] to resolve conflict peacefully, and we need to help them grow in this area. Sadly, my generation has not always set a good example."

A Fortune 50 corporate executive in New York was so outraged by the behavior of young black sorority sisters at her alma mater that she held anger management sessions on campus to keep these women from literally beating each other up when they disagreed. Her comments in our interview were telling: "Because many black women have forgotten how to use our full range of emotions, we go straight to anger whenever we're upset, frustrated, or annoyed. That doesn't give us much to work with when a sister friend hurts us or doesn't come through on a promise. Our emotions seem a lot more difficult to manage when another black woman is at fault because we expect her to know better than to let us down."

To underscore this point, I interviewed another fabulous sister who works in the nonprofit sector dealing exclusively with black women's health and emotional well-being. She told me:

> We need to be very focused now on the proper teaching and emotional management of young black women in their twenties and thirties who will be our next generation of business, university, and government leaders. More and more, we are seeing the use of abusive language and actions as an acceptable means for black women to deal punitively with each other. The ramifications are repressed anger, depression, low self-esteem, and women who wall themselves off for fear of being taken advantage of by other women. If we don't teach these young women how to better manage their emotions now, we are going to have a mess on our hands.

We have to let this next generation of black women know that they have permission to feel their emotions, and we must provide help to work through them in a healthy and healing way that will strengthen our relationships rather than destroy them.

As Kelly Saulsberry says, we need to take inventory of our lives and get to the root of our pain and conflict so that we don't recycle it to others in our communities. One of the things I admire about the Jewish community is the way they embrace the mantra "Never forget."[11] To honor the memory of their ancestors who suffered in the Holocaust, they've vowed to never forget their collective history, struggle, and commitment. Out of their tragedy, they built a legacy of community that has sustained their people since World War II. I compare this experience to slavery in a 2001 opinion piece for the *Washington Post* titled "We Need to Put Slavery in Its Place."[12] We should take a page out of the Jewish handbook, dear sisters, because we also have a history of struggle and endurance in the face of unspeakable tragedy and brutality, as we discussed in detail in Chapter 2. We've failed this generation coming up behind us in the most negligent of ways—we failed to teach them their value, their history, and the struggle and triumph of the people who sacrificed so that we could be the accomplished, wealthy, well-educated women that we are today.

In a nutshell, it is imperative for us to love each other, support each other, and work together collaboratively in ways that advance us *all*. It's time for all of us to take a look at the woman in the mirror and ask her to change her ways.

## Conflict Resolution Skills Required

So how do we learn to react appropriately to stressful or hurtful situations when our emotions are fired up? One conflict management expert I spoke with suggested that we reflect on the steps below and keep them posted in our hearts and minds when we disagree with one another:

1. See conflict not as a problem but as an opportunity to clear the air and draw closer.
2. View the other person not as your adversary but as your partner in solving the problem.
3. Be fair, and take your share of the responsibility for the conflict. It takes two to cause conflict, and you must be willing to start there, or resolution will not happen.
4. Take the risk of truly listening to the other person, knowing that you may be changed for the better in the process.
5. Be curious instead of critical, compassionate instead of condemning.
6. Appreciate differences rather than feel threatened by them.

7. Refrain from judgment and criticism. Choose instead to share how you're affected by the other's behavior.
8. Disclose your vulnerable feelings rather than blaming the other for causing them.
9. Express your needs as requests instead of demands.
10. Trust that the other person has as much goodwill participating in this process as you do.
11. Balance your desire to prevail with your desire for a mutually satisfying relationship.

## Yes, We Can: The Redefinition Revolution

I STARTED THIS book by saying, "Some say we have conquered the world as accomplished black women. I say we have yet to conquer ourselves."

So, we've now come to the end of this book. I pray that the journey I asked you to come along on has helped you think clearly, ask questions, explore, assess, reconsider, and redefine life for you on healthier and happier terms. If you've vowed to address even one area of your life that troubles you, congratulations! You're on your way to conquering yourself.

My journey in writing this book has revealed many things. For one, I've learned that how we treat others is usually a reflection of how we feel about ourselves. Dr. Gayle Porter said it best:

> We must stop accepting as a universal given that black women have negative relationships with each other. Instead, let's uplift the loving, lifetime friendships that we see around us. Let's talk about and promote the history of black women taking care of and supporting each other as the role model we want to emulate. We must get past this negativity.

*So now what? Where do we start?* Let's start by rejecting centuries-old myths and stereotypical ideas about who we are and how we behave. I reject the all-too-common practice of us tearing one another down in front of others to justify our own actions in a failed relationship.

I reject the myth that we can't start businesses together, collaborate together, network, and grow million-dollar enterprises together without somehow damaging our friendships and love for one another. We can, and it's happening all around us, sisters.

I reject the ugly caricatures and stereotypes that paint a picture of angry, bitter, mean, depressed, materialistic, uncompromising, hyper-sexual, hypocritical black women, who relentlessly compete against each other, backbite, put each other down, steal each other's men, go to church and praise God while harboring hatred in our hearts, and continuously and recklessly fail to care for ourselves most of all.

I reject the myths and stereotypes, sisters, because at our core, this is *not* who we are. As I write throughout this book, we have to relearn the meaning of "value." Unless and until we begin to see each other's value as human beings, we'll never be able to accomplish all we're destined to be as strong black women. The time has come for us to stop messing around and embrace all that is *right* with us. After all, many of us are Christian women, right?

I wholeheartedly support the notion that we as powerful and accomplished black women can love, nurture, support, challenge, uplift, care for, and even lovingly rebuke each other as an everyday practice.

I wholeheartedly support the view that we can learn to survive and grow from our disagreements as sister friends and colleagues without ending our relationships. We do this in our jobs and in our relationships with the men we love, so why not give a sister the benefit of the doubt, write the apology note, call her up, have dinner, work it out, live by the Golden Rule, and *forgive her as you yourself want to be forgiven*?

I wholeheartedly support the idea that we can learn to be vulnerable with one another and still emerge strong.

Sisters, I end this book by asking you a series of questions that I've asked myself. These questions have helped me develop the plan that has led me to the deeply satisfying life I'm building today. I want you to take a long, hard look in the mirror and into your soul and decide who you want to be in this revolution I'm calling for.

- Will you agree to treat yourself with respect, work through past hurts, learn how to forgive, and let your heart heal?
- Will you agree to treat all black women with respect?
- Will you commit to learning how to incorporate conflict resolution skills into your life so you can resolve disagreement without strife?
- Will you be a Titus 2 woman and mentor younger women?
- Are you willing to let the Titus 2 women in your life advise you?
- Can you be woman enough to admit when you're wrong and apologize sincerely?

- Will you try to be more open to constructive criticism?
- Will you commit to honoring your word?
- Will you take a pledge to simply smile and say, "Good morning" the next time you pass another sister?
- Will you promise to give a simple and gracious thank you when a sister offers a kind word, sends a card, sends money, or stands in your corner without flinching?
- Are you willing to lighten up, soften up, and open up to make deeper connections with the men you want in your life?
- Can you reconnect with the joyful and playful side of your personality?
- Can you be woman enough to face your demons and shout, "Do your worst, because I'll do mine!"
- Will you promise to take care of yourself and rest? To exercise at least two days a week? To treat yourself with love and kindness?
- Will you promise to live out your faith in your actions? To stop walking through the motions of religious ritual? To stop using trite phrases like "too blessed to be stressed" when you really need to ask for help?
- Will you learn that forgiveness is essential for any human being?
- Will you fill your love with the love of a child if you're childless? Adoption, foster parenting, volunteering, and getting involved with the children already in your family are all wonderful options.
- Will you commit to building a more loving relationship with your daughters and not just your sons? And to you single or divorced moms, will you pledge to be fair when you talk about men to your children, even if their father walked out on all of you? Your children deserve better than hearing your rant about no-good black men.
- Will you commit to being your sister's keeper day in and day out, even when it's hard? And will you strive each day to live the Golden Rule—to treat others as you want to be treated?

If you can answer yes to the questions that are relevant to your life, take the following pledge with me. You can also sign our pledge at http://www.redefinitionrevolution.com and the new book website, at http://www.blackwomanredefined.com.

## Redefinition Pledge

I, _____, pledge that I will first and foremost love and take care of myself and stand up for what I want, need, and desire. I will no longer allow myself to be defined by myth, stereotype, or limitation. I promise to make meaningful connections and spend more time with the people I love and care about. I promise to honor my spirituality and religious beliefs by putting compassion, civility, honesty, and love into action each and every day. I promise to honor my body as my temple and engage only in those actions that bring health and wellness to my soul. I promise to live out my faith in a way that draws people to me, not pushes them away from me. I promise to bring joy into my life and into the lives of others. I promise to treat myself by spending quality time alone, listening to music, taking a stroll, or doing nothing. I promise to guard my financial health just as closely as I do my physical health. I promise to apologize and ask for forgiveness when I am wrong. I promise to be a role model and mentor other women. I promise to respect and support black women and to practice friendship, civility, compassion, honesty, and kindness within the sisterhood of all women.

Signed_____

Witnessed by_____

Witnessed by_____

# BONUS FEATURE

*Celebrity and Distinguished
African American Essays and
Sage Wisdoms*

## BLACK WOMAN RE DEFINED

Original written by
poet/author Monda Raquel Webb—© 2010


How Do You Redefine a Black Woman?
Full of Grace
Wisdom for the Ages
Timeless Beauty Etched on her Face
Turning the pages
Of a History contrived
with negative images
Perceptions and lies
To the Now, a Future, a Permanent place in time
Of a true Black Woman—organically Re Defined

Black woman
Do you know who you are?
Plucked by God from the Heavens
Rare and beautiful, bright as the North Star
When others look upon you they see diamonds
You see lumps of coal
What will it take for you to feel whole
Reach new heights, surpass impossible goals
and finally realize your power, recognizing God in your soul?
Black Woman
Why do you succumb to the myths

As your mental Master cracks the whip
On your inbred insecurities?
Even though you nursed their children raised generations
and carried heavy loads that broke you down to your knees

Black woman
It is your turn to shine
As you thoughtfully, purposefully take time to Re Define

# AUTHOR'S NOTE

*I* hope you have enjoyed reading this book as much as have I enjoyed working on it for the past several years. The section that follows is my personal favorite, and I think you will treasure it too! I cannot begin to thank the fabulous men and women from all walks of life who enthusiatically jumped at the chance to send messages of love, inspiration, guidance, encouragement, and hope to a new generation of aspiring black women, as well as the rest of us at "mid-life"who are entrepreneurs, moms, wives, singles, professionals, caretakers, and community servants still working to make our dreams come true.

What I found most striking about each contribution is the honesty each person willingly shared. Some shared insights on family, love, relationships, and career; while others focused on our spirt, sexuality, faith, self-care, finances, education, service, and success. But the common theme running throughout each contribution is our collective love and sincere desire to see the next generation of young folks do better than we did and to learn from our mistakes as well as from our successes.

The essays that follow include six features on what I call the core values of our lives: self-care, spirituality, career, finances, and relationships. Then there are the short essays and wisdoms penned by some very famous faces that we all know as well as some *new faces* that are in the trenches everyday working to build a stronger African American community and *redefine* the way we as black men and women relate to one another. I know you will enjoy reading them as much as I have.

I encourage you to keep these essays and wisdoms handy throughout the course of your life because I promise you that the simple and profound wisdom here will bring you much perspective and guidance as you reflect back on them from time to time as you travel on this journey called life. There will also be some overflow essays available on the book website only for those contributions that were in an earlier draft of the book or those that came in past the publication deadline.

Thank you for purchasing this book and for your interest in positively redefining the way in which strong accomplished black women are viewed in our society and in our community. I look forward to seeing you on the book tour this summer and throughout 2011.

# A TRIBUTE TO THE LATE DR. DOROTHY IRENE HEIGHT[1]

By the honorable Alexis M. Herman

23rd United States Secretary of Labor

(1997-2001)

"My experience has been that many black women struggle with the ideal of self-love. We often feel that taking care of self is somehow selfish or insensitive. We've been taught that value and self worth stem from nurturing the emotional and physical needs of others. Yet, I've discovered during my ninety-three years of living that taking care of *self* is at the core of a meaningful life."

—DOROTHY IRENE HEIGHT,

from the book *Tomorrow Begins Today* (2006)

hen Sophia asked me to write a brief tribute to my friend, teacher, and beloved mentor Dr. Dorothy Irene Height, I was glad that she felt it important in our time as modern-day women to include such an important civil rights pioneer in her work on "redefining" the image of a new, young, gifted generation of black women in America.

---

[1] Author note: Dr. Height had graciously agreed to write a short wisdom for this book in the fall of 2009. Being the wonderful perfectionist that she was, she was still working on tweaking her submission when she fell ill and died suddenly in April 2010. Because of my deep respect and admiration for her as the ultimate "accomplished black woman in America." I asked her dear friend, protégé, sorority sister, and confidante Secretary Herman to offer a brief tribute of her life that would inspire us all to follow in her footsteps.

As you all well know, Dr. Height was very interested in the advancement of black women (or as we were called in her day, "Negro women"). Up until the time she left us in 2010, she was a dedicated servant and supporter of all things black and female. She was committed to ensuring that we live our lives out with purpose—not focused on what we lacked, but instead focused on the gift of life itself.

She spent her life dedicated to the principles of justice, equality, freedom, and economic success for all people, but she had a special place in her heart for us as black women. She understood struggle. She understood strength. She understood having to be twice as good. She understood what it meant to be admitted to Barnard College in 1929, and when she arrived, to be denied admission because of the color of her skin.[2] However, she was not one to lament or allow denial to stand in the way of destiny. She moved forward and completed her undergraduate studies at NYU. She would later successfully lead the National Council of Negro Women at a time when Negro women were not highly respected or valued in the workplace or corridors of power.

Dr. Height was above all a lady—she was the quintessential Renaissance woman, which really enabled her to achieve all that she did—in the presence of men, who often tried to silence or marginalize her. She was truly a family person and a friend. Her humanity was not just based on others but with her friends and family—she had a great laugh and was a great "laugher." Those of us who were blessed to call her friend or family knew her as the person, not the icon. She was down-to-earth and real.

As I thought about what guidance and wisdom I could share with you younger sisters of Gen X and Gen Y, I would start with something Dr. Height believed in firmly: God has given each one of us an assignment of who we will be and what we will represent. Life is about choices. And no matter what happens to us, what we may lose, or what we may never have that we desired so greatly—your life, my young sisters is a gift, so use it in a way that honors yourself, your family, and others.

I learned this lesson well from my mentor. Without her, I would not have become the woman I am today. Dr. Height dedicated her life's work to inspiring people and giving them the tools to move forward and work together for the highest good, and although she is gone from us, that work is continuing at the National Council of Negro Women and in the lives of the many women she mentored, taught, and inspired.

---

[2] A wrong that was righted by Barnard College seventy-five years later.

Let me end by saying this to you, the young women in the prime of your lives, on college campuses, and entering into the workforce: *Now is a time to be connected to one another as sisters.* This is the time to be connected to each other as women who can accomplish so much more together than any of us can do alone. Dr. Height used to quote her mentor, Dr. Mary McLeod Bethune. She would say, "If I touch you with my one finger nothing happens—but if I ball up my fist you will feel the impact." We need to work together so the world can feel our impact. My humble advice to you on how to life a happy and fulfilled life is to learn from the wisdom of your elders.

They are wiser because they have already forged and walked the paths you now follow. They can offer you guidance, a listening ear, a shoulder to lean on and direction that so many of us coming before you did not often have available. Draw closer together and collaborate, build business success, form new agendas, create new visions and in doing so you will honor your ancestors and the legacy of strength that we as black women have always embraced. This is something I know Dr. Height would want you to achieve more than money, fame or fortune. She would want you to be the wonderful, beautiful women you are, and to take care of and nurture yourself most of all.

# FEATURE ESSAYS

## Relationships
### Dr. Audrey B. Chapman

*Dr. Audrey B. Chapman is a nationally renowned expert in male-female relationships, a family therapist, and author. She is also the host of* The Audrey Chapman Show, *which airs weekly on WHUR-FM in Washington, D.C.*

### *Attracting Love When Prince Charming Is Hard to Find*

African American women, more than any other group of women, must face the dreaded reality that they may never marry. According to the Joint Center for Political and Economic Studies, only 50 percent of black women expect to marry by age twenty-eight. Only 32 percent of black women remarry within five years of divorce. To effectively change these bleak statistics, African American women must shift their beliefs about men who are available as potential partners. Black women must challenge and adopt new principles to cancel out the early programming taught by elders in their families and communities.

Early childhood social messages are so damaging and powerful because they last well into adulthood, making the possibility of mating more difficult. Many black women are fed messages to be self-reliant, aggressive, and controlling in order to survive. They are also taught to mother everyone, particularly men. As a result, they are not as strategic about their own survival. For single black women, the greatest challenge is not other women or the lack of enough black men, but whether or not they are willing to make internal shifts in their expectations, change their paradigm about the perceived shortage of black men, and cross the cultural line by dating men from other ethnic groups. To be more con-scientious and to increase their love options, black women will need to reprogram and get on track.

1. Gain Clarity
   **When women meet men, they should not rush to judgment. Allow a reasonable amount of time,** *at least 90 days,* before identifying what you want in the relationship. Discuss your goals for the rela-tionship and urge your partner to share his. You should not try to be aggressive or lead the discussion, but rather work on being a team participant.

2. Stay Present
   Do not bring up old painful relationships or rehash past negative behaviors that left you wounded. Stay present and learn to state what you need in the "here and now." This should enhance the new union and teach both of you how to solve problems more compas-sionately.

3. Choose a Man for His Character
   Remember, men come in various sizes, colors, and traits, so have an open mind and an open heart. Explore men of various ethnic groups, classes, and education levels. Choose a man based on his spirituality, values, and traits, not just his looks.

4. Declare What Won't Make It and What Will
   Remember no one will show up in your life that is perfect. After at least six months of dating, discuss together what you both would like to change and take turns providing feedback. Each partner should have an opportunity to make suggestions about what he or she thinks will work well. You are learning about each other, and you are exploring whether the relationship is a good emotional fit.

5. Don't Be Shallow
   Learn to accept him as he is. His personality, values, and ability to be caring matter more than his bank account. Don't pass or fail a potential partner based on how good-looking he is. Often women discover that a regular-looking Joe is the positive, loving person they have always wanted. Be realistic and openhearted. How he looks is not the best barometer of a positive relationship.

6. Re-check Your Stuff
   Check to see if your old patterns have shifted and if you can move on to new ways of relating to a partner. Also, it's valuable to work

on strengthening your self-esteem; we tend to attract people who are in the same place emotionally as we are. If you are still resisting change, this is a good time to seek professional help from a life coach, therapist, or pastor. Once you own your stuff, re-check it, and make adjustments, you're ready for commitment with Prince Charming.

# Relationships: A Man's View
## Dr. Marc Lamont Hill

*Dr. Marc Lamont Hill is a professor at Columbia University. He is also an author, host of Black Enterprise's* Our World, *a nationally syndicated newspaper columnist, and father.*

## A Window into a Brother's Soul

My Dear Sisters,

Although I've had more professional success than I ever expected, my experiences on the personal front have been met mostly with failure. Some of this can be attributed to my crazy schedule, bad timing, or just plain bad luck—all of the excuses that we use to avoid looking in the mirror. But I've come to realize that the biggest issue has been me. Despite my best intentions, I have never been truly available to the women I've pursued, dated, and even loved.

After considerable prayer, meditation, reading, and, yes, therapy, I rummaged through my past in an effort to make sense of things. This process helped me recognize the many sources of my difficulties: parents who stayed together but never showed any signs of intimacy or affection, role models who taught me that "real" men didn't reveal any emotion other than anger, a media world that equated black masculinity with violence and hyper-sexuality. The more I dug, the more I realized how much about the world and myself that I had to *unlearn* in order to be a healthy partner for someone else.

While my past is my own, it is similar to that of countless brothers I've encountered throughout my life. Like me, they have been fed a steady diet of patriarchy, misogyny, and homophobia. Few have had access to strong and healthy romantic relationships. Even fewer have had functional models of black masculinity at their disposal. Still, against these considerable odds, many brothers are fighting to *unlearn* a lifetime of seductive but dangerous lies. Many of us are fighting to re-imagine ourselves and the world in ways that will make us better lovers, better fathers, better friends, and better partners.

To do this successfully, sisters, we need your help. Only together can we craft spaces in which men and women safely practice new ways of being, new ways of living, and new ways of loving. Only together can we begin the painful but necessary project of *unlearning* everything the world has taught us about who we are and who we can be.

Of course, in a world that remains beset by racial and gender-based violence, economic inequality, and dehumanization, black women already carry an unimaginable load. It is not my intention to put more on your plates or to prioritize male development over female suffering. Rather, I believe that the most urgent issues confronted by both black women and black men can only be resolved at the moment when we have fully committed to understanding, loving, supporting, and healing each other. While brothers must pull their own weight, we will not be successful without your help.

Sisters, we need you to resist the same troublesome ideas, expectations, and anxieties that have crippled us. We need you to help create space for brothers to be open, honest, and vulnerable. We need you to demand the very best from us without compromising the ethics of care, empathy, and patience that have sustained us through the worst of times. We need you to *unlearn* with us. If we commit ourselves to this work, there is literally nothing that we cannot do.

# Education and Career Development
## Dr. Julianne Malveaux

*Dr. Julianne Malveaux, economist and author, is the fifteenth president of Bennett College for Women. As she likes to say, "Bennett . . . is an oasis where we educate and celebrate women and develop them into twenty-first century leaders and global thinkers."*

## A Word for Young Sisters—You Are Enough

I like to tell my students at Bennett that men are like icing, and women are like cake. You can have cake without icing, but not icing without cake. This means they have to understand that they are enough, sufficient, ample, whether they are partnered or not. This is an important message to deliver in a patriarchy, where men are so much more relentlessly promoted than women are. We need to figure out ways to promote and lift up our women. With confidence at their base, they can do anything.

We must have conversations about gender relations, sex and sexuality, and relationship choices so that young women are not blindsided by the swirl of emotions that come with the transition from girlhood to young womanhood. We must also talk about the social construction of gender and ways that it affects our lives. And we must encourage our young women to find and trust friends, and to identify other helpers (including physicians and mental health professionals) when they find life overwhelming. If we remind young women that they are *enough*, then they will understand that every need they have can be met. The sense of being *enough* is also a deterrent to making poor relationship choices, even in the face of social pressure.

Our love must be a love that fosters excellence. We absolutely must infuse the highest academic standards on our young women, including excellence in written and verbal expression. We must not hesitate to be gently corrective when we observe our young women failing to embrace concepts of excellence in their spoken and written word, in their physical appearance, and in their interactions with others. While we fully understand that adolescence is tumultuous and sometimes encourages young people to test themselves against the world, it is always our job to encourage young women to be their highest and best.

Most importantly, we must make allowances for mistakes, because all human beings make them. We must create "roads back" from poor choices, and keep open options for all possibilities for our young women. It is never too late to go to college, never too late to try something new. Having a child too early may make college or career more difficult, but it certainly will not make it impossible. Messages to our young women must always include the richness of possibility.

Young African American women must be reminded of their ancestry, of the strength from which they come. The life stories of women like Ida B. Wells, Harriet Tubman, Sojourner Truth, Dr. Willa Player, Dr. Phyllis Wallace, Nannie Helen Burroughs, Dr. Dorothy I. Height, and so many others are stories of tenacity and achievement. In reviewing the lives of women who succeeded against all odds, young women are reminded that they face fewer odds and with persistence and preparation, many possibilities for having successful and fulfilling lives.

So many of our young women simply want affirmation. They want to hear, "You can do it." We play a key role in lifting them up and affirming them, but our affirmation must be honestly appraising. You can't go to med school if you can't master biology; you can't be a writer if you won't master English. We have to create maps for young women to help them get from where they are to where they want to be. And we must do it while, and by, embracing our foundations.

We must also teach young women an appreciation for diversity and a kindness for each other. To appreciate diversity we must acknowledge our differences—we are light and dark, gay and straight, and we are diasporically connected through the African continent differently—as Caribbean-Americans, African-born Americans, and with different links to the continent. There is also a class distribution among us that must be acknowledged. When we teach appreciation for our differences, we give each young woman permission to soar in her own right. And when we teach and model kindness, we remind them of the very highest and best in our interactions with each other. We must remind young women that "hurt people hurt people" and teach them the resilience that they must develop to navigate human relations in an age that the artist India Arie describes as "graceless."

Spirit and spirituality are an integral part of the message that we want to send you young women. Faith in a Mother/Father God or in a higher power to which we are subordinate is essential in putting each of our lives in context. The Desdirata of Happiness reminds us that there are always people who have more than we do and always people who have less. Again, faith reminds us that we always have *enough*, and that each of us, simply, is *enough*. We want our young women to have a dynamic sense of possibility. The richness of community relations and the sweetness of sisterhood helps to make every possibility attainable. We must surround our young women with the possibility of excellence—academic, personal, physical, and spiritual. We must be an antidote to the patriarchal messages that lift up men and ignore women.

# Life, Love, and Transformation after Forty
## Michel Martin

*Michel McQueen Martin, host of* Tell Me More, *a nationally syndicated news and talk program on National Public Radio, is from Brooklyn, NY. Before joining NPR, Martin worked at ABC, and covered state and local politics for the* Washington Post *and national politics and policy for the* Wall Street Journal. *She has won many awards for her work in journalism, including an Emmy.*

"It is never too late to fall in love."

—ANONYMOUS

A few months after I started dating the man who would become my husband, he surprised me with the kind of crazy thing you hear about but think never actually happens in real life: He took me out to dinner and—handing me two tickets with a flourish—asked me to go on a weekend jaunt to the Caribbean with him in celebration of my birthday.

I was too through. I was already smitten with him, so of course I said yes.

Now going away for the weekend with a man I had only known for a few months was not, shall we say, my usual style. When I was growing up, the rules were—and I suppose still are—that "nice girls" and smart women are not impulsive. They take their sweet time letting a man know they are interested, especially coming out of a divorce as I was. But from the moment I met Billy, I knew that was "it." And by "it" I don't mean I could have predicted with certainty there would be marriage and kids and all that later, but rather, a relationship with him was what I wanted, and I was willing to take what came, even if it led to heartbreak.

By this time, my heart had been broken more than once—and I can say with assurance I had also broken a heart or two. I had experienced career triumphs and setbacks. In fact, when we met, the news program I was working on was cancelled, and to make things even more challenging, my contract had expired. I was still working at the network but without a net—I could have been let go at any time. On top of that my parents were undergoing a health crisis. I knew what it was like to be up against it and so did he.

Reading this, you might think that Billy and I were clinging to each other as if each was some kind of life raft. But that is not so. Our relationship was relaxed, fun, and for the most part, without a lot of anxiety. There was the occasional grand gesture—the Caribbean jaunt was spectacular—and there was the occasional big blowout. But with my recent divorce and his second daughter still in college, our dates were mostly laid-back, and we tried to keep things drama free. We did typical things together—making homemade pizza, watching the Final Four, or taking trips to the driving range. Our courtship was more like a sexy friendship. And you know what? It's still that way. We like going to the dry cleaners together (almost) as much as a jaunt to the Caribbean, and a late night run to the ice cream parlor will do us just as well as a fancy black tie soirée. We just like each other's company, and we respect each other's judgment, even when we don't agree with it.

People often have this idea that when you get older, women especially get anxious about relationships because their biological clocks are ticking. But what they don't seem to realize is that being older can also make you more resilient. By the time we met, we were both living proof that what doesn't kill you will make you stronger. We both knew who we were and where we were headed, or at least where we wanted to go. For my part, I also knew from the very beginning that even if our relationship did not end well, I did not want to miss whatever it was going to be on the way.

When Sophia asked me to write this essay about finding love and having a family later in life, I realized that Billy and I generally do not talk to people, other than our children, about our relationship. This attitude is partly personal (Billy was a prosecutor for years and most of my family members are cops, so we are both used to keeping our own counsel), partly cultural (black people in general, I think I can say this, do not like other people in our business), and partly because we're superstitious. *It just seems like bad luck.* You see people on Barbara Walters telling people their business and the next thing you know there's some tattoo model popping up. Plus, we've both been divorced, so who are we to tell other people how to live? But the truth is we learn our best life lessons from our challenging moments, or as Sophia writes in chapter ten "in the midst of our storms."

One of the things we learned from both our individual and collective storms is that you really do need to keep hope alive: hope that love is out there and worth it. It seems to us that professional black women and men still need hope around the ability to have positive intimate relationships. My husband and I are saddened by what we hear relative to the love quotient in our community. So many people, even young people, are cynical about relationships. They have such low expectations that they don't seem to even try to get to a place of deep connection. So after some discussion, Billy and I agreed that if our story might inspire someone, sharing it was worth it.

Notice how I am saying "we." I can honestly say that when I was younger, I would have viewed consulting with my husband about whether or not to write an essay as demeaning to me as an accomplished black woman. My attitude would have been: I am the writer; you are the lawyer, so stay in your lane. But time has a way of smoothing some of those edges—and making some things less of a big deal. Now I know why I felt that way: I grew up in a household with very little money and even less mutual respect. My father thought nothing of belittling our mother in front of us, even though she is quite bright. Even more tragic, she's bright in ways that would have complimented his talents if he had permitted her to do so. For my mother's part, she also clung to very rigid and traditional ideas about the roles men and women were supposed to play in a household—to her own detriment. By the time she went back to work and started earning her own money she was both grateful to have it and resentful for having to do it.

With that example—and coming to age at a time when black women started doing so many exciting things—I think I got the idea that partnership equals *put me in my place.* The only problem was that I did not have a clear idea of what exactly I did want, what partnership could be.

Eventually I figured out that I wanted to be with somebody who made me laugh but who let me make him laugh, who would row the boat and also let me row as I am able, and even let me steer when appropriate. For me, Billy is that man.

Now Billy would be the first to tell you that he was not always so progressive. In his earlier years, he has admitted to me that he had a lot of, shall we say, opinions about a lot of things, including women's hairdos— I wear mine in a natural style. Today, however, he understands that being the head of our household does not mean that he needs to put his stamp on everything. Recently I was thinking about cutting my hair again, and I asked him his opinion. After much throat clearing he allowed as to how he liked it longer. I cut it anyway. When I came in that way, he just shook his head and laughed.

He also respects what it takes to make it as a black woman in the work world and cheers me on constantly. He's my biggest fan, and I'm his.

I recently read *As Time Goes By*, a book about finding love in mid-life by Abigail Trafford, former *Washington Post* health columnist. And I discovered that my experience with Billy is, if not typical, not strange. People who fall in love later in life are often actually more open and more tolerant than they might have been when they were younger, in part because it may take awhile to realize that being with someone who has the "right" resume or who their friends think is right for them is bullshit and has nothing to do with making them happy. On the downside, their openness may be one reason they can be taken advantage of, by handing over the credit cards or the house keys a bit too soon.

There were times during my courtship with Billy that I went out on a limb for him—in ways that surprised even me. For example, I helped his daughters throw a big surprise party for him at a time when our relationship was strained. We had been dating for a couple of years, and I had decided I really wanted to get married again, but he was still hesitant. I worried that if I decided to help his daughters throw the party and we wound up breaking up that I would look like a fool. But by then I had really come to love the girls, the young women actually—one was in medical school by then, and the other was working as a chemist and herself engaged to be married. I really wanted to help them with something that they really wanted to do. That's when it struck me: What if I did look like a fool? Who was looking at me, except me?

**But here is the lesson, sisters:** life is not over at forty or fifty or at whatever age you may find yourself. Life is only over when you decide to stay stuck where you are and stop taking wise and meaningful risks for love. My story is like countless women I know and who you know—women who found love after age forty and who had children in their forties as did I. If I hadn't taken a chance on love, even when it was a bit "iffy," I would have missed out on helping to throw a really great party that night. I would have missed out on two wedding rings, one mortgage, two small children (of my own), two sons-in-law, two grandkids (and counting). By being willing to risk my heart once again, by being spontaneous, and by being open to love—I can tell you that I would have missed one incredible piece of this journey—the fabulous journey called my life!

# Self-Care and Spirituality
## Mikki Taylor

*Mikki Taylor recently retired as beauty and cover editor of* Essence *magazine after thirty years of service. Currently an editor at large for the magazine, she is also president and creative director of Mikki Taylor Enterprises, LLC.*

"She knows who she is because she knows who she isn't."

—NIKKI GIOVANNI, POET

There's an old saying: home is where your story begins. As I move forward in life, I've come to learn the depths and the richness of the term *home*, and I realize that home is what lies *inside of you*. It's what you play forward, the foundation that you walk in everyday and the truth by which you measure your quality of life. It is a sacred space—one that's not up for grabs or violation. The same holds true for our bodies, our unique life vessels that we must honor and regard in the highest order. I can always tell a woman who lives from "home"; she walks purposely through life because she lives from the inside out as opposed to outside in.

To my young sisters: your sense of self and what is and is not acceptable to you must always be clear if you are to navigate this journey called life successfully. Never let others define your way of being. A woman who knows who she is always carries herself with the utmost respect for her temple (body) and celebrates her distinct beauty to the fullest because she loves the skin she's in. Whether you are just starting out in your twenties or if you are at mid-life in your 40s, your most precious resource is *you*. So be about the business of setting and keeping a standard that is affirming and honors all that God has done in uniquely creating you.

My dear friend and mentor Susan Taylor once told me, "You have to give yourself *to yourself* before you give yourself away." I have come to embrace her words on a much deeper level over the years as I have watched sisters struggle in their interpersonal relationships and in the workplace with the notion of self-care and self-love. In other words, I have watched us struggle with knowing where our *home* is and how to honor its unique value.

My thirty-plus years of working with my sisters at *Essence* and of walking my faith as a Christian have taught me that none of us can move through life acting in isolation—it only leads to anxiety, depression, and self-pity. Too many strong, accomplished black women fail to see how important it is for us to be connected. Instead we compete, we fight, we tear down, and we leave broken places that cause us to go inward and wall ourselves off.

Ironically, the research for this book showed that more than 90 percent of black women place an extremely high value on their relationships with other black women, sister friends, and female matriarchs in the family.[3] We need to be true to our instincts, which tell us to value each other and our relationships. Although we know best how to shape our destiny and define our value and worth, we need each other to make it through, sisters. No woman is an island. The easiest way to self-care also centers on keeping your truth close to your heart so that you don't lose it. When we lose sight of our truth, we make mistakes. For example, we welcome the *unwelcome,* those people who are abusive, users, or who willingly disregard our value. As a mother, sister, and lover of all things black and female, some of the findings in this book frankly gave me pause. The statistics that show we are giving our

---

[3] See appendices quantitative research n=540, pp 336-339

bodies away as "buddies" or "jump offs"—and throwing away all our gifts just to attract men—concern me.[4]

Sometimes I think how unfortunate it is in these so-called "modern times" that we don't know what to do with each other besides have sex. Perhaps, I am just an old-fashioned girl. After twenty-eight years in a very passionate marriage, I can tell you with certainty that there is value in having a man who will court you, and a man who will honor your home.

The crux of any meaningful relationship begins with *your mind*. True relationships are formed over time and are worth their weight in gold. Too often today people treat one another as if they are cars on a lot to be bought and sold. Clearly the Creator didn't design "test drives" or "short-term leases" for human beings. Man did, which should tell you a lot. But I say to you, hold onto your value: Don't become someone's "used" ride.

If ever there was a time to keep your head on straight about self-love and knowing who you are, it's now. This is the greatest period in the history of women of African descent. One of my favorite life-lines comes from the Old Testament, and it's found in Proverbs 4:23, which says, "Above all things guard your heart for it is a wellspring of life." The directive is this: Guard your mind with meticulous care, for it is the center from which your every action comes. Remember, your purpose in life cannot be altered unless *you allow* other people or things to control you. So your role as you travel this journey is to be the gatekeeper to your sacred space and keep home ever before you.

---

[4] See results, pp 336-339

# Financial Wellness
## Michelle Singletary

*Michelle Singletary is a nationally syndicated columnist for* The Washington Post *and author of* The Power to Prosper: 21 Days to Financial Freedom.

### *The Pursuit of Financial Happiness*

It's not how much you make that matters, but
how you make do with what you have.

That simple but profoundly sophisticated statement should be a money mantra for everyone, especially black women. It was advice I received from Big Mama, my grandmother, who was the best financial adviser I've ever known.

My grandmother worked as a nursing assistant at a hospital in Baltimore, and with her small salary she paid off her home before she retired, bought cars that she paid off early, and managed her money the way our government should—without ever creating a deficit. But despite her financial acumen, Big Mama worried about her finances. She stressed about them not because she wasn't a good manager but because she knew that the financial odds were against her.

Truth be told, the odds are still stacked against many of us. Statistically, African Americans are more likely to be low-income earners, have higher unemployment rates in both good times and bad, have lower homeownership rates, lack adequate health care, and have less money saved for retirement. On all major economic indicators—income, wages, employment, and poverty—African Americans were worse off in 2007 than they were in 2000, according to a study by the Economic Policy Institute.

So it isn't surprising that financial security is the biggest concern for women in general and for black women in particular. In a survey conducted for this book, 540 professional black women with a bachelor's degree or higher were asked what concerns them most.

Overwhelmingly, the survey found that they are more worried about their finances than they are about their health, well-being, or love life. Sixty percent of survey respondents said that financial pressures and debt affect their emotional health or cause depression.

Black women are stressed about money, in part, because they are more often than not the major providers for their families. They are more likely to be single, divorced, or widowed. They are more likely to be raising children without a father (or his paycheck). And finally, they are more likely, especially in their senior years, to be taking care of extended family members or their grandchildren.

The survey found that 30 percent of black women earning less than $50,000 a year considered fiscal stability central to their life state. Money is key for 19 percent of those bringing home $50,000 to $100,000 per year, as well as for 24 percent of those making more than $100,000 annually. The challenge for our society, and for black women in particular, is to avoid confusing our net worth with our self-worth. Financial stability is critical, but we must not allow it to define us.

I cringe when those in my community talk as if blacks are genetically predisposed to overspending on cars and clothes. I communicate with hundreds of consumers of all ages, races and economic backgrounds, and it's clear to me that America—not just black America—is a nation of conspicuous consumers.

The path that avoids financial stress and that leads to prosperity is to follow Big Mama's advice and live below your means. My grandmother didn't spend every dollar that she earned. And because she didn't, this black woman, who never earned more than $13,000 a year, retired with more savings and financial strength than other folks I know—black, white, Hispanic or Asian—making ten times what she earned in any given year.

My grandmother also didn't confuse wants with needs. We are constantly bombarded with messages that tell us to upgrade—our wardrobes, cars, homes, and even our spouses. If you aren't happy, get rid of it and get something newer and better, we are told.

But to what end is this endless search for more? Where is the balance?

The pursuit of financial happiness should begin by defining what's most important to you. For me, it's faith, family, and friends. It's community service. Your money will follow your values. I don't see my money solely as a means to self-enrichment but also as a way to build a net worth used to lift up others. The pursuit of stuff alone will not give you internally what will satisfy you.

Bottom line: nothing is wrong with wanting more. But once you achieve financial stability, don't keep moving up the bar. Learn to be content with what you have.

# Connecting Your Sensual and Sacred
## Marcia L. Dyson

*Marcia L. Dyson is an ordained minister, political strategist, writer, and social activist. Her novel* Don't Call Me Angel *will be published in 2011. She is a contributor to* New Deal 2.0, *womensradio.com and theroot.com where she addresses issues concerning race, gender inequality, and national concerns.*

### You Are Beautifully and Wonderfully Made

Too many of our beautifully and wonderfully made black women have dimmed their sensuality in one of two extremes: they have either become completely carnal and sexual, treating their bodies with little regard and value; or they have cut themselves off from love, affection, touch, and intimacy. Many have gone so far inward, often under the guise of "religion," that they have lost their connection to their most precious gift—their true spirit. Too many of our young women have traded their integrity for meaningless sex: jump offs, friends with benefits.

As Sister Sophia writes so well in chapter six of this important book, we have confused our religion for our spirituality. We have called Jesus "Our Man" instead of rightly understanding his place as our "Lord and Savior." They are different beloved ones. As I stated in my interview for this book in chapter six, the Bible tells us that we were made for companion and union. Not for isolation and a rigid walled off faith that denies us our most basic humanity: the right to love, be loved, be touched, and to be sexual beings.

Sadly, we are not talking about this important issue in the open as we need to be in the church. And out of loneliness, as the data in the ABW survey shows, some of our sisters find themselves in what I call "situational sex," which includes experimental lesbianism. Our spirituality and our sensuality are intricately linked. We were designed that way, sisters. Our Creator intended sensuality and sexuality to be a blessing in our lives, not a burden. The poet T.S. Eliot said it best in *The Four Quartets*. He uses time, flowers, and the change of seasons as a metaphor for our sensuality. He speaks of "emptying the sensual with deprivation" which "cleanses affection from the temporal." Without true and meaningful light, love, touch, affection, and warmth in our lives, we wither, and we die.

Black American women hail from a very unique context and experience relative to our sexuality. Many of us have not been taught to be sensually free and available. Because so many black women have been sexually abused and misused, their sensuality has faded. We need to find peace within ourselves that allows us to reconnect with our sensuality.

When all is said and done, we need to understand that sex is more than a physical act. Sex is, as the Word says, a "knowing," having a deep understanding, a meeting of body and soul. When we can learn to dwell in a place of sensuality, instead of raw sexuality, when we learn that our sacred is special, we will experience a deeper connection with the spirit and attract the true love we want and desire.

# SHORT ESSAYS

## WISDOMS AND STRAIGHT TALK YOU CAN STAND ON

### Define Yourself for Yourself

By Rep. Terrie Sewell (D-AL)

First African American woman elected to Congress from Alabama

Define yourself for yourself—if you don't the world will. The single most important life lesson I have learned is that I am the master of my own thoughts. No one can get in my head unless I let them. The world will seek to define you by your race, your gender, your religious beliefs, and your socioeconomic background. As a black girl growing up in Selma, Alabama, it would have been easy to see life's limitations. My mother would say, "So a person thinks, so is she—if you think you can be a lawyer, doctor or entrepreneur and you carry yourself like one, you will become one." I had to believe that I could be a Congresswoman long before I became one.

People will make assumptions about you based on their own and societal perceptions of who you are and what you represent. It is because of the prejudices of society that one's own self-worth must be high. It requires a tough mental attitude to see the possibilities of life and to create the success you want to be. If your mind can conceive it, you can achieve it!

In life, I have seen my obstacles as challenges to be conquered. I found strength in the perseverance and determination of others before me. It was because of their courage that I had the audacity to believe that I could become the first African American Congresswoman from the state of Alabama. We all stand on the shoulders of undeterred, tenacious black women—some known and many unknown—who were unwilling to allow society to define them. You must remember from whence you come, sisters, and in doing so you can become anything or anyone you dare to dream.

# It's All About Strategy, Ladies

## By Soledad O'Brien

### CNN Special Correspondent and Host of *Black in America*

I'm a journalist by day and a strategist by heart. I have had a strategy for both my personal life and career for as long as I can remember. I have given them both equal weight and attention. As a result, my life has balance—as much as one could hope for.

I believe in setting goals, setting a path, and achieving what I have set out to do. Most of my success has not come easily. I put the work in. I knew early on I wanted to have a successful career, but I also knew I wanted to be a wife and mother. I wanted a big family like the one I grew up in. I also knew the kind of man I wanted to marry and to be the father of my children. I was very clear that integrity mattered. I never cared about the kind of car a guy drove or if he could even afford to take me out on a date. If he wasn't trustworthy, I did not linger. I knew the relationship would go nowhere.

When I met my husband in college, we were friends first. We shared similar values. There was no game playing, and we built a relationship based on mutual trust and respect. That foundation has been the key to my successful marriage and career. He stands behind me one hundred percent. Strategy, for me, doesn't work without core values. Integrity, honesty, graciousness, and loyalty are the values I live by and treasure in others. I work hard at being a good wife, a good mother, a good friend, and a good citizen. I carry these values with me in my work as a journalist, and they have served me well.

# My Admiration for Strong Black Women
## By Rep. Jesse Jackson, Jr. (D-Ill.)

I must have been an adult before I realized that all women were not strong and independent. Or that the larger society often placed limitations on them. Because I had grown up around mostly African American women who defined strength and independence on their own terms, I assumed all women lived this way. I always found strength to be a good thing—when did it become bad in the eyes of so many? The black women I knew judged beauty, intelligence, and talent by their own rules. They defined themselves, for themselves.

One strong independent black woman stands out for me: my mother, Jacqueline Jackson. She has an unfailing commitment to what she calls "doing what's right." In 2001, for example, she made headlines when she was jailed in Puerto Rico for protesting Navy bomb tests on the island of Vieques. She stood tall when she walked out of prison—as I believe all generations of black women have stood tall through the most challenging of life's events.

I admire my mother's strength and independence, just as I appreciate the countless black women who exhibit these same qualities every day. I see evidence of these women's resolve in everything from the businesses they start to the churches and community organizations they help to thrive. I see it in our children who are raised at the hands of phenomenal sisters mostly on their own. I believe that whenever fate calls the roll up yonder every strong African American woman —Harriet Tubman, Sojourner Truth, Ida B. Wells, Fannie Lou Hamer, Rosa Parks, Shirley Chisholm, Barbara Jordan, Jacqueline Jackson, Michelle Obama—should likewise add her name to the list. I may not know who she is, but I know she's out there. And I love her for the work she does and the strength she brings day after day to make our world a better place.

# Meeting Twenty-first Century Challenges with our Legendary Strength and Perseverance

## By Congresswoman Eleanor Holmes Norton
### (D-District of Columbia)

Almost everything about being a black woman today has changed, except for our ability to adjust to the challenges that are thrown our way. Swift, and sometimes mystifying, these challenges affect every aspect of the lives of African American women today—from their rise in education and jobs to the decline many are experiencing in marriage and family. But black women come from a long line of women who have preferred to resist rather than acquiesce. Black pioneers, such as Rosa Parks and Shirley Chisholm, are well known for their perseverance. Less celebrated are our mothers and grandmothers in whom perseverance and independence also are deeply rooted. These qualities are the lifeline that young black women today can call upon as they take on a vexing set of new challenges: from an economy undergoing tough structural changes to HIV and AIDS, an unwelcome new factor in relationships. As bewildering as today's developments are, they will not overwhelm young black women. Young women can look to icons that confronted daunting crises. Even closer to home, and most obviously at 1600 Pennsylvania Avenue, black woman are likely to see one source of their strength in the rich traditions of African American women who surround them.

# Be the Light in the Tunnel

## By Taraji P. Henson
Academy Award-Nominated actress, *The Curious Case of Benjamin Button* (2008), *Date Night* (2009), *The Karate Kid* (2010)

We've all heard the phrase "the light at the end of the tunnel." As accomplished black women, we often have so many things pulling at us all at once: our careers, our families, our relationships, our commitments and our ambitions that we are drained of our own light. The truth is many of us live harried and hurried lives.

So often we feel stressed instead of knowing that we are blessed. I go through this too. We talk about seeing the light at the end of the tunnel, instead of learning to be the light in the tunnel. Life rarely goes as we plan—it will challenge you, throw you curve balls, and bring about the unexpected. But through it all if you keep your faith, walk in the light, and trust that what you put into your life, you will get back, you can make it through any test or difficulty.

*What am I saying?*

No matter who or what may upset you it is your job to walk in what I like to call the "love light." Just know that in the darkest moments of your life you will often need to learn to *be the light* in the midst of the struggle or tragedy you are facing. And most of all remember this: others are always watching, and sometimes the only God others will see out here in this world is the God they see in *you* dear sister—so be the light that brightens the way for others who may follow your path.

*I luv me some you!*

# Embrace Your Fears and Turn Them into Your Success

## By Sherri Shepherd

Author, Emmy Award-winning co-host of ABC's *The View* and host of *The Newlywed Game*

One of the things we as black women are taught early on is what we should fear: "That is not for me—or they can do that, but I cannot." I understand that we all experience fear. Fear can be very normal, but my advice to sisters everywhere is to run as fast as you can to that thing you fear the most because the thing we fear the most often holds us back from our destiny. You all know what I am talking about because we have all experienced it. "Fear" shows up as a knot in our stomach, that voice that says "I don't deserve this," the well-meaning friend who says,

"What if you fail?," the naysayers who rant, "You are not good enough." All of this for us as black women comes from being told we are not "good enough." It is time for us to change that way of thinking once and for all.

Many of you know my story. I did not go to college. I am not a lawyer or doctor by training. I was raised in a very religious family, and to be honest I feared God at times thinking that if I made a mistake he would punish me. I now know that is not the God I serve. My mom always wanted to go to college, but she never saw her dreams realized. That breaks my heart to this day. I think that is what propelled me to such great heights. I did not want to leave this life without making all my dreams come true. So when I reluctantly took my friend Star Jones' seat on *The View*, I told her I was afraid. *What could I possibly bring to the table I thought?* She encouraged me. She told me I had a lot to bring and that God would not have brought me to this place if that were not so. There was a sister who was moving on, and she was encouraging me through my fear.

To be candid, sisters, my entire career has been running toward my fears but that fear started in me as a child. Like many of us I was raised with limitations. I started as a stand-up comic in 1991 at *The Comedy Act Theatre* in Los Angeles and I was scared to death—my back was to the audience almost the entire time. I got booed and heckled. DL Hughley encouraged me to get back on the stage despite my fear, and Eddie Griffin said the same thing. It was the hardest thing I ever had to ever do—to go back on that stage. But I did and look where God has brought me. He can do the same for you—ability without faith means nothing sisters.

One last word: I too once lived, ate, and breathed my career. It was everything until I had my son. Why? Because I had dreams and wanted to accomplish them. I saw friends with these knuckle heads, and I had to make a choice—did I want a legacy or a career? I had to put my career on hold, but I trusted that if God put both desires in my heart, my career and a desire for family that I could have both. God knows what he has for you. Fear and faith cannot reside in the same place. My hope for each of you is to run toward life with all of your heart. Live it boldly and courageously. Know that no matter who you are, or where you may be starting your life's journey that you do bring something to the game. Let go of lack, sisters, and embrace the possibilities for your life. When I faced the fear and stepped out on faith, the things God desired for me came into fruition.

# Black Women, What do You Want? Better Yet, What do You Need?

## By Roland S. Martin

Award-winning journalist, nationally syndicated columnist, and host of TV-One's *Washington Watch*

The fundamental problem most men and women have is that they don't know what to distinguish in a potential mate. I've met countless women who have a "want" list that could fill a legal pad. Yet when you ask them what they "need," you get a confused look—as if you're talking to a two-year-old.

No woman will ever know what she needs in a man until she takes a personal inventory to understand who she is; why she behaves the way she does; where she has come from; what has gone right and wrong in her previous relationships; and what God's will is for her life.

I took such an inventory after my divorce eleven years ago, and it helped me recognize what I needed in a partner. After the split, I dated several women who had the potential to be fantastic mates. But as I was in prayer, God revealed to me that they were not what I "needed." As He began to reveal my future, He began to show me the kind of woman I "needed," and eventually I met that woman.

We typically only assess ourselves after we have gone through traumatic situations. But I implore every single man and woman to take inventory—to learn who they are, where they are going in life, and what kind of mate they need for the journey. The man or woman for you may not be the doctor or lawyer you had in mind. The right person could be a minister making $2,000 a month or a mechanic who will love you unconditionally and not be jealous of your career. It's time we cut the crap about degrees, houses, cars, and bank accounts. I thank God that He sent me a spiritually prosperous woman with a loving heart, rather than a cold-hearted one with a large 401K.

# We Aren't Intimidated, Sisters— Just Show Us the Real You

## By Finesse Mitchell

Author, speaker, and *Essence* contributor

It is often said that black men won't approach educated, successful black women because they're intimidated. *That is simply not true.* Most dating men will tell you that their assumption is that a sister already has a man— not intimidation—and that keeps our motor in neutral. Dating men will also tell you that they're *turned off* by the sense of entitlement that some accomplished women exude. Nonetheless, black men and black women perpetuate stereotypes about each other that have definitely influenced the game.

But black women need to know that black men who are about something *want* smart, accomplished women with inner and outer beauty. They don't mind if you're the CEO of a Fortune 500 company or a neighborhood nail technician, as long as they see that you are as affectionate and nurturing at home as you are driven at work.

So if your search for a man of equal status keeps landing you in Heartbreak Hotel, *try something different.* Don't hang on to a man who looks good "on paper" but doesn't click with you spiritually or make you laugh. Dating men who have something more to offer than a driven, competitive nature isn't settling. It's widening your horizons. So if your hard work has led to financial success, enjoy the fruits of your labor. But avoid becoming cocky or selfish—lose your sense of entitlement. Finding and keeping love is hard, but being lovable makes it easier.

# Love Doesn't Have to Be Hard

### By Lamar and Ronnie Tyler

*Essence* bloggers and founders of BlackandMarriedWithKids.com

Young sisters, as you transition into the full-fledged, beautiful journey of womanhood, remember to follow your heart but also your head. Many a young woman's life has been altered by not listening to her intuition, the amazing gift that God has blessed her with. Think of the years of schooling, the hard work, and everything else that has gone into making you the beautiful person you are today. It can be instantly washed away by making the wrong choices in your personal life.

In your personal relationships remember, above all else, that love doesn't have to be hard. Often we hear others say that going through the bad parts of a relationship makes a couple stronger or that the first few years of marriage are tough. *Really?* Don't subscribe to what others think a relationship should be; remain steadfast in the belief that God has his best reserved for you.

# Sisters, Tap into Your True Power: Lead the Brothers by Example

### By Warren Ballentine, Esq.

Nationally syndicated radio talk-show host, *The Warren Ballentine Show*

When I think of strong black women, I think of the women in my family first.

I owe my success as an attorney, activist, and radio show host to three such women: my grandmother, my mother, and my aunt. Just watching these amazing women showed me the strength of independent women and also gave me the strength to be the man that I am today. These women taught me how to be self-sufficient, caring, and loving. They also taught me the kind of woman I deserve to have in my life. They taught me to love the sisters who may be overlooked by society as too strong, too independent, too much of this and too much of that—the sister doctors, lawyers, and other professionals.

I have such admiration for First Lady Michelle Obama and for all the sisters out there who do it all every day—raise their kids, hold down careers, and love their men. Most women don't get the power that you have over us as men. A woman can make a lazy man work and help change a boy into a man. Sisters, you are queens. It's in your DNA! It's up to you to tap into that DNA and teach your special brand of compassion, strength, and loyalty to the next generation of queens and kings. My mother, aunt, and grandmother did not have a formal education, but they tapped into their DNA daily with strength, grace, and love that showed the harsh world everyday that they were in fact queens. The question is, will you?

# The Healing Power of Intimacy

## By Omar Tyree

NAACP Award winner, best-selling author

My mother and my aunts were self-sufficient women. My mother, the oldest, showed her sisters the ropes by graduating third in her high school class, acquiring an academic scholarship to college, and finishing pharmacy school on time. She accomplished all of this before buying her own home at the tender age of twenty-six, without marrying my handsome but shiftless father. So, I was used to independent, intelligent, hustling women who did whatever it took to progress. Because my mother was a go-getter, I tended to date women in the same vein. If a woman didn't have her own life or make her own money, I wasn't interested.

But I learned along the way that my attraction to women like this, however, only goes so far. *Intimacy* seems to be a non-issue for most driven women I know. Perhaps so many juggling-it-all sisters have had to do so much as single moms, caretakers, and providers that it has left them too tired for love. This is something real that we need to talk about across the gender lines. But for me, and, subsequently, for the woman in my life, intimacy—the need and desire for it—is a major requirement for fulfillment.

So, how do independent women manage to work, raise kids, excel in their careers and still have me-time, and find time to be intimate with their men—who definitely want and need to be intimate with them? I don't have an answer. But committed men have to juggle multiple activities during the day like their women do. They work, pay bills, raise and discipline kids, and find me-time without losing their need, their desire, for the human healing of intimacy. So regardless of what is going on brothers and sisters during the day, men and women alike need to find time to be intimate in order to sustain a healthy and happy relationship.

# Giving Him Something He Can Feel

## By Harold T. Fisher

WHUR radio host and author of the romance novel
*Two Weeks to the Rest of My Life*

Sisters I want you to think along these lines in the romance department: ask yourself other than great sex and financial success, what do you offer a man that he can't get from other women?

It's a hard but important question for black women searching for a mate. I ask because my heart goes out to single black women, many of whom are hurting because they haven't found their heart's desire. Too often they ask me, "Where are the single guys?" or "Why is it so hard to find a *good man?*" I always answer with questions that make them think: "Are you a good woman?," "How do you define 'good'?," "What qualities do you offer?"

Women often discuss what *men* must bring to a relationship, as if they all have *it* together. Educated, accomplished, sexy, fashionable divas are *a dime a dozen*—and they're two dozen for a nickel on their way to church on Sunday mornings. Just kidding with you, sisters. All kidding aside, there is nothing wrong with being an independent woman. If a man is secure, your success won't be an issue, but don't beat him over the head with it.

Men also discuss what they're looking for in a mate. Many, for example, say they want a woman whose personality glows from the *inside*. But she's hard to find. So I ask you, "Are you genuinely kind?," "Do men *really* enjoy your company?," "Are you friendly?," "Do you smile easily—or do you look as if you've been sucking lemons?," "Can you make a man laugh—with you, not at you?," "Are you affectionate?," "Are you easy to talk to?" Answering yes to these questions *is a good beginning*.

# We Need to Learn the "Value" of Each Other

## By Jeffrey Johnson

MSNBC/TheGrio.com special correspondent, *Tom Joyner Morning Show*, award-winning activist, journalist, motivational speaker, and author of *Everything I am Not, Made Me Everything I Am*

I hate to say this sisters but I know a lot of brothers who simply don't like women. No, not like that—they want to "possess" women for what they can bring to their lives, but not value women for who they are independent of "us." I know this to be true, because I was that kind of selfish brother once. We can all speculate and hypothesize about what has gone wrong between black men and black women but at the end of the day it really isn't that complicated. The challenge as I see it is that we all need to relearn the concept of "value." *We live in a throw-away culture.*

Our conditioning and modeling as black men has not been to place value on being a husband or on building a successful friendship with women we love because far too many of us simply have not seen it modeled. So, we place value on what can she do for me instead of where it should properly be on a woman's heart, her calling, her love of children, or in how she inspires me as a man to be my best self. The same goes for you, sisters. You often place value on the wrong things in the men you seek. You value his job, his degree, his car, his success, instead of valuing *first* how he will treat you, love you, honor, and protect you. You turn him into a resume instead of looking at his intrinsic value and worth as a human being with whom you can build a life. This needs to change for both men and women—we need to communicate and start valuing one another for who we are, not what we have.

# Choose Balance Sisters

## By Angelo B. Henderson

Pulitzer Prize-winning journalist, Detroit Radio One talk-radio host

Many women—and men, too—make the mistake of expecting too much from their jobs. Supervisors are not hired to make you feel appreciated, loved, supported, or nurtured. Companies are not designed to define your value and significance or to make you feel whole. Employers are not designed to caress your cares or soothe your fears. And coworkers should not be confused with friends. Learn to separate your worlds!

Someone once said: "Show me how you spend your time, and I'll show you what you value." As you invest your time in ascending the ladder of success, remember that what you do *is not* who you are. Learn to create balance in your life. Work hard, but remember to make time for God, family, and friends. The opposite of balance is bitterness—you choose.

How will you create this balance? First, I recommend a loving relationship with the Lord that will keep your priorities ordered, as well as your steps. I also encourage you to have multiple streams of income—don't depend solely on one job as Sophia writes in chapter ten. I also believe that marriage and motherhood are two wonders of the world that every woman should experience.

Finally, in relationships, always remember the power of the purr. Strong black men appreciate and applaud successful, accomplished, competitive—and often vocal—black women. But to attract and keep us, leave that aggressive "do-it-my-way" roar at the workplace. *Vulnerability is sexy.* When you're home, put away your cares of the workday. Relax, and *purr* in our arms.

# It is Possible to Have it All, Sisters

## By Kimberly Elise

Award-winning actress, *Woman Thou Art Loosed, Diary of a Mad Black Woman,
The Great Debaters, Gifted Hands: The Ben Carson Story,* and *For Colored Girls*

I am a living testimony that it is possible to have career, family, and marriage at the beginning of one's life, in your twenties if that's what you desire. But the key to having it all is self-care first. We've all heard the airline stewardess say, "in case of an emergency put on your own oxygen mask first before tending to others." That, for me, has been the secret to my success: taking care of *self* first.

Young sisters, if I can provide any guidance to your generation I would tell you the following: First, make yourself a priority. Take care of yourself spiritually, emotionally, and physically so that you are able to hear your inner voice (your God voice), and make decisions and choices that serve you best. When you do this in divine order, it will in turn serve everything and everyone else in your world positively as well. Second, if you choose to marry young and start a family then you and your spouse must work as a team. I chose to put my family before my career and based every decision I made on that structure. Yes, it was challenging at times but we made it work with the help of a great support system.

I have also found throughout my life's journey that when I am true to my inner voice and spirit all of the pieces of my life work well and in balance. Because I took care of myself, I was better able to offer my family more of me. I was able to be a happy, vibrant, fully alive, and available wife and mother for my family. And although my husband and I eventually divorced, there are no regrets. I was able to sustain an amazing sixteen-year marriage, as well as have a fabulous career.

Sisters know this, that sometimes despite your best efforts, and despite still loving one another, your relationships can change. The key thing for me and my ex-husband is that we love our children, and our oldest daughter is now a powerful young woman attending college in Paris, and our youngest is blossoming beautifully in her own right. Yes, my life is happy, my career is thriving and most importantly my spirit is shining and alive!

Remember this: It is possible!

# Achieve Higher Heights, Boldly and Confidently

## By Florida Lieutenant Governor Jennifer Carroll (R-FL)

The first African American to be elected to that office in the state of Florida

Many women stand on the shoulders of the brave work and sacrifices of women like Harriet Tubman, Sojourner Truth, Mary McLeod Bethune, Madame C.J. Walker, or Dr. Condoleezza Rice.

All of these women paved the way to battle many laws and rules that oppressed women. Because of their hard work, society changed, mentality changed, policy changed, and a clear path was made to make the journey to ascension much easier for women.

From early on in my military career, I realized that being a woman in a man's world was not going to be easy. There were times when it seemed as if it would be best for me to lose my femininity to get along or to fit in. At times, I thought it may be best to get as rough and tough as the men just to fit in. What I discovered was that to achieve success in a man's world, I needed to take a different path—be myself. I believe that all women should not be afraid to showcase their talents, intelligence and confidence to achieve excellence. This excellence will emanate where it cannot be ignored.

The skills, talents, flexibility, forward-thinking acumen that women possess are attributes for the professional world, and for this women should embrace their God-given gifts and use it to achieve higher heights, boldly and confidently.

# Be a Sister Mentor: It Changes Lives for the Better

## By Cory Booker, Mayor of Newark, New Jersey (D-NJ)

As Mayor of Newark, New Jersey, I am inspired and encouraged by the talent, intelligence, and spirit of the young women I see every day. More and more I see how our young women can truly blossom when exposed to mentors who are also gifted, experienced, wise, and visionary. In the black community there is a powerful history of women leaders—courageous women of strength and determination—who helped sustain, transform, and empower our larger community. This tradition must continue. Yet, the challenges our young women face grow more vast and complex. While men often receive empowering messages from the larger community, black women often receive—from the media, the work place, and even amongst peers—disempowering messages that attack their spirits and seek to undermine their potential. Yet, black women still demonstrate an incredible capacity to "do it all."

I applaud Sophia for dealing with these issues in a candid and uncompromising book. More than this, she celebrates the lives of black women and enables readers to draw lessons, inspiration, and strength from the examples she highlights in her writing. Finally, she calls all readers to answer the call of our ancestors, to continue our tradition and meet our societies current challenges through service, leadership, and a steadfast commitment to improving oneself through helping others.

Finally, life is not a spectator sport. We cannot allow ourselves to simply sit on our couches and give passionate color commentary about what is happening in the community around us and how it must change, yet do nothing. Being a mentor in a young girl or woman's life can make all the difference. If we want the world to change, it must start with us as individuals and our own actions. If we want young sisters to make better choices, get a good education, and make a positive contribution to society then they have to see that first modeled in us as adults.

# What is Your Vision for Your Life
## By Valorie Burton
Life and executive coach, author, speaker, *Essence* and
*O Magazine* contributor

What do you want your life to look like twenty years from now? In other words, what's your vision—not just for your career and bank account, but for your *life?* It can be easy to pour your energy into the area of your life where you feel you have the most control: work. But if you don't pour as much energy into laying the groundwork for a healthy relationship, the life you end up with twenty years from now may look quite different from the one you imagine.

In my work with women, especially high-achieving African American women, many of us have figured out how to excel at work. More and more, we have fabulous career role models who look like us. But even at the highest levels, we too often don't have what we want in love. Whether you didn't have a strong model of a healthy, happy relationship growing up or your relationships as an adult have left you unsure of yourself, now is the time to lay the foundation for a happy relationship.

My challenge to you: Face your fears. Deal with your issues (and we all have them). Don't just look for a mentor who will guide your career. Find a mentor who has succeeded at love. If you need to overcome past hurts, be as tenacious about becoming whole and healthy, loving and desirable, as you are about furthering your education, excelling at work, and growing that paycheck.

# Make the Most of Small Opportunities
## By Fredricka Whitfield
### CNN Anchor

Everyone starting out in life likes to think big—*big* as in opportunity, a paycheck, or a lifestyle. Well, wanting and getting aren't always in sync. And honestly, I'm so glad that incongruence was there for me in my early twenties, just before I graduated from college.

I fantasized—no, not fantasized—I felt with unabashed assurance that I'd land my first on-air reporter job in a big American city, such as Washington, earning a healthy salary of $35,000 or more per year (that was a lot of money back then). I was just a green sprout, but I didn't think that at the time. I thought that because I believed in my ability and my vision—and because as an undergraduate I had held six internships at publications and television and radio stations—that I was ready. I thought I could hang with the big dogs, as I never even considered failure.

I thank my parents and my first gymnastics coach for my bluster. They discouraged me from ever saying or thinking "I can't." But I was due for a comeuppance, which came after an interview for my first on-air job in Charleston, South Carolina. After being offered the gig for $13,000 a year, I wanted to say, "No way, I'm worth more than that." Afterwards, I called my mom on the payphone at the Charleston airport to complain. I expected her to say, "Baby, you're right. They don't know your value. Something else will come along." To the contrary, Mom said, "And you're taking it." That sent me right back down to earth. I knew Mom was right. You've got to crawl before you walk. Bigger and better come later—after you've *earned* it. That job in Charleston, the one with the skimpiest paycheck, rewarded me with the richest of learning experiences—both professionally and personally.

# The Formula for Success: Confidence and People Skills

## By Gloria Mayfield Banks

### Entrepreneur, motivational speaker, and Mary Kay executive

Two life and career values that will help you succeed are *confidence* and *people skills*. Your confidence will draw people to you. Your people skills will move people to want to be in your space. Both of these are learned skills—and with attention they can be your greatest assets.

Confidence is important, so work to grow yours. Confident people share their wisdom, look you in the eyes, and have a steady voice and humble spirit. Confident people serve and lift up others. While you're working to increase your confidence, it's okay to "fake it 'til you make it"—as long as you do so with integrity.

Good people skills are invaluable. Perfect the art of making *everyone* you meet feel important. When you concentrate on what is important to the people in your space, they may not remember what you said, but they will remember how they felt in your space.

I define success as *joy*. Because I always radiate confidence and practice my best people skills, I bring success and joy into my life and my career.

# Inspiration to Pursue a Career in the Performing Arts

## By Rae Dawn Chong

Actress, *Soul Man*, *The Color Purple*, and *Constellation*

Pursuit of a career in the arts is a fascinating journey. You become a communicator, a teacher, a friend, and a lover. These are the things you become because of a performance, a gesture, a word or words spun into a mystical magical love infused moment. It is all about a "moment." Never forget to live in the moment. Oh sure, we as women have to worship our bodies as best we can, and maybe not taking care of our bodies is also a statement. I am not going to demand thinness from young women who take this path; in fact the only thing I will demand is *true connection* and *total commitment* and *fearlessness* in *whatever* you are presenting or cre- ating. In life, don't stop *at less* than *your all*; *give it your all* whatever it is that you do. Commit completely to your art *fearlessly*. If you do this, I promise you that you will be successful because when you love you and pursue your craft with passion, you will attract others to you and make what you do irresistible.

# Time Management is Everything!

## By Sirena Moore-Thomas

Entrepreneur, mom, and motivational speaker

As a young woman who started out as a teenage mother, sometimes it is hard to believe that I am now a CEO, mother, and wife all at once. Time management has truly been key to my success. We are all given the same twenty-four hours, and it's all about how you use them. Most small busi- ness owners, like myself, have a family, other business ventures, church obligations, community obligations, school obligations, so we have a lot to balance. The first thing that you must do in order to get the most out of your day is create a list of "time-wasting activities." These are activities that can in no way help you reach your goals such as mindless telephone conversations, viewing friends' pictures on Facebook, watching television for hours at a time, and the list goes on. Once you identify what you waste time doing, you can now consciously avoid those activities in an effort to boost your productivity.

Here are a few time-management techniques that I use. I schedule outside meetings on Thursdays and Fridays only. On these two days I try to schedule as many meetings as possible. I call it "meeting marathons." In essence, I don't take meetings in the middle of the day, come back to the office, try to get something done, go back out for another meeting, come back again to answer phones calls, check e-mail, and so on. Those interruptions just slow down productivity. So I commit only certain days to meetings. Here's another, within my office we have instituted something called "productivity hour." From the hours of eleven to twelve each day there is absolutely no talking in the office. We use that time to focus on the projects that have made it to our to-do list. Allow me to explain: people do not do projects—people do tasks, so it's important that you review your to-do list and remove the projects. For example, *Plan Upcoming Staff Meeting* is *not* a task—it's a project— it requires several tasks in order to be complete so I encourage my office staff to set aside that one hour—from eleven to twelve—to focus solely on completing one project.

Always remember time is not just money, time is *everything*! It is the one thing in this world that you cannot recover once wasted.

# Loving Others Starts with Loving Yourself
## By Dr. Michelle Callahan
Psychologist, author, TV personality, *Women's Health* magazine columnist

Oh, how powerful and committed we are as mothers! We watch over our children with such care and concern for every aspect of their lives. We teach them how to care for themselves, making sure that they master personal grooming, brush their teeth twice a day, get a good nights sleep, eat well-rounded nutritious meals, and stay physically active. We insist that they study hard every day, do well in school, and make eager plans for the future. And most importantly, we tell them how beautiful, smart, funny, blessed, special, and loved they are because we want them to feel empowered to do and be their best.

But do we walk the talk? Are we walking shining examples of all that we tell them to be or have we stopped loving ourselves in the very way we know we must be loved in order to not only survive, but thrive? Are we taking time out each day to carefully watch what we eat, get a good night's sleep, exercise, or invest time in our own personal growth? Are we telling ourselves how beautiful we are? Are we looking enthusiastically into the future or walking through each day with dread? In order to be successful at work, at home, and in the community, you must nurture your mind, body and spirit. You cannot successfully lead, raise, or take care of others until you take care of yourself. You cannot properly love others until you love yourself enough to tell yourself all the things you need to know to march through each day hopeful, with your head held high no matter what you have to face. If you love your kids enough to do it for them, love them enough to do it for you. They need you to be all that you need them to be. It's never too late to redefine and rebuild— start by loving and nurturing *yourself* first.

# Don't Diminish the Greatness Within

## By Avis A. Jones-DeWeever

### Executive director of the National Council of Negro Women

Somewhere someone said, "You can't have it all." I implore you: do not accept that precept as your reality. Instead, understand that life is not always linear. It is not a rigid path that we embark on at birth, and march through unwavering in our destination until we draw our final breath. In my estimation, it is perhaps more accurately thought of as a series of interlocking circles; cycles that each represent ever-evolving aspects of all of those distinct characteristics, abilities, and possibilities that in the end, create that one special being that the world knows as you.

This realization is key. For it reminds us that while today we may not have checked off every little box that we think we need to find "happiness," the reality is, maybe the box that we covet isn't yet supposed to be in play. That's not to say you'll never have what your desire. Nor does it imply that in time you won't come to reassess the value of what you now believe to be of exceeding importance. It just means, not today.

Perhaps there is no aspect of life that is more likely to get us "stuck" in this way, than the quest for love. It breaks my heart to hear young sisters—beautiful, intelligent, vibrant, and capable young sisters question the wisdom in truly being all that they can be for fear that it will limit their romantic possibilities. To that young sister I say, consider the degree to which you would not only limit yourself, but would also inhibit the world's ability to experience the unique greatness that you alone possess. Also, imagine the life that you would be sentencing yourself to if forever you had to be careful not to be who and what you were truly meant to be? Instead, take solace in the fact that perhaps it is just not time yet for him to walk into your life. My parents provide for me a living breathing example of this principle. Each was over thirty-five when they married and my mother was forty when she birthed me. Today, in their eighties, they are still loving each other, caring for one another, and enjoying life with the zeal and zest that many would ascribe to individuals half their age. They were patient.

And though their love did not come on the traditional time-line, particularly in the era in which they met, it came at the *right* time. At a time when they each knew themselves, knew what they wanted out of life, and knew what they needed in a life-long partner. In the meantime, they were both accomplished and independently successful. But together, they were unstoppable! Yes, they now have it all. It was worth the wait.

# A Few Simple Tidbits for Success in Your Life's Journey

### By Jill Nelson

*New York Times* best-selling author, journalist, and speaker; her latest book is titled, *Let's Get it On*

Choose work you love.
Find exercise you enjoy.
Surround yourself with people you love and who love you.
Be authentic, and the universe will handle the details.

# Take it One Day at a Time

### By Lonnae O'Neal Parker

*Washington Post* reporter and author of *I Am Every Woman*

You can have the best hand in the world but still play yourself badly. You can pursue your career to the exclusion of all else. But do that, and you neglect relationships with family and friends. You won't eat right or exercise, and your health will suffer. You will lack time for reflection, and your self-worth will feel predicated on achievement and acquisition. Even the most ambitious life is about balance, seasons, and finding your reset button, so mark your time wisely.

Decide the hours, days, and years that you will give yourself fully to work, and go hard! Then, just as intentionally, make time to set that work aside. Find spaces to connect with other passions and people, and all the things that make you most beautifully human. This will give your work, when you return to it, more focus and meaning. Take the time, because no one will ever give it to you. Recognize when you are out of balance (or just plain tripping) and check yourself: meditate, exercise, breathe, pray. Learn to hit your reset button—daily if you need to—because we all fall down. But the crying shame is to stay there because we haven't developed the resilience or tools or knowledge of self to get back up. Run from negative voices, especially the ones inside your own head. Speak love, and wait for all the love that comes back your way.

And remember, you can have it all—*just rarely on the same day.*

# The Sister Revolution is Now
## By Michaela Angela Davis
### Image activist, cultural critic, and writer

What a time this is: a real time, a touchable time, and a time that feels like it belongs to us. A time we imagined, and then we built. It's finally our time sisters. And who are we? We are the "significant others," the ones who have the color, the ones who have the children. We are the ones who've been working and waiting. We've been waiting to get to our real work. The work of this generation, this woman, this person of color is to heal.

This is the time to untangle our nappy web of historic wounds. Time to no longer lengthen our legacy of pain. We've been paid for by those who died so that we could live, vote, and not be burned or hung from trees. Those who struggled left us debt free so we could rap about Ladies First and be First Ladies. Time to let the blood of past battles dry, for a fresh gash needs our tending. Our aching minds and our injured spirits cry out for our care. This time it's not about standing on a picket line, it's about lying on a therapist's couch, and kneeling before an altar and having a relationship with a power greater than our fears. Like our ancestors we must be fearless, tireless, and focused on our future brothers and sisters. This time, *healing* is the revolution!

# To Live Well: Show Up Ready
## By Terrie M. Williams
Author of *Black Pain: It Just Looks Like We're Not Hurting*

Our lives are already written—all we have to do is show up. What I've learned the hard way is that *that* is the most difficult part. I don't mean us being physically present—I mean being genuinely true to ourselves. We have nothing—and cannot be all God has called us to be—without our mental and emotional health. Have the pure courage to listen carefully to your heart, your inner voice. It always tells you what to do, but too often, we ignore it or second-guess what we have sensed and heard. Be you. I can promise that if you don't, you will learn that spiritual suicide is death just the same.

Too often we go through this life thinking and doing but not *feeling*—wearing a mask, going through the motions, trying to be superwoman (it's a myth, and you will die trying to be one). However, real power is when your presence—your actions and words—awakens something inside of people, influences them, and transforms their spirit. I love you too much to say anything less than the truth, as I know it—straight no chaser. What I know is that I can't be who I'm supposed to be until you become who you are supposed to be. *Stay strong—and share your light.*

# Activate Your Worthiness
## By Dr. Tricia Bent-Goodley
Professor of sociology at Howard University

You are worthy. As Black women we give so much of ourselves to the people around us. Some of us are emotionally depleted, our spirits hemorrhaging and no one seems to notice. Well I want to remind you that you are worthy. Knowing you are worthy is not just about loving yourself. It means honoring yourself with your choices and who you choose to allow in your circle. Knowing you are worthy is a verb. It means not settling for a man because others think you need to be with somebody. It means loving yourself enough to not let anyone hurt, harm, or hinder you. It means standing on the principle of the matter when it does not feel good but it is right for you. It means honoring your intuition, which, I believe, is God's way of quietly speaking to us at critical moments. You are worthy of yourself definition and not how others conveniently compartmentalize us as black women. You are worthy of relationships that love, affirm, and respect your mind, body, and spirit. You are worthy of being cared for, pampered, and the silence of sacred moments. Activate your sense of worthiness and honor the *you* that God created.

# Redefining the Meaning of Sexual Freedom: You Are Worth the Wait

By Dr. Lindsay Marsh Warren

Anesthesiologist, inspirational author, entrepreneur, and founder of Worth the Wait Revolution, Inc.

Of all the things you may learn in this life, nothing is more valuable than knowing your *value*!

You are precious. Your price is far above rubies. Your body is God's temple, and when you truly understand your price, you'll never give out another discount. This is my call to inspire you to recognize that *you are worth the wait*. I know. I waited and was a virgin (in my thirties) until my wedding day which took place last October 2010. My journey with my husband has been chronicled in newspapers and media nationwide. Waiting changed us both. We were both attractive, vibrant, whole people who made the commitment to wait. Sex is a beautiful experience created by God to be enjoyed by two people committed in a covenant of marriage. This is a special gift that you and your husband can enjoy, together, one amazing day. Don't promise this gift to someone undeserving. Don't allow the media, the mainstream, and the misguided to pressure you. Virginity is beautiful. Waiting is admirable. I challenge you to pursue virtue, integrity, and purity while keeping your own beautiful "swagga." Sophia has nailed it in this book, you can be sensual and sacred all at once. Your spirit will shine all the brighter when you embrace this truth. Then, the man who truly respects and honors you will be willing to love, not just lust after, you. He will prefer you to himself. He will treasure you above his desires. The man who truly deserves you will recognize that *you are worth the wait,* and so is he.

# Show Your Body Some Love
## By Kacy Duke
Author of *The Show It Love Workout,* fitness expert, and cofounder
of Equinox Fitness Clubs

I believe that since we ask so much of our bodies—to be sexy, to be powerful, to be strong—that we must take time to respect and nourish our physical beings, especially as African American women. We are doing more with our bodies as mothers (many times as single mothers), as career women, caretakers and providers. But do we take the time to really develop a personal relationship with our bodies?

We treat it like a stepchild and drag it along, as opposed to treating it like a friend. But I believe that the most important relationship we can have in this world is with ourselves, and that includes taking the time to develop a relationship with our bodies and show it love. We are so busy developing relationships outside of ourselves and being the friend, the mother, the significant other. However, in order to reach our full potential, we have to have a better relationship with ourselves—our mind, body, and spirit.

The process of appreciating and honoring your body is something that all women, especially African American women, need to do right now. Exercise: it's that exertion of energy that makes you think in a different way. It gives you a better foundation. Forget about all of the diet and fitness trends that failed you in the past. Move on. Understand and accept that the past is your teacher. It is not baggage. The present is your creation. How are you developing yourself and creating great things so that you can glow and grow?

The future? The future is your inspiration. What do you see that's inspiring you to take care of yourself? Do you ever look at what you want as far as being healthy and fit and living a long life? Being honest with yourself and tap into your inner strength. Stand in the mirror and look at yourself. Acknowledge the fact that you are more than a pair of thighs. You are more than a belly. You are a heart and a mind and a spirit. Your thoughts and feelings affect your body. Know that you are powerful, loved, and capable. You are one beautiful and complete entity. Now go create your beautiful body!

# Are You a Mammy:
# Stop Taking Care of Everyone but You

## By Rhonda Joy McLean, Esq.

Deputy General Counsel, Time Inc., and coauthor of
*The Little Black Book of Success*

Do you rush to assist others in your personal and professional lives, without taking good care of yourself? Are you known as the "go-to" person to "fix things" or "get things done" in your family and workplace? While it is admirable to be helpful to others and essential to be responsible, you may be doing yourselves a disservice.

If you find that you do not have time to handle your own personal business in a timely manner—getting your bills paid on time (knowing where they are), going to the doctor(s) regularly and maintaining a healthy regimen (healthy diet, regular exercise, appropriate rest, spiritual attention, etc.)—when you may be just a little too helpful to others and not helpful enough to yourself.

Sometimes we become overwhelmed not only by our own job duties and family responsibilities, but also by additional things we have promised to do for others, including some things that they could do themselves. When you find that your plate is a bit too full and most of the items on that plate are for other people, then you may be in danger of becoming the "Mammy," according to *The Little Black Book of Success:*

*Laws of Leadership for Black Women,* by Elaine Meryl Brown, Marsha Haygood, and Rhonda Joy McLean (Random House/One World Press, March, 2010). You need to step back and take a look at how and why you are taking on too much.

Women in general and women of color in particular have been charged throughout history to take care of others, whether their own or someone else's children, households or businesses. We are genetically programmed to set the needs of others above our own, and it can be quite difficult to talk ourselves off the ledge of "giving ourselves away." Especially where we are responsible for children, parents, other elderly relatives or incompetent or overly needy colleagues, we have to learn to *put that foot down!*

You can actually improve your ability to help others if you help yourself first—whether by learning to say "no" and mean it, deciding to delegate, managing your own expectations as well as those of others, or just seeing yourself and your role(s) differently. If you are taking on too much in order to impress others, you might be surprised to learn that they may see you as disorganized and not a good manager, since you're probably stretched too thin with all of those other people's tasks to perform as well as your own.

One thing is certain. If you do not respect yourself and your time, no one else will.

Don't be the "*Mammy!*" Nurture yourself instead and find new ways to move forward.

# Suporting Our Military with a New Generation of Military Spouses

## By Mrs. Lucille Pittard

Educator and wife of Major Gen. Dana J.H. Pittard (USA)

The Army motto is: "There is strong . . . and then there is Army Strong."

I am an educator by profession but I am an Army spouse by choice. I have spent over twenty years in the classroom educating our youth, but it is my role as an Army officer wife for the past twenty-five years that has brought me to the pages of this book.

The military expects much from their leaders. It's one of the few career fields where the spouse can be a major asset. But lines are blurry and not easy to navigate in this new world as there is no textbook. It's a life where there are expectations, but at the same time all work is voluntary. Over the years, more and more spouses have chosen to work outside the home which translates to creativity when trying to juggle home, work, and family . . . and unit volunteering. Yet, many of us have done it and done it well.

Sure, over the years I have struggled as a woman to find the right balance between the above. In this current *optempo* of dual wars it is even more difficult. I am proud of the growth I have made over the years and that I have seen in the young women I have mentored. It takes a special person to live this life. And we as black women are becoming more and more of a force within the U.S. Military force. Know that if you choose this life, no two days are the same. With deployments the unexpected is always just a "knock on the door" away. I am hopeful that a new generation of young women will likewise lead as officers themselves but also as the devoted spouse of an officer or enlisted personnel. You have no idea how valuable you are to our service members and to our nation.

I recently spearheaded the *Resilient Leader Spouse Academy* here on our post. It provides an opportunity for leader spouses to learn resiliency and bond with fellow spouses at the same time.

I believe being a military spouse is a calling . . . for you young women who are living this life—I applaud you, and can only say . . . HOO-AH!

# You Are Never Too Young to Make a Difference

## By Rep. Alisha Thomas Morgan (D-GA)

Youngest member of the Georgia House of Representatives, wife,
mother, speaker, and author

Never apologize for being young. If you don't see a space for yourself in the world you choose, create one. Never ask for permission to walk in your destiny. Some people will tell you that you're too young. That is their problem. But be patient: As you go about doing what you've been called to do, people will adjust to you being there. Earn the respect of your older colleagues by creating a niche for yourself. Become an expert in a particular area so you are the go-to person. Earn the reputation of a hard worker, and people won't focus on your age.

If a mentor doesn't seek you out, ask someone you admire to advise you. Having a mentor, however, doesn't mean you are bound by his or her worldview or limitations—you simply build on the foundation he or she provides. Everyone's needs are different, so be honest with yourself and respect your intuition. As women we can exercise our options to include marriage, children, and successful careers. Don't be afraid to work toward fulfilling your desire, if it's what you truly want.

Sisters, you can have it all—but you can't be everything to everyone at once. Give whatever moment you are in 100 percent of your attention. If you are being a wife at the moment, be the best wife you can be. Be that trusted sounding board after a hard day's work, a partner in parenting, and someone to plan and share your financial future. When it's time to be a mother, give your all to your children. While at work, give it your all. Strive to be your best, and continue to walk in your destiny. Success will surely follow.

# Redefining Success for a New Age
## By Rolonda Watts
Actress, radio personality, and voiceover expert *Judge Mathis Show*

My advice to my younger sisters of a new time, in a new age, is simple: Always believe in yourself, have faith in your dreams, and live your life with passion, maintaining a positive attitude and perspective as you do it. There is tremendous power in having faith in yourself.

Much of success is how we think, so keep your thoughts optimistic and focused on positive outcomes. Good thoughts attract good things. Keep your inner eye keenly focused on all that you are most grateful for—all that you already have and all that is already all right—so you can soar to even greater heights.

Live life with passion! The great George Bernard Shaw said, "Happy is the man who can make a living by his hobby." And that applies to women too! There is nothing more delightful than seeing someone who is energetic and enthusiastic about their life and work. When you are happy, the money will follow.

Work hard. There's no substitute for hard work and no success comes without going the extra mile. So many people are under the sad spell that success happens overnight or—as seen on TV—in an hour. I often measure my many successes in my various fields by how much I had to give up to get them. Every success comes with some sacrifices, as well as from burning the midnight oil and putting in a lot of elbow grease. Success also comes from having integrity in your work and being a lady when it counts. Pretty is as pretty does in any business, circumstance, or situation.

Smile. It's the ultimate antidepressant, plus it makes you pleasing company around others and boosts your positive energy flow. Surround yourself with people and things that make you smile—even better that make you laugh. Laughter is fun, bonding, and healing. It's like antifreeze for the soul. Laughter also prolongs your life, so do it often.

Pray and exercise, as your faith, spirit, body, and mind are mighty partners in this thing called life. As challenges arise—and they will—you will be better prepared to stay centered and true to yourself no matter what. And keep your Karma good—what you put out you get back.

Give back and ask others how you can help them along the way. We don't do anything alone in life and the more you give—the more you get, so network with others who may become part of your mastermind group, sharing similar goals and resources in a common dream of success. You show me your friends, and I'll show you your future.

Never stop learning and trying new things as you discover and learn more about yourself and the beautiful gifts God gave you. I believe that God gives us all many wonderful gifts and it's our gift back to God when we use them. At the end of your spectacular life—let's hope you are all used up!

Now, go out there and conquer the world.

# Follow Your Heart . . .

## By Tamron Hall

Fill-in correspondant for the *Today* show and *Weekend Today*

When I think of the advice I want to offer you all, I end up at the same place—listen to advice but follow "your" heart.

I want you to bravely walk this journey, uncertain about the future but not afraid of making a mistake. Taking too much advice can sometimes prevent us from doing what I see as the most special part of this journey, *living*.

To feel life's joy, pain, passion, and honesty, *we must live*. This of course does not mean we can't learn from each other. Some of the most wonderful advice I have received is from people who would have never believed the impact they had on me; people I passed in the blink of an eye but their wisdom lingered for years.

Be clear, I too have made great mistakes and missteps on my life's journey but they have made me a better person. Sometimes despite the great advice I received, I spent too much money, loved the wrong man, and mixed up my priorities. I am blessed to have survived those bad calls and I am better for it. In my twenties I led with my heart and not my head; but it was the best way for me to learn. I don't regret it a single bit.

As African American women we are often seen as strident, rigid, and unwilling to take chances. This could be for any number of reasons, but for the most part we as black women are often on our own, which makes it harder to take risks. *I understand!* Bottom line, sisters: don't fear mistakes, learn from them. No one holds the key to perfection. The "secret book of answers" *is a myth*. The joy of life is the "mystery." The uncertainty of life, challenges us to live for each moment despite the possibility of it not working out the way we planned.

To me that is a life both fulfilling and one worth living.

# RESEARCH APPENDICES

*From the
Researchers Methodology
and Summary
of Key Findings*

# BOOK RESEARCH METHODOLOGY AND KEY FINDINGS SUMMARY

---

## LETTERS FROM THE LEAD RESEARCH TEAM

### Professional Black Female and National Research Statement

Kellyanne Conway

President and CEO, the polling company™, inc./WomanTrend

Sophia Nelson and I share a kinship that is part choice, part coincidence. We were born fifteen days and a few towns apart in Southern New Jersey, raised as only daughters by single, divorced moms. We are attorneys by education and political junkies by acquisition. I love her and admire the moxie, vision, intelligence, and introspection with which she has written this important book. The polling company™, inc./WomanTrend was fortunate to be included in such a timely and consequential research endeavor on behalf of *Black Woman Redefined*.

In the fifteen-year history of the company, we have conducted a plethora of qualitative and quantitative research projects aimed at understanding how women think, feel, and behave with respect to lifestyle and decision-making. Sophia's project presented unique opportunities to research and connect with professional black women, a vibrant and remarkable, yet culturally and politically underexamined, cohort.

Sophia contacted us in 2006 to share her ideas for a book on professional black women. We were tasked with helping her understand and collect data on their personal experiences, aspirations, and attitudes, and the broader expectations and implications of their lifestyle choices. It was a task that excited and inspired us.

Sophia's approach and passion for uncovering the challenges and triumphs that professional black women face in their workplace, relationships, aspirations and lives was unparalleled. After extensive discussions with Sophia, the polling company™, inc./WomanTrend developed a customized research program, which included qualitative and quantitative methods. Based on our experiences within this specific cohort of women, we understood that some unique, yet surmountable, challenges existed with respect to connecting and engaging black women and men to participate in our research exercises.

The polling company™, inc./WomanTrend utilized a series of creative methods to recruit individuals to participate in the surveys or focus groups. First, we contacted potential participants in Sophia's extensive personal and professional networks that might qualify for the online survey or focus group studies. Second, we encouraged those participating in the survey research to send on the invitation to promote a higher response. Third, we screened online survey and focus group participants according to race, gender, education, and professional occupation and drafted a customized questionnaire for this specific audience of professional black women. A full methodological description of the research program is included in the appendix of this book. We developed the research program to be methodologically and statistically sound while addressing the objectives of the project and with special consideration for the audience of professional black men and women.

We recognize that while significant, Sophia's research and analysis in the area of professional black women is just one step in understanding the unique challenges this demographic cohort faces and the momentous contributions they will continue to make to their families, peers, communities, and larger society. We were delighted to be part of this undertaking and celebrate the dynamic, soulful way professional, black women are redefining themselves and reinvigorating so many people and pathways in that pursuit. They will author the next chapters of this ongoing journey.

# Black Male Sample Research Statement
## Dr. Silas H. Lee, III, PhD, Xavier University Chair

As a researcher, I am always invigorated by the challenge to explore the issues that are familiar as well those that that present a challenge to conventional thought. This often provides an opportunity to explore the opinions and thoughts of people, the contours of their beliefs which expose the depth of their emotions and actions toward each other. I also know that very few people are willing to step onto the research battlefield to open themselves to the criticisms of many who wish to express their own points of view.

When Sophia Nelson was introduced to me by a mutual friend, the first attribute I noticed about her was her passion to learn more about the barriers which interfere with black men and women enjoying and experiencing the fullness of love and how to build the emotional bridges to nurture one another. Rather than be content with writing a catalog of stories retelling love won and lost, Sophia sought to incorporate and elevate the voices of those who have been touched by the angels of love or still feel the pain of an unsuccessful relationship. She wanted more than to quantatively measure the penetration of the experiences and opinions of black men and women in their relationships with each other, but to start a discussion to reconcile the differences. What distinguishes *Black Woman Redefined* (hereafter referred to as Redefined) is the fact that we now have a statistical baseline assessment of the experiences, attitudes and perceptions that African American men and women have about their relationships and the physical and psychological impact of those unions on the partners.

Because one goal of Redefined was to measure the opinions of black males and gain some perspicacity about their experiences in relationships, Dr. Silas Lee customized a questionnaire that was conducted via social networking sites. To ensure that respondents met the criteria to participate in the survey, potential participants were screened by race, occupation and education. After the completion of the survey, an online focus group was conducted with selected participants to further explore the thoughts and experiences of black males in their journey for a soul mate.

*Black Woman Redefined* opens the window for readers to inhale the diverse fragrances of opinions and experiences that compose the rainbow of life we often see but seldom feel with each other. This book represents the quest for all people to experience the ultimate fulfillment of life—to feel fully human and embraced by the love of another. *Black Woman Redefined* is an awakening of the mind and spirit to encourage people to do two things that often suffocate many of us from living talk and trusting one another.

# POLLING METHODOLOGY AND RESULTS[5]

One of the challenges of our research was that we knew going in that high-earning, accomplished black women in particular would be *very reluctant* to share their personal information or "business" with close associates, much less with pollsters and authors. We also worried about how to ensure that we would engender as much candor as possible on both qualitative and quantitative analyses. The research team discussed this challenge with the author in detail and as a result we decided to use some new, yet scientifically valid methods of data collection and analysis for this book.

We used what is called a national "convenience sample"[6] versus "random sample" for the black male and female quantitative research as the best way for us to hit our very specific target demographic and to be able to "over sample" the black professional population.[7] However, for the nationwide omnibus quantitative sample we did a "random" phone poll which was

---

[5] *Editor's Note:* You can find a more comprehensive overview of the research instruments, topline data, cross tabular findings, charts, focus group transcripts, and video (where authorized) via the book website www.blackwomanredefined.com in June 2011.

[6] Defined as: (sometimes known as *grab or opportunity sampling*) is a type of non-probability sampling which involves the sample being drawn from that part of the population, which is close to hand. That is, a sample population selected because it is readily available and convenient. It is also used in exploratory research where the researcher is interested in getting an inexpensive approximation of the truth. As the name implies, the sample is selected because they are convenient. This non probability method is often used during preliminary research efforts to get a gross estimate of the results, without incurring the cost or time required to select a random sample.

[7] By oversample we mean to say that if we were doing a statistically sound national poll of between 400-600 professional women, black women would only be about 10-14 percent of that number; the same rule applies to our black male survey, and that is why we oversampled there as well.

done by purchasing lists and having call centers contact people. We also utilized some new survey methods such as social networking mediums and the internet, which allowed black professional women and women alike to take the survey confidentially online. The way that we approached successfully sampling the black male/female groups was done very methodically and with the collaboration and help of many national organizations and groups. Our unique approach was as follows:

1. We defined "professional black women" as narrowly as we could by only allowing women with four-year college degrees or advanced/professional degrees to receive the survey and/or respond.
2. For the professional black male sample we broadened the education categories to allow black men with a trade (electrician, paralegal, dental tech, etc.) to be included in the sample as we knew this population would be much harder to reach and sample successfully.
3. For the white male/female, nationwide sample we agreed to attach five (5) substantive subject matter questions about the views and perceptions of white collar, white professionals about black women onto a national survey.
4. Our target age demographic was 24-34 and 35-44 because we wanted to know what GenXers and Millenniums were thinking across race and gender about black women; and we sampled older respondents 45 and up to get cross generational views and insights. Cross tabulations were professionally prepared by demographic markers to tell us how people responded to questions by age, race, gender, income, profession, and marital status.[8]
5. Respondents for this survey were selected from among the author's personal network/platform as a national media pundit and commentator and as president of iask, Inc., which is an international organization for professional black women as well as a number of prominent African American Professional networks such as National Bar Association (black lawyers), Black Doctors Association, Black Engineers, Jack & Jill of America, Coalition of 100 Black Women/Men, the black Greek lettered sororities and fraternities, Black

---

[8] This data and crosstabs are not available in the appendices section of the book along because of the size and length of the findings; however, there will be a dedicated book website that will launch in the June 2011 that will include the cross-tabular analysis or media may request such and we will provide copies at cost.

Chambers of Commerce, and regional black professional networks in Atlanta, Chicago, Philadelphia, New York, Los Angeles,
Washington, D.C., Indianapolis, San Diego, Dallas, San Antonio,
Miami, Newark, Detroit, Richmond, and Charlotte. Then they
were e-blasted or "snowballed" in order to further randomize the
sample.[9]

6. Potential respondents were screened to ensure they met the criteria
   for participation and were logged into the correct survey (e.g., professional black women were taking the survey with questions about
   them as black women and black men about their opinions and attitudes about black women).

7. We had built in "traps" to the survey that would immediately screen
   out women and men who were not part of our target demographic
   if they answered certain questions wrongly. Respondents had no
   advance knowledge of such questions or of the survey contents.

8. The sample as previously mentioned was drawn utilizing a *convenience sample*; and this is "a non-probability sampling design
   whereby people are selected for interviews because they are easily
   available," as defined by the American Association of Public Opinion
   Research. Had we used a probability sample, every person in the
   eligible universe (all black professional women, for example) would
   have the same non-zero chance of being selected. Since the surveys
   used a non-probability sample, it was not randomized in development or contact.

9. The professional black women survey instrument contained 40 questions, including twelve demographic queries. The professional black
   male survey contained twenty-two questions and five demographic
   queries. Each final questionnaire was approved by the book's author
   Sophia A. Nelson prior to fielding.

---

[9] The data have not been weighted to reflect the demographic composition of the general
black or white populations. Because the sample is based on a convenience sample rather
than a probability sample, no estimates of sampling error can be calculated. All sample
surveys and polls may be subject to multiple sources of error, including but not limited
to sampling, coverage, and measurement error.

## KEY FINDINGS—
*Black Male and Female Online National Survey Samples,*
*Regional and National Focus Group Findings,*
*and Nationwide Omnibus Findings*

We started our official research studies in May/June 2009 with qualitative focus group research to set the basis for how we would go forward with the quantitative surveys and national online focus groups. The author commissioned two in person 10 to 12 person focus groups of professional black women, which was hosted at a certified focus group facility in Washington, D.C., and run by professionally trained focus group moderators. Sessions were video and audio taped and transcripts were provided. These two focus groups were selected so we could better draft the quantitative survey tools and interviews to follow.

These regional focus groups had participants who resided in the state of Maryland, Virginia, and the District of Columbia.[10] The worldwide focus groups (which were conducted in fall 2010 online through itrack technology) included participants from Indiana, California, Atlanta, Philadelphia, Georgia, Texas, New York, Washington, D.C., Maryland, Virginia, New Jersey, and the UK. The black male worldwide focus group (which was also conducted by itrak online) included men serving in the U.S. Military Abroad (Iraq), Maryland, Washington, D.C., Indiana, Philadelphia, Atlanta, New York, Los Angeles, and Chicago. The first two test groups were *all black professional women* in the workforce and were broken down into two distinct groups. Group A was single professional black women only. Group B was married or women who had been married with children. The following online focus groups were broken out as follows: Group C was a national sample of single women or single moms who were in the workforce. Group D was a national sample of black professional men both married and single. White males and white females were interviewed extensively for this book in "informal" groups to add some measure of depth to the quantitative findings in the nationwide omnibus survey.[11]

---

[10] A summary of findings from these groups can be found in the bibliography section of the book—a professional analysis was provided in a thirty-six page report by thepollingcompany™/WomanTrend to the author in July 2009.

[11] Small groups of professional white males, females, executives, thought leaders, etc., were interviewed by the author to provide more insights and analysis to the data collected in the national random samples.

To view the topline data and questions asked in both the convenience and random sampling methods, please see the book website http://www. blackwomanredefined.com.

The summaries that follow are of "key findings" *only* and for a more comprehensive, cross-tabular analysis you can request the research reports from the publisher, research team or view them on the official book website online as of June 2011:

KEY FINDINGS—
*Black Female Focus Groups, June 2009*

Key=PBW (professional black women)

- PBW were positive toward being "Black in America" today, and many spoke to their personal educational and professional accomplishments as paramount to this observation. In fact, beyond their personal perception of the current and optimistic state of their culture, PBW believed their successes (as a demographic group) were being recognized by "mainstream" America through the media, and this new outlook was—and will continue to be—promulgated through the opportunities experienced by their daughters (and sons).
- When asked to reflect upon their definition of the "American Dream" and whether or not they believed they could achieve it, married participants certainly felt they "had it all," as did single participants, even though they had not yet reached all of the "traditional" markers of success. Many women discussed that education is a key component to living the dream and accomplishing one's goals. What's more, married participants did not necessarily feel pressure to achieve the typical definition of the "dream" (though many had), a sentiment that research has shown is typical among women of all races. The single discussants, however, were more apt to say they did *want* to achieve the goals set forth in the traditional list for most Americans.
- Both younger and older PBW experienced stereotypes in the workplace and in educational arenas due to the color of their skin. It was perseverant across both discussion groups that PBW felt they needed to take extra steps to prove themselves in these

situations. Married women commented, more specifically, that children were more of a delineating factor in the workplace over their race or marital status. Married participants seemed to ignore the plight of single PBW, signaling a disconnect between their present and past lives and an oversight of their need to prove themselves in the office as a single black woman. When pressed further about their own daughters facing challenges, they seemed uncaring—almost as if they are taking a "that won't happen to me" stance since their daughters will have the opportunities that higher education provides and the "push" needed not to experience the "single black women's plight."

- Across both discussions, PBW spoke to the real effect facing challenges in the workplace had on their personal health and well-being. The desire to prove oneself was so strong in this group that some in the session drove themselves to hypertension, shingles, and other complications.

- Health issues, such as fibroids, breast cancer, and depression had touched most participants in some way. With regards to depression, participants in both groups felt simple awareness of its treatability, and acceptance of therapy and medical staff was the key to battling the disease. Participants agreed that the hardest thing for many black women is to ask for—and seek out—help when needed; as for some, it would be admitting defeat.

## KEY RESULTS—
*Black Male Quantitative (n=211) and Focus Group Findings*

The survey was available to respondents from August 24 to September, 2009. Potential respondents were invited to participate in the survey or were directed to a website of the survey via social networking sites such as Facebook, African American organizations, and professional associations. To qualify for participation, prospective respondents were screened by occupational demographics to ensure that they met the criteria for this study. The professional black male survey instrument consisted of twenty-three questions including seven demographic questions. The final questionnaire was approved by Sophia A. Nelson, Dr. Silas Lee, and Kelly-anne Conway prior to fielding. The data have not been weighted to reflect the demographic composition of the general black male population.

- An unexpected percentage of professional black men identified work-related stress (hypertension) at 72 percent as major challenge confronting them in the workplace. This is a groundbreaking revelation that has not been discussed in mainstream media and reflects the silent agony experienced by many black men in society.
- The descriptions selected by the male respondents to describe black professional women reinforced their experiences, perceptions, and some stereotypes. The most frequent words used to describe the women accentuated their success, such as independent (72 percent) and accomplished (66 percent). This contrasts with the second set of descriptors focusing on less than flattering personality traits such as controlling (39 percent) and angry (22 percent).
- More than seven of ten (75 percent) respondents "strongly/somewhat agreed" that Michelle Obama is reconstructing the image of black women in society by exposing America to a successful black woman who reflects the dominant values of society.
- Irrespective of their education and professional status, being stereotyped as lazy or criminal (30 percent) was identified as the biggest problem facing black men in America today.
- The four qualities that attract professional black men to black women are personality (72 percent), emotional stability (69 percent), a sense of humor, and compassion (65 percent each). Interestingly, these characteristics were not listed in the descriptions of black professional women by the respondents.
- Nearly half (48 percent) of the respondents "strongly/somewhat agreed" that to have a successful relationship with a professional Black woman, compromises are necessary. However, there was a split decision that "professional black and white women maintain themselves equally." Forty-one percent "strongly/somewhat agreed" and 38 percent "strongly/somewhat disagreed."
- White women are perceived as less sexually conservative than professional black women by 45 percent of the respondents and 51 percent believe a professional black woman's devotion to her religion can interfere with a relationship's intimacy.
- Of the black professional males who have dated white women (54 percent), the respondents noted that personality (62 percent) and physical appeal (57 percent) attracted them to her the most.

- The election of President Obama has not altered their perception of professional Black women as independent and accomplished (87 percent).
- Admitting their shortcomings, the respondents identified the two primary barriers to professional black women having a successful relationship as: Past hurts at the hands of other black men—55 percent. Differences in career and/or life goals—49 percent.
- One-third or more of the men questioned if "they can enhance the quality of life for a professional black woman (35 percent) or make her happy (33 percent)."
- Possessing a combination of intelligence (89 percent), the potential to be a good wife and mother and refreshing to be around (83 percent each), emotional stability and sexual compatibility (82 percent each) were identified as the secrets to capturing the affection of Black professional men.   This reaffirmed some of the characteristics that men desire more women to exhibit.
- Of the married respondents, a combined 79 percent would "definitively/probably remarry" their present wife. However, less than half (48 percent) "strongly/somewhat agreed" that their marriage is sexually gratifying to them.

### KEY FINDINGS—
*Black Female Quantitative (n=540)*

The survey was fielded from August 13 to September 1, 2009. Prospective respondents were either emailed an invitation and link to participate in the survey, or directed to a website containing the survey link (social networking websites including Facebook). Potential respondents were screened to ensure they met the criteria for participation, including race (African American), age (over the age of 18), and work function (employed in some type of professional capacity).

The professional black women survey instrument contained 40 questions, including four demographic queries. The final questionnaire was approved by Sophia A. Nelson and Dr. Silas Lee prior to fielding. A convenience sampling method was used.

- Professional Black women admired First Lady Michelle Obama for her intelligence (40 percent) and accomplishments (35 percent) and many name her a role model or inspiration. In total, 87 percent credited Michelle Obama with *dispelling stereotypes* about the achievements of Black women in America.
- In the workplace, PBW pointed first to limits on opportunities for advancement (38 percent) and next to racial (29 percent), more so than gender, (10 percent) discrimination as hampering their ability to succeed. In fact, women in professional or executive positions were more apt than white collar workers to have perceived prejudicial behavior based on race in their work environment (32 percent vs. 19 percent).
- PBW recognized many challenges faced by Black women in the workplace beyond that experienced by their White counterparts, including getting ahead in the office (68 percent), earning respect from male colleagues (58 percent), being viewed as competent (54 percent), and hitting the "glass ceiling" professionally (52 percent). Exploring the social implications of these difficulties in the workplace, the majority of PBW believed Black women disproportionately confront the challenge of providing for their families (66 percent).
- Mental and emotional stability (42 percent) as well as financial security (23 percent) were key to PBW when considering their overall well being. Smaller proportions of Black women selected factors related to physical health and relationships as important for personal contentment. Financial pressures or debt was the "number one" factor that would negatively influence PBW's mental health, including causing depression, for 60 percent of respondents.
- When "feeling blue" the majority of women (66 percent) turn to their faith to get them through the difficult time, while smaller proportions reach out to friends or family members or engage in other activities to distract them from the pain. A small percentage of PBW (12 percent) would seek medical or therapeutic help for their depression and nearly the same number would just "wait for the feelings to pass." This is especially worrisome as the majority of PBW (64 percent) categorized "stress-related diseases" as something that affects Black women more so than White women.

- The majority of PBW (66 percent) reported that they would rather be alone than enter into a relationship with someone who is below their standards for the sake of companionship. More than three-quarters of PBW (78 percent) believed that "finding a 'suitable' husband" was a challenge that is faced by Black women more so than their White counterparts.
- Intimidation was pegged by 67 percent of PBW as the main impediment to Black women's abilities to start and sustain healthy relationships with Black men. For the words or phrases that they believed Black men would use to the describe them, PBW selected those that express the PBW's ability to be successful on her own ("independent," 70 percent or "self-sufficient," 70 percent) or those that negatively describe her attitude or personality ("standoffish," 51 percent; "arrogant," 48 percent, "snob," 46 percent, "distant/ aloof," 32 percent; and "angry," 30 percent).
- Beyond romance, nearly all PBW (92 percent) expressed the importance of forming and maintaining relationships with other Black women, including family members and friends for their personal fulfillment and happiness.
- In questions asked only of those PBW who were currently married, three-quarters (75 percent) reported bliss with their current husbands, and relatively smaller proportions (62 percent) disclosed that they were feeling sexually fulfilled with their spouse. On this topic, nearly one-half of all survey participants (47 percent) disclosed that being in an intimate and committed relationship was not necessary for personal well-being.
- While over one-half of PBW (56 percent) had engaged a "friends with benefits" at some point, 41 percent were not comfortable with the experience, and an addition 25 percent said they would not consider such an arrangement.
- Three-quarters of PBW (75 percent)were raised to believe that engaging in intimate acts outside of marriage was indecent, especially those who professed to be more religiously-minded in adulthood. In a separate question asked of these participants who confirmed traditional views with respect to sex, one-third of participants (33 percent) believed this was constructive for their adult relationships.
- In spite of relationship difficulties many PBW would not delay taking their own steps to have a child or form or build upon

existing relationships to satisfy their familial needs. A portion of PBW were open to adoption (56 percent), artificial insemination (13 percent) or seeking a father for their child (15 percent) to add to their own family, while others would be content to spend more time with nieces and nephews (40 percent) or volunteer with children (36 percent).

- Interestingly, faith and religion played a larger role in some of the more vocal single participants' romantic relationships and daily decisions than in their married counterpart's lives. In fact, some women discussed having to choose between their commitment to God and their standards for men, implying that one would have to be compromised in a relationship. Others were comfortable in their faith and current situation, even if it meant that they did not have male companionship.
- Both groups of women respected and admired the First Lady, Michelle Obama. The younger and single were more apt to view Mrs. Obama as a role model, the married and older ones, more like a peer. In fact, several married women claimed that they had accomplished as much—if not more—than Mrs. Obama, even as they appreciated that Michelle was helping their accomplishments be recognized outside of their community. Some of the single women, on the other hand, commented that she was setting the bar too high, and making it difficult for other PBW to live up to her standards.
- The two groups of women responded very differently when asked about the "angry Black woman" stereotype. Those in the married session felt strongly that if someone was angry, they probably had a reason to feel that way, while the single ladies accepted that sometimes they were perceived as angry due to stereotypes, and there was nothing they could do to change it.

## KEY FINDINGS—
*National Omnibus Sample (n=1000)*

The survey was fielded October 22–25, 2009 at a Computer Assisted Telephone Interviewing (CATI) phone facility using live callers. The 1000 person national sample was drawn utilizing a Random Digit Dial (RDD), where phone numbers were generated by a computer to ensure that every household in the nation with a landline telephone had an equal chance to be surveyed. A total of five close-ended questions that were specific to the central theme of *Black Woman Redefined* were added to a national omnibus survey. Sampling controls were used to ensure that a proportional and representative number of adults were interviewed from such demographic groups as age, gender, race and ethnicity, and geographic region according to the latest figures available from the United States Census. The final questionnaire was approved by Sophia A. Nelson prior to fielding. The margin of error is calculated at +/- 3.1 percent at the 95 percent confidence level, meaning that in 19 out of 20 cases, the results obtained would differ by no more than three point one percentage points in either direction if the entire adult population nationwide were to be surveyed. Margins of error for subgroups are higher.

## ◆ Women in the Workplace

The first substantive question in the survey asked respondents if "trouble getting respect from male colleagues at work" was experienced more often by black professional women or white professional women. A solid majority of respondents (62 percent) felt that this problem is an equal opportunity challenge for both black and white women in the workplace. Another 17 percent said black women were affected more by this, and 6 percent said white women had it the toughest.

Fourteen percent could not or would not choose either answer and said instead "I don't know."

## ◆ Affirmative Action

In a separate question, respondents were also asked how black women might have been *helped* in the workplace, specifically by affirmative action. In fairness to respondents, and recognizing that the term "affirmative action" may be beyond the ken and everyday lexicon of average Americans, a definition was supplied, if requested.[12]

Fully 60 percent of respondents felt affirmative action had helped black women to advance professionally. The intensity varied: with 22

---

[12] If requested, the following definition of Affirmative Action was supplied: "Affirmative action is an active effort to improve the employment or educational opportunities of members of minority groups and women."

percent saying it had been a "very big" factor and 38 percent calling it out as "somewhat" of a factor. In contrast, 30 percent rejected the notion that affirmative action had such a nexus to black women's advancement. In fact, 13 percent said it only had been "a little bit" of a factor and 17 percent maintained that it had no impact at all. Only 7 percent were unsure.

## ◆ Qualities of Women in the Workplace

In order to further understand how respondents felt about accomplished black women, all were asked to choose one or more words from a list of nine that described African American women in their own places of work. "Intelligent" and "capable or skilled" tied for first, with 57 percent selecting each of those phrases as illustrative. Coming in a close second was "independent" (54 percent); and "accomplished" (49 percent) rounded out the top descriptors. The more negative attributes, such as "controlling," "angry," "arrogant," "unfulfilled," and "lonely" were cited by 15 percent or less of respondents. Interestingly, the majority (55 percent) of black respondents supplied a negative characterization of black women in the workplace, more than double the number of whites who did (24 percent), and higher than Hispanics as well (40 percent).

## ◆ Romantic Relationships

The survey switched gears from the boardroom to the bedroom and asked respondents if they had ever had a romantic relationship with an African American. As shown in the nearby textbox, 28 percent of respondents had dated a black man or woman, while 63 percent had not. The deeper responses were most revealing: 28 percent would consider it, but have not had occasion to do so yet, and more than one-third (35 percent) of all those surveyed admitted they would *not* consider such involved with an African American. By race, 88 percent of African Americans surveyed had been involved with someone of their race; 9 percent had not, and 6 percent would not even consider it.

## ◆ Michelle Obama

In a question that was posed to respondents in the online survey of 540 black professional women in 2009, as well as nationwide on this survey

in 2009, participants were asked to choose which of the word(s) provided best describe(s) First Lady Michelle Obama. "Wife and mother"
was the most popular response, with more than four-fifths (82 percent)
choosing this. Other top responses included "intelligent" (76 percent),
"strong-willed" (71 percent), and "accomplished" (70 percent).

The responses across genders, all races, age groups, geographic
regions and even political affiliations to describe Michelle Obama, whose
approval ratings were 50 percent[13] at the time of this writing in 2009,
while her husband's have dipped to 51.5 percent[14] were mostly positive.
In fact, all responses provided were selected by a majority of respondents except for "made-over," which just 16 percent selected. However,
10 percent did select "all of the above," which would include this seemingly negative response. See the snapshot below from both samples.


## MICHELLE OBAMA RESEARCH SECTION SNAP SHOT
*National Sample of 1,000 (all races—men and women)*


◆ Michelle Obama

In a question that was posed to respondents in the online survey of 540
black professional women earlier this year, as well as nationwide on this
survey, participants were asked to choose which of the word(s) provided best describe(s) First Lady Michelle Obama. "Wife and mother"
was the most popular response, with more than four-fifths (82 percent)
choosing this. Other top responses included "intelligent" (76 percent),
"strong-willed" (71 percent), and "accomplished" (70 percent).

The responses across genders, all races, age groups, geographic regions
and even political affiliations to describe Michelle Obama, whose approval
ratings are 50 percent[15][1] at the time of this writing, while her husband's
have dipped to 51.5 percent[16][2] were mostly positive. In fact, all responses
provided were selected by a majority of respondents except for "made-
over," which just 16 percent selected. However, 10 percent did select "all of

---

[13] *New York Times*/CBS News Poll, September 23, 2009. Favorability rating.
[14] Real Clear Politics, Average of all Polls. November 6, 2009. President Obama Job Approval.
[15][1] *New York Times*/CBS News Poll, September 23, 2009. Favorability rating.
[16][2] Real Clear Politics, Average of all Polls. November 6, 2009. President Obama Job
Approval.

the above," which would include this seemingly negative response.

Men were 7 points more apt than women to say Michelle Obama was "made-over" (20 percent vs. 13 percent), whereas the reverse was true for "accomplished" (75 percent women vs. 66 percent men), "role model" (69 percent women, 63 percent men), and "inspiring" (64 percent women, 51 percent men).

By race and gender, black women were equally likely to say Mrs. Obama is "inspiring," "intelligent" and "wife and mother" (all 85 percent).

White men, however, were much more likely than all others to say the First Lady had been "made over" (21 percent vs. 15 white women, 3 percent of black men, and 4 percent of black women). While "wife and mother" was a top of mind response regardless of race or gender, while "inspiring" responses varied wildly by those respondent characteristics—with just 49 percent of white men saying so, compared to a whopping 85 percent of black women.

## PROFESSIONAL BLACK WOMEN SURVEY
*(540 completes)*

◆ Professional Black Women Praise the First Lady's Aptitude and Achievement

When asked, First Lady Michelle Obama first and foremost describes herself as "Malia's and Sasha's mom" according to the White House's website. While 28 percent of professional black women in the online survey echoed this self-assessment, higher proportions of PBW associate her with "intelligent" (40 percent) and "accomplished" (35 percent). Nearly half of PBW (49 percent) selected descriptors for Michelle Obama that centered on her status as an exemplar, including those that called her "inspiring" (26 percent) and a "role model" (23 percent). Twenty-nine percent of PBW selected words to reflect Michelle's authority such as "strong" (18 percent) and "powerful" (11 percent).

Just 6 percent of professional black women believed that Michelle Obama reflected their own personality or characteristics. In the focus group research conducted with PBW on behalf of Sophia Nelson, the polling company™, inc./WomanTrend found that younger generations of black women assigned Michelle Obama a "rock star" status, while older black women believed they had accomplished as much as the First Lady had.

In a separate question, fully 87 percent of PBW credited First Lady Michelle Obama with dispelling stereotypes about the accomplishments and actualities of being a black woman in America in 2009. What's more, the majority of survey takers (62 percent) were in strong accordance with this idea. Just 3 percent of PBW in total disagreed with the message Michelle is sending about PBW, while 9 percent abstained from judgment on the matter.

- PBW in white collar positions were more apt than those in professional or executive roles to strongly agree with this statement about Michelle Obama (66 percent vs. 60 percent).
- Those age 35-44 were more apt than PBW generally to be in enthusiastic accordance with the positive effect of Mrs. Obama's accomplishments (67 percent vs. 62 percent overall).

Reflecting more generally on the perception of professional black women and the stereotypes with which Michelle Obama must contend, fully 91 percent of respondents believed that black women are typecast as being "angry" or "pushy" compared to just 1 percent who reported the same for White women. Seven percent of PBW said that this stereotype was applied equally to women of either race. No demographic cohorts were more likely than the average survey taker to attribute this prejudicial statement to black women.

# ACKNOWLEDGMENTS

It is never possible to thank all of the people who help us along our life's journey toward success and achievement. But I will do my best here:

To Master Ethan Frick Armstrong—the cute little blue-eyed boy next door who saved my life one day when he told me to "put my helmet on" (you can read that story on the book website).

To my immediate and extended family members (too many to name—you know who you are). Thank you for the prayers and encouragement along the way. To my Xi Omega sorority sisters, and my beloved Alpha Kappa Alpha sorority, Inc., "we help each other"—love you all!! To the sisters of iask, Inc., you made the dream a reality—thank you! To my Church of Christ family at 13th Street, Falls Church, Manassas, Princeton, and nationally, your love and prayers lifted me!

To my dearest friends who made me laugh along the way, encouraged me with cards, flowers, and lots of wine when needed: Lynda Dorman and Beverly Kirk thank you two for everything! Rhonda Lambert Parson (you are the best gift giver in the world), Talaya Simpson (you are my girl), Dani Keemer Edmond (the best friend I will ever have), Melissa A. Young (thanks for being my big sister), Mike and Janet Spokony (my second mom and dad), the late Fran Robinson, Soror Dawn Baskerville (you are a true sister friend), Soror Melanie Burney, Senovia Ross, Dedra McCannon, Dominque Evans (for your great assistance when I needed to heal), Dr. Joi Martin, Dr. Marie Anderson, Dr. John Bruchalski, Dr. Grace Keenan and Dr. Holly Harris (for keeping me well), Ray Cotton (you have been a true mentor), Fred and Sandy Steinberg (love you two), Brian and Nicole Bradley, David and Marilyn Troung. Stephen Williams, EJ, Ann Caggins, Angela Trammel and Myles Caggins, Glynda Mayo Hall, Andy Morris, Sherylyn Strong, Vickie Writt, Dee Dean, Val Meekins, Sheena and Shaun Meekins, Christi Rich, Soror Roz Parker, Soror Camilla McKinney, Gywndia and Michelle Hawkins, Sam and Venesa

Bates, Angela Cobb, Herb Lowe, Kym Taylor, Victoria Jackson, The Don Smith Family, Vanessa Allen, Dr. Floyd Hayes III and Charlene Hayes, Valerie Manuel, Tiffani Lee, my former H&K assistant Claire Pierce, my neighbors Jeff and Sarah Armstrong, and Meredith and Bobby Blanco. And so many more who I love and cannot name here (but you know who you are)!!!

Soledad O'Brien and Roland Martin (you two were my first supporters and did all I asked of you and then some—thank you forever!!)

To the Ascendant Group family and Team Sophia: Raoul Davis, Candace J. Reese (Publicist), Kimberly S. Reid, Seun Ariyo, Erica Bennett, Annika Murray, Davida Pitts, Cheryl Carr, Robin McDougal, Jamaal Bell, and Don Cottner (websites) and my SAN Enterprises partner Gregory Campbell, I could NOT have done this without you ALL. Love you all like my family. Thank you.

My pollsters Dr. Silas Lee of Xavier University, Kellyanne Conway, Katie Musolino, Danielle King, and Ashley Koonce at Woman Trend/ Polling Company, and Nicole CrawfordTichawonna for early editorial support. Thank you!!!

Mikki Taylor, I can never thank you enough for the fabulous book cover image that you selected from day #1 and brought the rest of us along. I will always treasure the spiritual sisterhood that is ours. Congrats and good luck on your own book release this fall!

To my photo shoot, hair, make-up, styling team summer of 2010: Damon D. Moore (you are a great photographer), Jeanette Moore (hair and make-up), Rachel Grante (color), Dusan Grante (cut), Monica Barnett (styling), Karen Millen Summer 2010 collection (Tyson's Corner, VA Store), Gulick Homes (VA), Nicole Miller (Tyson's Store), Zoey Reed (the best Brit I know), Shapes Spa & Salon (hair products), KLS Studio (Reston, VA), and Salon Daniel (Tyson's, VA).

Claudia Menza, my literary agent. Thanks for sticking with me all the way!! What a journey for us both!

My publisher BenBella Books. Thank you for believing in me and this project. And for getting it to print on an impossible timeline. It was a rough road for us all, but we did it!

My literary attorneys at Holland & Knight LLP, Chicago Office Bob Labate, Joi Thomas, and Vic Henderson. And my personal attorney Patricia E. Tichenor, Esq. Thank you!!!!

My Johnson Publishing Company Colleagues, Ms. Mira Lowe (former editor-in-chief) who brought me on as a feature columnist at *JET* in

2010. You give me renewed faith in "the sisterhood" woman—I love you and thank you!

Candi Meriwether, Avis Weathersbee, Amy DuBois Barnett, Rod Sierra, CEO & Pres Desiree Rogers, Chair of Board Linda Johnson Rice—thank you, thank you for the wonderful platform you all gave me as a columnist and political writer for *JET* in her 60th year!

My MSNBC Family, Yvette Miley, Shanta Covington, David Wilson, Monica Leas, Dax Tejera, Chris Jansing, Michele Loschiavo, and Patty (make-up in DC N. Cap Bureau)!

And finally to those who worked tirelessly on this project and provided support during the summer of 2009-2010 during the research and writing phase: Jill Harner, Aaron Dom, Vasama Williams (personal assistant), Krishan Trotman, The Management and staff at Wild Dunes Resort-Isle of Palms, South Carolina, Charleston School of Law, Boone Hall Plantation-Mount Pleasant, South Carolina, Loudoun and Fairfax County Public Library staffs, American University Washington College of Law (my alma mater), and to those men and women who were interviewed for the book as experts, to those who contributed essays, and to those who participated in our regional and national focus groups thank you very much!

# ENDNOTES

## PROLOGUE

1. "Michelle Obama Inteview: Our Life in the White House," *People* magazine, February 25, 2009, March cover feature.
2. "The World's 100 Most Powerful Women," *Forbes*, October 6, 2010.
3. David Yermack, "Vision Statement: How This First lady Moves Markets", *Harvard Business Review*, November 1, 2010.
4. Michelle Obama poll numbers analysis from the following publications: Gary Langer, "Michelle Obama: Bragging Rights," *ABC News*, March 31, 2009; Nia-Malika Henderson, "Michelle Obama's Poll Numbers Slide," *Politico* Forum, November 9, 2009; Lymari Morales, "Michelle Obama Outshines All Others In Favorability Poll," *Gallup*, July 22, 2010; Michael O'Brien, "Michelle Obama Hits Campaign Trail with High Approval Ratings," *The Hill*, October 13, 2010; AP-GFK Poll, conducted by Roper/GFK Public Affairs and Corporate Communications, January 2011, show Mrs. Obama at 72 percent favorable ratings.
5. Maureen Dowd, "She is Not Buttering Him Up," *New York Times*, April 25, 2007.
6. Barry Blitt, "The Politics of Fear" (cover art), *New Yorker*, July 21, 2008.
7. Sarah Palin, *America by Heart: Reflections on Family, Faith and Flag* (New York: Harper Collins, 2010), 26.
8. "Rafting and Dog Mushing," *Sarah Palin's Alaska*, TLC December 19, 2010.
9. Jenna Goudreau, "How to Shine Like Michelle Obama," *Forbes*, November 12, 2010: Liza Mundy, *Michelle: A Biography* (New York: Simon and Schuster, 2008).
10. "First Lady Michelle Obama," WhiteHouse.gov, http://www.whitehouse.gove/administration/first-lady-michelle-obama.
11. See Appendices A: Research Section, Key Findings on Michelle Obama.

## INTRODUCTION

1. Amanda Sesko and Monica Biernat, "Prototypes of Race and Gender: The Invisibility of Black Women," *Journal of Experimental Social Psychology*, 46 (2010): 356–60. Issue 2, Pages 356-360, March 2010.

## CHAPTER 1

1. Mark Hugo Lopez, associate director, Pew Hispanic Center, Paul Taylor, executive vice president, Pew Research Center and "Dissecting the 2008 Electorate: Most Diverse in U.S. History," April 30, 2009: "Election Center 2008: Exit Polls," CNN, http://www.cnn.com/ELECTION/2008/results/polls/#USP00p1.

2. Sophia Nelson, "Moving Black Women Beyond 'For Colored Girls' to Discovering Love, Happiness, and Fulfillment," Huffington Post, November 8, 2010, http://www.huffingtonpost.com/sophia-a-nelson/moving-black-women-beyond_b_780388.html; Sophia Nelson, "It's Time for 'Colored Girls' to Move Beyond the Pain," TheGrio.com, November 14, 2010, http://www.thegrio.com/entertainment/its-time-for-colored-girls-to-move-beyond-the-pain.php?page=1.

3. Offical transcript, Imus in the Morning, MSNBC, April 4, 2007.

4. Rob Tannenbaum, "John Mayer: Playboy Interview," *Playboy*, March 2010, http://www.playboy.com/articles/john-mayer-playboy-interview.

5. Mortimer Zuckerman, "Why 'Ho' Is So Hurtful," *U.S. News & World Report*, April 22, 2007, http://www.usnews.com/usnews/opinion/articles/070422/30edit.htm.

6. Allison Samuels, "John Mayer Is Not Alone," *Newsweek*, February 16, 2010, http://www.newsweek.com/2010/02/15/john-mayer-is-not-alone.html.

7. John Jurgensen, "Just Asking: Decoding Jay-Z," *Wall Street Journal*, October 21, 2010, http://online.wsj.com/article/SB10001424052702304023804575566644176961542.html.

8. Danielle Belton, "'Bitch Is the New Black' Author Gives Public Apology," Essence, December 6, 2010, http://www.essence.com/entertainment/hot_topics/bitch_is_the_new_black_author_helena_andrews_sheila_bridges.php.

9. Jayson Rodriguez, "Lil' Kim Disses Nicki Minaj Again," *MTV News*, January 3, 2011, http://www.mtv.com/news/articles/1655171/lil-kim-disses-nicki-minaj-again.jhtm.

10. The South Atlantic region comprises Delaware, Washington, D.C., Florida, Georgia, North Carolina, South Carolina, West Virginia, Virginia, and Maryland. Thirteen percent of respondents were from the Mid-Atlantic states (New Jersey, Pennsylvania, and New York), 20 percent were from the Central and Western states (Illinois, Texas, Indiana, Missouri, Ohio, Wisconsin, Kansas, Minnesota, North Dakota, South Dakota, Arkansas, Oklahoma, Louisiana, Kentucky, Alabama, Mississippi, and Tennessee), 5 percent were from the Pacific region (California, Alaska, Hawaii, Oregon, and Washington), and less than 2 percent were from New England and the Mountain states.

11. Fifteen percent of our survey respondents had an associate's degree for licensed professionals, which we considered "professional" because registered nurses and some technical professionals require only a two-year degree.

## CHAPTER 2

1. Henry Louis Gates, Jr., "Ending the Slavery Blame-Game," *New York Times*, April 22, 2010, http://www.nytimes.com/2010/04/23/opinion/23gates.html.

2. Barbara Ransby, "A Response to Skip Gates' Call for Slavery Absolution," *NewBlackMan* blog, May 5, 2010, http://newblackman.blogspot.com/2010/05/response-to-skip-gates-call-for-slavery.html.

3. Rachel Swarns and Jodi Kantor, "In First Lady's Roots, a Complex Path from

Slavery," *New York Times*, October 7, 2009, http://www.nytimes.com/2009/10/08/us/politics/08genealogy.html.

4. Ibid.
5. Harriet Jacobs, *Incidents in the Life of a Slave Girl* (Clayton, DE: Prestwick House, 2006), 38.
6. Ibid., 103.
7. Truth delivered this speech in 1851 at a women's convention in Akron, Ohio.
8. Chris Murray, "Single Moms Step up to the Plate to Keep Blacks in Baseball," TheGrio.com, September 1, 2010, http://www.thegrio.com/sports/single-moms-step-up-to-the-plate-to-save-blacks-in-baseball.php.
9. Stephen Steinberg, *The Ethnic Myth* (Boston: Beacon Press, 2001), 293.
10. Ibid.
11. Andrew J. Cherlin, *Marriage, Divorce, Remarriage* (Cambridge, MA: Harvard University Press, 1992), 110. See also Herbert G. Gutman, *The Black Family in Slavery and Freedom, 1750–1925* (New York: Pantheon, 1976). For a review of this and similar studies, see Stanley L. Engerman, "Black Fertility and Family Structure in the U.S., 1880–1940," *Journal of Family History* 2, (1977): 117–138.

## CHAPTER 3

1. Catalyst, "Census of Women Corporate Officers and Top Earners of the Fortune 500," December 2008.
2. Ibid.
3. See the explanation of the unconscious bias theory on page 47 of this chapter.
4. ABA Commission on Women in the Profession, "Visible Invisibility: Women of Color in Law Firms" Chicago: American Bar Association, 2006, 5. Emphasis added.
5. Ibid., 9.
6. From the poem "Invictus," written in 1875.
7. ABA Commission on Women in the Profession, "Visible Invisibility: Women of Color in Law Firms," 9–10.
8. Executive Leadership Council, "Black Women Executives Research Initiatives" Alexandria, VA: Executive Leadership Council, 2009, 2.
9. Ibid.
10. U.S. Bureau of Labor Statistics, "Black Career Women Fact Sheet," 2007–2009, http://www.bcw.org/facts.shtml.
11. See Research Appendices: Polling Methodology and Results. ABW study respondents earning $60,000 to $69,000 and professionals/executives/business owners reported the highest incidence of stress-related challenges, at 91 percent and 83 percent, respectively.
12. Executive Leadership Council, "Black Women Executives Research Initiatives," 2.
13. Ella L. J. Edmondson Bell, *Career GPS: Strategies for Women Navigating the New Corporate Landscape* (New York: HarperCollins, 2010), 88.
14. Rosewood Victims v. State of Florida, HB 591 by representatives De Grandy and Lawson Claim of Arnett Goins, Minnie Lee Langley, et al. v. State of Florida, March 24, 1994 at http://afgen.com/roswood2.html.
15. Chesterfield Smith was president of the American Bar Association from 1973–1974 during the Watergate Investigation. He was a partner at the Law Firm of Holland & Knight LLP until his death in 2003. See *Washington Post* article at

http://www.washingtonpost.com/wp-dyn/content/article/2003/07/18/AR2005
111001243.html.

16. Sophia Nelson, "Haley Barbour Is the True Face of the New GOP," *The Root*, April 14, 2010, http://www.theroot.com/views/haley-barbour-true-face-new-gop.


## CHAPTER 4

1. Steve Harvey, *Act Like a Lady, Think Like a Man: What Men Really Think About Love, Relationships, Intimacy, and Commitment* (New York: HarperCollins, 2009).
2. Shanae Hall and Rhonda Frost, *Why Do I Have to Think Like a Man? How to Think Like a Lady and Still Get the Man* (Las Vegas: Farrah Gray Publishing, 2010).
3. Hill Harper, *The Conversation: How Men and Women Can Build Loving, Trusting Relationships* (New York: Gotham Books, 2009).
4. "Why Can't a Successful Black Woman Find a Man?," *Nightline Face-Off*, ABC, April 21, 2010. The panelists for this episode's debate included Sherri Shepherd, cohost of ABC's *The View*; Jacque Reid, star of VH1's *Let's Talk About Pep*; Hill Harper; and Jimi Izrael, author of *The Denzel Principle*.
5. James Harrison, George Jackson, Terry Lewis, James Wright and Chante Moore, "Chante's Got a Man at Home," Moore, perf., *This Moment Is Mine*, MCA, 1999..
6. Natalie Nitsche and Hannah Brueckner, *Opting Out of the Family? Social Change in Racial Inequality in Family Formation Patterns and Marriage Outcomes among Highly Educated Women* (New Haven, CT: CIQLE, 2009).
7. "Marriage, Family on the Decline for Highly Educated Black Women," Yale Office of Public Affairs and Communications press release, August 8, 2009, http://opac.yale.edu/news/article.aspx?id=6815.
8. Ibid.
9. Nitsche and Brueckner, *Opting Out of the Family?*, 1–2.
10. Adam Isen and Betsey Stevenson, "Women's Education and Family Behavior: Trends in Marriage," February 2010.
11. "Black Men/Black Women: Has Something Gone Wrong Between Them?" *Ebony*, August 1977, 160.
12. Ellis Cose, "The Black Gender Gap," *Newsweek*, March 3, 2003, http://www.newsweek.com/2003/03/02/the-black-gender-gap.html.
13. For more on this idea, see Audrey Chapman, *Man Sharing, Dilemma or Choice: A Radical New Way of Relating to the Men in Your Life* (New York: William Morrow, 1986).
14. Excerpted with permission from Mybrotha.com.
15. Joy Jones, "Are Black Women Scaring Off Their Men?" Gillis Triplett Ministries, http://www.gillistriplett.com/rel101/articles/scaring.html.
16. Michaelericmarkland, March 9, 2010. comment on *Ebony* "The biggest lies about Black male and female relationships," BNet, March 2002, at URL http://findarticles.com/p/articles/mi_m1077/is_5_57/ai_83450359/pg_3/?tag=content;col1.
17. See Research Appendices: Polling Methodology Results.
18. Ibid.
19. Ibid.
20. Mark Stibich, PhD, "Top 10 Reasons to Smile"; About.com Guide, February 4, 2010.
21. Jam Donaldson, "He's Not Intimidated, He Just Doesn't Like You: The

Intimidation Doctrine," *Conversate Is Not a Word* blog, May 4, 2009, http://www.conversateisnotaword.com/?m=200905. See also Ms. Donaldson's original short essay for this book, titled "It's Not All about You," in the Bonus Feature section.

22. "Simplify Your Life," *The Oprah Winfrey Show*, March 2, 2009.
23. This does not mean just being able to have children. It means people who are well and radiate life.
24. David Brooks, "The Sandra Bullock Trade," *New York Times*, March 29, 2010, http://www.nytimes.com/2010/03/30/opinion/30brooks.html.

## CHAPTER 5

1. Natalie Nitsche and Hannah Brueckner, *Opting Out of the Family? Social Change in Racial Inequality in Family Formation Patterns and Marriage Outcomes among Highly Educated Women* (New Haven, CT: CIQLE, 2009).
2. Valorie Burton, *How Did I Get So Busy? The 28-Day Plan to Free Your Time, Reclaim Your Schedule, and Reconnect with What Matters Most* (New York: Broadway Books, 2007), 2.
3. Carlos Greer, "Overdose No Accident, Says Fantasia—'I Wanted Out,'" *People*, August 23, 2010, http://www.people.com/people/article/0,,20414919,00.html.
4. The alienation of affection claim charges that the defendant has willfully and maliciously interfered with the marriage. The criminal conversation claim simply charges that adultery, or seduction, was committed—with or without malice. Even in the few states that haven't abolished "home wrecker" statutes, most courts are reluctant to reward damages for these claims.
5. U.S. Census Bureau, 2008.
6. "Many Cheat for a Thrill, More Stay for True Love," MSNBC.com/iVillage, April 16, 2007, http://www.msnbc.msn.com/id/17951664/ns/health-sexual_health/.
7. "I'm the Other Woman," *The Oprah Winfrey Show*, June 9, 2010.
8. "'The Anatomy of Adultery," Family Talk With Dr. James Dobson.
9. See Research Appendices: Polling Methodology Results.
10. Ibid.

## CHAPTER 6

1. In several of the interviews I conducted with black female clergy, parishioners, and laypeople, the interviewees used the term "bondage" to describe the strict teachings in black churches led by both men and women. They believe it is having a detrimental effect on young and middle-aged single professional black women most of all.
2. Deborrah Cooper, "The Black Church: How Black Churches Keep African American Women Single and Lonely," *Surviving Dating!* blog, June 14, 2010, http://survivingdating.com/black-churches-how-black-churches-keep-African American-women-single-and-alone.
3. Proverbs 5:18–19 (New International Version).
4. Song of Solomon 1:2–4 (New International Version).
5. Song of Solomon 6:2–3 (New International Version).
6. 1 Corinthians 7:1–2 (New International Version).

7.   Hebrews 13:4 (New International Version).
8.   Healthy Marriage Initiative, "What is HMI?," U.S. Department of Health and Human Services Administration for Children and Families, http://www.acf. hhs.gov/healthymarriage/about/mission.html#background. Some HMI data was taken from Institute for American Values, *Why Marriage Matters: Twenty-Six Conclusions from the Social Sciences*, 2nd ed. (New York: Institute for American Values, 2005).
9.   Barna Group, "How the Faith of African Americans Has Changed," 2009, http://www.barna.org/barna-update/article/13-culture/286-how-the-faith-of-African Americans-has-changed.
10.  Harlem Health Promotion Center, "Harlem Word: Dr. Hilda Hutcherson—Sex Is Taboo: The Black Church and Sex in the African American Community," October 14, 2008, http://www.gethealthyharlem.org/articles/harlem-word-dr-hilda-hutcherson-sex-taboo-black-church-and-sex-African American-community.
11.  Susan Newman, *Oh God! A Black Woman's Guide to Sex and Spirituality* (New York: Ballantine, 2002), 34–35.
12.  Barna Group, "How the Faith of African Americans Has Changed."
13.  Excerpted with permission for use granted by Jacqueline Mattis, "Religion and Spirituality in the Meaning-Making and Coping Experience of African American Women: A Qualitative Analysis," *Psychology of Women Quarterly* 26, (2002): 309–321.
14.  Ibid.
15.  Ibid.
16.  Harlem Health Promotion Center, "Harlem Word: Dr. Hilda Hutcherson—Sex Is Taboo: The Black Church and Sex in the African American Community."
17.  Natalie Angier, Cristina Garcia, and Elizabeth Taylor, "Sexes: Finding Trouble in Paradise," *Time*, January 28, 1985, http://www.time.com/time/magazine/article/0,9171,959268-1,00.html.
18.  Celinda Lake and Kellyanne Conway, *What Women Really Want: How American Women Are Quietly Erasing Political, Racial, Class, and Religious Lines to Change the Way We Live* (New York: Free Press, 2005) 127.
19.  Phyllis K. Davis, *The Power of Touch: The Basis for Survival, Health, Intimacy, and Emotional Well-Being* (Carlsbad, CA: Hay House, 1999), xxiv, xxv–xxvi.
20.  1 Corinthians 7:9 (New International Version)
21.  .Elijah Wolfson, "12 Ways Sex Helps You Live Longer," Healthline, January 29, 2010, http://www.healthline.com/hlc/12-ways-sex-helps-you-live-longer.

## CHAPTER 7

1.   See Research Appendices: Polling Methodology Results.
2.   Carolyn M. West, *Sexual Violence in the Lives of African American Women: Risk, Response, and Resilience* (Harrisburg, PA: VAWnet, 2006), 3, http://new.vawnet.org/category/Documents.php?docid=578&category_id=695.
3.   "Who Are the Victims?," RAINN, 2009, http://www.rainn.org/get-information/statistics/sexual-assault-victims.
4.   Robin D. Stone, *No Secrets, No Lies: How Black Families Can Heal from Sexual Abuse* (New York: Broadway Books, 2004), 58–59.
5.   Deborah Caldwell, "Now, Ladies and Gentlemen . . . T. D. Jakes on Film," Beliefnet, October 2004, http://www.beliefnet.com/Faiths/Christianity/2004/10/

Now-Ladies-And-Gentlemen-T-D-Jakes-On-Film.aspx?p=1.

6.  Rachel Donadio, "Pope Issues His Most Direct Words to Date on Abuse," *New York Times*, May 11, 2010, http://www.nytimes.com/2010/05/12world/europe/12pope. html?adxnnl=1&partner=rss&emc=rss&adxnnlx= 1295932153-TJtyCCwmfaqq Tkj9+xm2Dg.

7.  "Accused of Molesting Her: Oscar Winner Mo'Nique's Brother Comes Forward," *The Oprah Winfrey Show*, CBS, April 19, 2010.

8.  Barabara Bogorad, "Sexual Abuse: Surviving the Pain," American Academy of Experts in Traumatic Stress, 1998, http://www.aaets.org/arts/art31.htm.

9.  Grooming can generate an unhealthy sense of comfort because it may feel good. This can be especially tempting for kids who are suffering from loneliness, neglect, and mistreatment. Grooming often sets off years of inappropriate sexual behavior by the victims. Victims of sexual abuse often deal with a crippling range of emotions—such as guilt, shame, and deep conflict—when they experience a normal physical response of pleasure to the unwanted sexual stimulation. This is a difficult situation to navigate, especially for a vulnerable child or teen.

10. "Childhood Sexual Abuse Predicts Female HIV," UCLA Health Sciences press release, April 5, 2002, on Newswise, http://www.newswise.com/articles/view/28889/ Gail E. Wyatt et al.; "Does a History of Trauma Contribute to HIV Risk for Women of Color? Implications for Prevention and Policy," *American Journal of Public Health* 92, no. 4 (April 2002): 660–665.

11. Iyanla Vanzant, *Acts of Faith: Daily Meditations for People of Color* (New York: Fireside, 1993), 21.

12. "The 12 Steps of SIA," Survivors of Incest Anonymous, 2007, http://www.siawso. org/Default.aspx?pageId=158755.

## CHAPTER 8

1.  *The Book of Common Prayer with the Additions and Deviations* (Oxford, London: University Press, 1928) This is *The Book of Common Prayer* adaptation of Matthew 6:12.

2.  Alina Cho, "Halle Berry's Help for Domestic Violence Victims Gets Personal," CNN, December 14, 2010, http://articles.cnn.com/2010-12-14/entertainment/ halle.berry.charity_1_domestic-violence-abusive-partners-abusive-relationships?_s=PM:SHOWBIZ.

3.  S. Tia Brown, "Balancing Act: Why Forgiveness Isn't Always Divine," *Essence*, March 4, 2010, http://www.essence.com/lifestyle/balancing_act/balancing_act_ forgiveness.php.

4.  Names have been changed to protect identities.

5.  Carolyn M. West, *Sexual Violence in the Lives of African American Women: Risk, Response, and Resilience* (Harrisburg, PA: VAWnet, 2006), http://new.vawnet. org/category/Documents.php?docid=578&category_id=695.

6.  Alanon Family Group Headquarters, Inc., *Al-Anons Twelve Steps & Twelve Traditions* (Virginia Beach, Va: Al-Anon Family Group Headquarters, Inc., 2005).

7.  Don Colbert, *Deadly Emotions: Understand the Mind-Body-Spirit Connection That Can Heal or Destroy You* (Nashville: Thomas Nelson, 2003), xi.

8.  "Black Women's Health Study," Boston University, http://www.bu.edu/bwhs/ index.htm: Centers for Disease Control at http://www.cdc.gov/women/index.htm.

## CHAPTER 9

1. Laura Bush, *Spoken from the Heart* (New York: Simon and Schuster, 2010), 103–105.
2. Karen S. Peterson, "Having It All—Except Children," *USA Today*, April 8, 2002, http://www.usatoday.com/life/2002/2002-04-08-execmoms.htm.
3. See Research Appendices: Polling Methodology Results.
4. National Center for Health Statistics, "Births: Final Data for 2008," *National Vital Statistics Reports* 59, no. 1 (December 2010), table 15, http://www.cdc.gov/nchs/fastats/unmarry.htm.
5. Brian Alexander, "Marriage Eludes High-Achieving Black Women," MSNBC, August 13, 2009, http://www.msnbc.msn.com/id/32379727/ns/health-sexual_health/.
6. Ibid.
7. John Black, "Single Black Women Choosing to Adopt," CNN, July 1, 2009, http://articles.cnn.com/2009-07-01/living/bia.single.black.women.adopt_1_African American-black-families-white-women?_s=PM:LIVING.
8. Proverbs 13:12 (New International Version).
9. "Mayo Clinic Definition Premature Ovarian Failure,"Mayo Clinic, http://www.mayoclinic.com/health/premature-ovarian-failure/DSS00843.
10. Steve Doughty, "Rise of the 'freemale': Number of Single Women Doubles in Three Decades," *Mail Online*, January 23, 2009, http://www.dailymail.co.uk/femail/article-1126658/Rise-freemale-Number-single-women-doubles-decades.html.
11. "From Schools to Jobs, Black Women Are Rising Much Faster than Black Men; What It Means for Work, Family and Race Relations," *Newsweek*, February 23, 2003.
12. First Lady Michelle Obama, WhiteHouse.gov, http://www.whitehouse.gove/administration/first-lady-michelle-obama.
13. Louise Hay (Hay House).
14. John R. Lee Medical Letter, "How to Treat Fibroids Naturally," Virginia Hopkins Health Watch, http://www.virginiahopkinstestkits.com/fibroiddemarco.html.

## CHAPTER 10

1. The story about the behavior of the American bald eagle has been used by many speakers to illustrate how we can survive the worst life throws at us. I first heard this story from evangelist Joyce Meyers in her DVD series *Mount Up with Wings as Eagles* and have adapted it here.
2. John McCormick, "Obama Social Secretary Has No Regrets Following Exit," *Bloomberg Businessweek*, April 29, 2010, http://www.businessweek.com/news/2010-04-29/obama-social-secretary-has-no-regrets-following-exit-update1-.html.
3. Jeremy W. Peters, "Desiree Rogers, Post Crash," *New York Times*, October 1, 2010, http://www.nytimes.com/2010/10/03/fashion/03Desiree.html.
4. "Minority Women's Health: African Americans," National Women's Health Information Center, May 18, 2010, http://www.womenshealth.gov/minority/africanamerican/.
5. "Leading Causes of Death in Females—United States, 2006," Centers for Disease Control and Prevention, http://www.cdc.gov/women/lcod/.
6. George Leary, "Black Women and Mental Health," Black Women's Health, 2006,

http://www.blackwomenshealth.com/2006/articles.php?id=56.
7.  Ibid.
8.  Linda Villarosa, "When Depression Strikes the (Black) Superwoman," *The Root*, February 24, 2010, http://www.theroot.com/views/when-depression-strikes-black-superwoman?page=0,0; Susan L. Taylor, "Clarification: Susan L. Taylor Talks Back to the Root," *The Root*, April 19, 2010, http://www.theroot.com/views/clarification-susan-l-taylor-talks-back-root. Taylor disputes the original article, saying she suffered bouts of the blues but never clinical depression.
9.  Eve Bender, "Depression Treatment in Black Women Must Consider Social Factors," *Psychiatric News* 40, no. 23 (December 2, 2005): 14, http://pn.psychiatryonline.org/content/40/23/14.1.full.
10. Insight Center for Community Economic Development, *Lifting as We Climb: Women of Color, Wealth, and America's Future* (Oakland, CA: Insight Center for Community Economic Development, 2010).
11. Mariko Lin Chang, *Shortchanged: Why Women Have Less Wealth and What Can Be Done About It* (New York: Oxford University Press, 2010).
12. Insight Center for Community Economic Development, *Lifting as We Climb*, 8.
13. Mariko Lin Change, *Shortchanged: Why Women Have Less Wealth and What Can Be Done About It*, 53.
14. Insight Center for Community Economic Development, *Lifting as We Climb*.
15. Barbara Ehrenreich and Dedrick Muhammed, "The Destruction of the Black Middle Class," Huffington Post, August 4, 2009, http://www.huffingtonpost.com/barbara-ehrenreich/the-destruction-of-the-bl_b_250828.html.
16. Liz Weiss, "Unmarried Women Hit Hard by Poverty," Center for American Progress, September 10, 2009, http://www.americanprogress.org/issues/2009/09/census_women.html.
17. Elizabeth Scott, "Sleep Benefits: Power Napping for Increased Productivity, Stress Relief and Health," About.com, July 7, 2008, http://stress.about.com/od/lowstresslifestyle/a/powernap.htm.
18. Elizabeth Scott, "Stress and Nutrition: The Link Between Strees and Nutrition Deficiencies," About.com, November 7, 2007, http://stress.about.com/od/dietandsuppliments/a/stressnutrition.htm.
19. Elizabeth Scott, "Exercise and Stress Relief: Using Exercise as a Stress-Management Tool," About.com, October 20, 2008, http://stress.about.com/od/programsandpractices/a/exercise.htm.
20. Elizabeth Scott, "Spirituality and Mental Health: Benefits of Spirituality," About.com, November 2, 2007, http://stress.about.com/od/optimism spirituality/a/22307_God_power.htm.

## CHAPTER 11

1.  Helena Andrews, *Bitch Is the New Black* (New York: HarperCollins, 2010), 81, 83, 93, 95–96.
2.  See Danielle Belton, "'Bitch Is the New Black' Author Gives Public Apology," *Essence*, December 6, 2010, http://www.essence.com/entertainment/hot_topics/bitch_is_the_new_black_author_helena_andrews_sheila_bridges.php.
3.  "Juanita Goggins—First Black Woman Elected to South Carolina Legislature Freezes to Death Alone," Ebony Inspired, March 13, 2010, http://www.ebony-inspired.com/?p=18757.

4.  Kelly Suzanne Saulsberry, "Are You Your Sister's Keeper or Overseer?" the *Reflections* blog, January 24, 2010, http://kelly-reflects.blogspot.com/2010/01/are-you-your-sisters-keeper-or-overseer_5690.html#more.
5.  "Imus Called Women's Basketball Team 'Nappy-Headed Hos,'" On the April 4, 2007, edition of MSNBC's *Imus in the Morning*, host Don Imus referred to the Rutgers University women's basketball team, which is composed of eight black and two white players, as "nappy-headed hos." MediaMatters for America, April 4, 2007, http://mediamatters.org/research/200704040011.
6.  Scott Kraft and Diane Pucin, "Tiger Woods Admits Infidelity, Announces Break from Golf," *Los Angeles Times*, December 12, 2009, http://articles.latimes.com/2009/dec/12/sports/la-sp-tiger_woods12-2009dec12.
7.  Audre Lorde, "Eye to Eye: Black Women, Hatred, and Anger," *Sister Outsider: Essays and Speeches by Audre Lorde* (Berkeley, CA: Crossing Press, 2007), 145–146.
8.  Kelly Suzanne Saulsberry, "Are You Your Sister's Keeper or Overseer?"
9.  *Sanctum sanctorum* is a Latin phrase that means "holy of holies." It was originally applied in a religious context to the most sacred place within a sacred building, such as a temple. However, in common usage, it can be applied to mean any reserved, private, or much-valued place.
10. Titus 2:3–5 (New International Version).
11. The Prophet Joel 1: 2-3 says "Hear this, you elders; listen all who live in the land. Has anything like this ever happened in your days or in the days of your ancestors? Tell it to your children, and let your children tell it to their children, and their children to the next generation." "If we wish to live and to bequeath life to our offspring, if we believe that we are to pave the way to the future, then we must first of all not forget." Prof. Ben Zion Dinur, Yad Vashem, 1956.
12. Sophia Nelson, "We Need to Put Slavery in Its Place," *Washington Post*, June 10, 2001, B1.